Jan in 35 Pieces

A MEMOIR

IN MUSIC

Ian Hampton

The Porcupine's Quill

Library and Archives Canada Cataloguing in Publication

Hampton, Ian, 1935–, author
  Jan in 35 pieces : a memoir in music / Ian Hampton. — 1st editon.

ISBN 978-0-88984-413-1 (softcover)

  1. Hampton, Ian, 1935–. 2. Cellists—Canada—Biography. I. Title.

ML418.H232A3 2018   787.4092   C2018-901023-1

Published by The Porcupine's Quill, 68 Main Street, PO Box 160,
Erin, Ontario NOB 1TO. http://porcupinesquill.ca

Drawings throughout the text are by the author.
Edited for the press by Barbara Nickel.

Represented in Canada by Canadian Manda.
Trade orders are available from University of Toronto Press.

We acknowledge the support of the Ontario Arts Council and the Canada
Council for the Arts for our publishing program. The financial support of the
Government of Canada is also gratefully acknowledged.

To my colleagues, heroes and heroines,
sung and unsung,
who toil for St. Cecilia

Contents

BOOK TWO

BT

Foreword

During my tenure at the Winnipeg Symphony in the 1990s, an elementary school student asked why orchestra musicians were not allowed to sit with their friends on stage. The late Jacob Gurevich, a veteran violinist who played with Erich Kleiber in Uruguay during the war, answered that we came to work to make music, not friends.

Clearly, this hasn't been the case for Ian Hampton whose long and extremely successful career as a cellist, chamber musician and teacher has seen him make legions of friends and acquaintances all around the world. To that roll call of accomplishment must be added 'writer' as Ian has conceived a brilliant way in which to share his favourite musical works alongside hundreds of anecdotes and period snapshots that bring his musical journey to life.

Unquestionably, this is one of the most interesting and absorbing memoirs of any musician I have ever read. I'll go even further and describe it as a mini-masterpiece. As I closed the final page I felt a great pang of regret that I hadn't been able to spend more time with Ian over the years. He is very funny indeed and incredibly perceptive.

Although we are from different generations, I was struck with the similarity of our lives. Like Ian (referred to in the third person as 'Jan' in this memoir), I began my career in London, working with many of the same musicians, though a little later in their careers. Our paths didn't cross professionally until I came to Vancouver Opera in 1992 (hilariously recounted in this book). Later, I witnessed the extraordinary contribution that Ian made to the Langley Community Music School, after a lifetime of music-making at the highest professional level.

A word of warning. If you read this book in public you are apt to burst into laughter or tears as the narrative takes hold. Beware Sibelius's farewell to the earnest conductor Sir Malcolm Sargent (probably the most politically incorrect moment in the book) and the hilarious pun on Kodaly's name that was said to the Hungarian composer's uncomprehending widow. You'll just have to read on ... no spoilers from me.

Ian belongs to that golden generation of British string players who came to the fore after the Second World War, their ranks boosted by European refugees who fled the fascists and came to live and work in London.

Players from the blossoming postwar U.K. orchestral life of the calibre of Simon Streatfeild, Norman Nelson, Philippe Etter, Raymond Ovens and Ian Hampton himself saw the opportunity to contribute to the ever growing Canadian scene and came to live and work in Vancouver during the 1960s and '70s, often with the encouragement of British conductor Meredith Davies, music director of the Vancouver Symphony Orchestra from 1964 to 1971.

Back in the day, the local branch of the Canadian Federation of Musicians was concerned these newcomers might take work away from the locals. While being interviewed for membership at the union local, one member of the committee remembered sitting with Ian in a cello section at a London performance of *Peter and the Wolf* in which they both finished a beat later than the rest of the orchestra. The committee member's exclamation of 'Oh crap ...' is one of those precious moments that would have been lost to posterity had Ian not set pen to paper. The recollection of this incident got Ian through the hurdle of union membership.

Meredith Davies and Ray Ovens eventually returned to the U.K., where, coincidentally, I met both early on in my career. After I arrived in Canada in 1989, I worked with Sydney Humphreys in Victoria and with Bob Growcott at the VSO, both part of Ian's narrative. More recently, I had the honour of being commissioned by the Elmer Isler Singers to compose a motet in honour of George Zukerman's retirement, the virtuoso bassoonist and impresario who forms a memorable part of Ian's story and who it might be argued, created the environment in which freelance musicians could flourish in British Columbia.

Simon Streatfeild later became Music Director of the Manitoba Chamber Orchestra in Winnipeg, where he and I first met. In Vancouver, Simon won our permanent gratitude as the man who persuaded the City of Vancouver not to demolish the Orpheum Theatre, now the VSO's precious home.

Although they would never have dreamt of using the term, it's pretty clear that all of these players were from an elite group of London musicians. Their contribution to Canadian musical life has been immeasurable. Today's Vancouver Symphony Orchestra owes an enormous debt to them for establishing the musical foundation for today's international orchestra.

Another member of this book's dramatis personae is conductor Sir John Eliot Gardiner, music director of the CBC Radio Orchestra (based in Vancouver) from 1980 to 1983. Jiggy, as he is universally known, makes several wonderful appearances, at least one of which he might prefer to forget. As principal cellist of this orchestra, Ian recounts many inspiring as well as hilarious moments. What a contrast with the dreary CBC of today which is involved with what Ian nails as a 'race to the bottom'.

Ian worked closely with legendary Canadian composer R. Murray Schafer. Indeed, I was reminded of Murray's love of the natural sound world in Ian's evocative opening and closing chapters. Many other composers benefitted from Ian's close attention as he commissioned new works in pursuit of a Canadian musical language that would benefit his adopted homeland. His proudest commissions are the cello works that he persuaded Nikolai Korndorf to complete before the composer's untimely death at the age of fifty-four.

Once, on a trip to Penticton, Ian ensured composer Barbara Pentland got paid after the Okanagan Festival failed to apply for public funding for a commission. A quick call to the Canada Council's Hugh Davidson (coincidentally, also a friend and mentor of mine) got the funds approved before the premiere. The reaction of the chair of the festival was appalling but, very satisfyingly, it's recorded for posterity in this book.

Being a composer is a lonely existence. Most days you sit at the piano (nowadays, at the computer and keyboard), eyes glazed over, staring at the empty musical staves. You're supposed to have a concept of content and form in your mind before setting off, but the reality is that ideas get flung down on paper and rejected at leisure for confusing reasons. Composing is just as much about making the right and wrong decisions as it is about being creative.

With chamber music there is the rare chance for musicians to debate these decisions in great detail.

Writing about the first performances of Jean Coulthard's Octet, Ian takes us into the rehearsal room where the players are initially baffled by obvious wrong notes. Jean herself seems uncertain what they should be but her biographer, David Gordon Duke, an excellent writer and composer himself, provides a way through the score.

These discussions often involve tiny aspects of music—whether to play staccato or portato, whether to play *pianissimo* or *pianississimo*, whether to accelerate or maintain the tempo. In any event, once a work is completed, the composer moves on to the next magnum opus and it's up to the musicians to figure it all out.

Ian Hampton has spent his life quibbling about such minutiae. On a daily basis he has participated in thousands of debates about emphasis and nuance. As a member of, first of all, the Edinburgh Quartet, then later the Purcell String Quartet (PSQ), Ian has sat and listened to his colleagues droning on about how such and such a problem should be solved.

The layperson cannot begin to appreciate how much patience is required to be a member of a successful string quartet. It's like being married to three people at once. You must get to know your colleagues so well that you can anticipate their next move without letting on that they're being predictable. When successful, you breathe new life into age-old works of art. When it doesn't work out, all you want to do is scream at their nauseating peccadilloes.

Ian seems to have worked with Job's patience alongside some very difficult people, although it's clear that in the case of the PSQ, a common English sense of humour empowered their harmonious music-making.

In time-honoured fashion, Ian has readily contributed to and enjoyed musicians' wit and wisdom. Whether waiting for a tour bus, getting on a tiny seaplane in a gale or just riding to a gig in the car, the witticisms flow. Ian Hampton is their Boswell, recording so many one-liners and amusing moments that you almost feel you're travelling with them. (I think I know who the timpanist was who left his stick case behind….)

At the same time—and this is the magic of this tome—we are taken into the waiting room of his first cello teacher, onto the train towards London, recoiling in horror at the air raid sirens that sent the citizens scuttling into cellars during the Blitz. He recounts the stimulating programming of the Oakland Symphony, back in the day considered a far more exciting environment than its near neighbour the San Francisco Symphony. Every destination is related afresh, as if it were yesterday.

Of course, as Shakespeare tells us, old men remember with advantages, but Ian's self-deprecating style lends the whole book an authenticity that is moving and profound. The Bard's dictum doesn't seem to apply in this case.

Ian's remarks about conductors are unsullied by vitriol, but they are direct. 'Toscanini, Szell, Solti et al. are all silent now. But they were never heard in the first place.'

My predecessor at the VSO, Maestro Sergiu Comissiona, has an unexpected encounter with birdseed. The tale of my discomfort at a performance of *Die Fledermaus*, and how it was unexpectedly stressful for Philippe Etter, is all recreated by Ian exactly as I remember it.

I'm writing these words in my study, underneath a woodcut by Walter Gramatté, the first husband of distinguished Canadian composer Sophie Carmen Eckhardt-Gramatté. It was a gift from her second husband, Dr Ferdinand Eckhardt. All three get a mention in *Jan in 35 Pieces*.

Reading Ian's thoughts on Elgar's Cello Concerto, we can see into the heart of this man. He has thought deeply about this music all his life. As he correctly ascertains, there were plenty of great performances of the Elgar before the famous Jacqueline du Pré recording with Sir John Barbirolli. And by the way, he was at school with Jacqueline's brother-in-law, Christopher Finzi, who married her sister, Hilary. And by the way, Christopher was the son of Gerald, one of England's greatest composers. And by the way, *Hilary and Jackie* became a controversial Oscar-nominated movie. All of this is part of Ian's narrative.

As well as by his musical erudition, I was struck by the sheer humanity of Ian Hampton, his love of music and devotion to his art and, particularly, by his tireless efforts to enhance the quality of life of people through music. His story captivates from start to finish. I was desperately sorry when the book ended, as it had to, as life has to.

Ian Hampton makes friends while making music. And he does it all at the highest level, with a ready wit and a welcoming smile—that's some legacy.

Bramwell Tovey
Vancouver, December 2017

Book One

The robin is the first bird to greet the dawn. He is staking his territory and guarding his spouse's nest and takes up his sentry duty at three locations, each nearer than the last to the bedroom window. 'Toodleloo, toodleloo' is relentless and gradually other avian sounds merge into it. Sometimes Jan hears what he once imagined was an owl making its last run of the night. Later he discovered that the call belongs to a loon out on the inlet. The fretting of the Canada geese on the muddy strand below eventually coalesces into regimented honking as squadrons of them take off inland to their feeding grounds. Two ravens begin calling one another as they circle the forest above. Occasionally, an eagle passes over the house, its cry seeming very uncharacteristic of such a magnificent bird—more like a sparrow. Finally, two red-breasted sapsuckers arrive to provide a percussive accompaniment to the ornithological chorus. They rat-a-tat-tat against the metal topping of the nearby telephone pole. It confounds reason how fast their short staccato bursts begin. In previous years, Jan imagined a single bird beating out a tattoo to look for a mate. This year the pair arrives every morning for at least a month to paradiddle the community. The family that pecks together evidently stays together.

Along with the woodpeckers, the sun arrives. It rises over the eastern mountain range and heralds the 6:20 a.m. West Coast Express—five trains that run every half hour taking commuters to Vancouver. In the late afternoon they will return their charges in similar half hours. Jan, snug in bed, listens to the characteristic horn chord that evokes Rimsky-Korsakov's *Scheherazade* before he knows absolutely that he has to get up.

A variety of trains run on the tracks that follow the Burrard Inlet up to Vancouver. There is *The Sorcerer's Apprentice* one, then the 'Britten' one, and the 'Glenn Miller' one. After Jan showers and pours his tea will be *The Rite of Spring* one, and after shaving while reading the newspaper headlines, the 'Varèse' one. Finally, after shutting the front door, is the 'Widor' one.

Sometimes, Jan lying abed speculates on the rich variety of these train horns. It's not just the predicted calls of the West Coast Express; add to them the infinite riches of the freight lines that tweak the ear day and night. Yes, they are invasive but they suggest, invoke, refer to, a series of sound images—from Verdi back to Mozart—from our Western musical heritage. Jan imagines, in his supine position, that some person of genius, perhaps appointed by the Canada Council, spends his or her days inventing evocative train horn chords. Something for everyone. For the unwilling émigré with few references, let's say a lonely sapper doing service in Rangoon, a melancholic E minor triad as diurnally sounded by the Canadian Pacific Railway will fill that person with resonances from a Canadian childhood to make him homesick for the rest of the day.

Over time, Jan's ears have moved from the nearby particular to the Burrard landscape as it opens up to Indian Arm, the water boundary, if you will, to the city of Vancouver. The process has been slow. Listening isn't necessarily easy in Vancouver. It rains. Not a gentle convalescing rain, but a vengeful rain that can soak you in seconds. As they say about Vancouver, if it's not raining, it's about to rain. When it's about to rain it can be foggy or very cloudy—not good listening weather.

Deep in his bed, Jan has become aware that the echoes of the train horns don't always perform as expected. There's the normal echo—a police siren passing you will immediately go lower by at least a semitone—what's known as the Doppler effect. But Jan begins to notice an unusual echo, that some train horns go up a tone instead. Trying to understand, Jan strains to listen. Which trains are approaching? Which are receding? Jan tries to judge the differing lengths of their calls and the reciprocal echoes. The process is frustrated by the sudden onset of local traffic sounds.

Why do some echoes go up rather than down? After weeks of listening, Jan conjectures that at a certain moment, the train receding on the opposite shore of the inlet to Vancouver pumps its horn. The sound is reflected back across the water and deflected by the mountains on his side of the inlet. The echo is thus nearer than the original emitted, a tone higher.

Jan remembers years previously flying to England and waking up the next day in a Yorkshire village on a Sunday morning to a symphony of clarion bells from churches calling folk to service. The churches hidden in the gullies of the Pennines created a rapturous landscape of a sonic surround.

The concept of a sonic landscape was revived for Vancouver's Expo in 1986. Tugboats were marshaled to sound their horns at intervals across the harbour. But R. Murray Schafer, the distinguished Canadian composer, did it best when he demanded that the true cognoscenti rise at dawn with their thermos of choice at Banff to witness a phalanx of trombones raising and lowering their slides like so many prehistoric pachyderms around the lake to greet the dawn.

Showering has always been a time for review. Back in the shower two decades earlier, Jan reviews his day. The morning will be spent in the CBC studio finishing off a recording of Ravel's *Le tombeau de Couperin*. The afternoon is reserved for a quartet rehearsal for a concert later in the week. Then, tonight, *Madama Butterfly*, the wrap-up of the opera season. There's always a party on stage afterwards. Jan knows he won't stay; early tomorrow there's a rehearsal right across the city for Monteverdi's *Vespers*. Did anyone remember to book a hotel for that quartet concert in Vernon? It's too far to come home afterwards, especially if there's a reception. Jan groans, drying himself as the first train horn of the day—*Scheherazade*—remains stubbornly in his ear, spinning her tales endlessly up the Burrard Inlet: 'Now I will tell you a story...'

INTERLUDE: THE AIRPORT

The Quartet is on tour. It seems that, as usual, its managers have planned this with the aid of a pinball machine. 'Kapow!'—you fly to the East Coast. 'Kapow!'—you ricochet to the Midwest. 'Kapow!' to Miami. 'Kapow!' to Juneau and finally dribble to LA and thence home. Jan worries every inch of the way. He has figured out that a lost flight could cause the whole enterprise to collapse. He takes on the responsibility of making sure his colleagues are in the hotel lobby with or without breakfast, bill paid, ready to take the airport limousine two hours ahead of the flight. Unfortunately for Jan, a musician's sense of timing is built into his DNA. Two hours ahead of the flight means setting the alarm. (There was a big reception after the concert the previous night.)

After a shower and confused packing, Jan arrives in the lobby to look for the courtesy cup of coffee and, joining the now long line to pay the bill, finds that he is not the last of the Quartet to arrive. Jan is beside himself. The limousine outside is filling up and scheduled to leave. The next one is in half an hour. Jan looks at his watch. Here comes Normsk. 'Morning, Janski!' Relief. Oh God, Normsk has to pay his bill. Luck of the Irish; a pretty girl opens up a counter, Normsk pays his bill and all four men get into the limousine. (Neither Normsk nor Jan can recollect when their names became Russianized but possibly it became fashionable when Stokowski with his fraudulent accent came to town—ordinary Anglo-Saxon names had 'ski' added. When Stokowski left town, Normski and Janski became merely Normsk and Jansk.)

The limousine takes a circuitous route to the airport, picking up people from important hotels around the city centre. At each stop, the driver unaccountably disappears inside the hotel. 'Probably getting a free breakfast at each place,' Fred suggests to the bus at large. Fred is a large man, who with his violin and suitcase, spills out into the aisle. Phil, smoking a pipe, looks out of the window. The bus gets on its way and after what seems to Jan an interminable journey, arrives at the airport. The Quartet checks in. Jan looks at his watch. 'We have half an hour,' he says.

Normsk leaves his violin case on the ground and disappears. The case lies on the concourse. Passengers avoid it by stepping over it. As cellist, Jan gets to pre-board because an extra seat has been bought for the cello. Jan is eyed with disapproval, his instrument strapped in as parents with young families brush by. Then the rest of the manifest gets in. Jan checks—there's Fred, there's Phil. Where's Normsk? Where the hell is Normsk?

'They were calling, "Norman Nelson, please come to the departure gate,"' Fred says cheerfully, 'as we got in. His violin was still where he left it.' A quiet time descends on the plane after passengers have forced belongings into upper racks or under seats and have belted themselves in. As they finger flight magazines, some late arrival hurls himself down the aisle, sweating, eyes bulging, trying to control excess cabin luggage. Behind him comes Normsk, blue eyes staring into the blue yonder, clutching violin in front of him.

'I had breakfast,' he explains, 'had to wait for the second cup of coffee. Excuse me ... window seat.'

ONE

Arlequin

Now that Jan is in his seventies himself, he likes to say that it is a long and perilous adventure that a student embarks upon from the first bowed open string to Dvořák's Cello Concerto. The stations on the way don't alter much—scales and arpeggios still lurk, there are as many studies out there as stars in the Milky Way. There are landmark repertoires: Bach's First Prelude, Breval's Sonata, Lalo's Concerto, Popper's 'Elfentanz'. 'Did you get to play Suzuki Book Ten? Did you play Kiwanis when you were a boy?' a student asks.

'It wasn't quite like that when I was a boy,' Jan replies. 'What are you studying in History at school?'

'The Second World War.'

'Has your teacher told you that "walls have ears"?'

'What do you mean?'

* 1 9 4 2 *

Down London's Baker Street, Jan and his mother, Elf, pick their way around shards of glass and pieces of masonry on their way to Jan's cello lesson. As they pass Madame Tussaud's, Jan notices that a landmark building has disappeared; the skyline beyond Marylebone Road looks different. Instead of the building, there's a gap through which Jan can see a cluster of barrage balloons like giant ears, straining on their ropes.

He walks with his mother in silence. London is often quiet after a bombing. Petrol is rationed and there is little traffic apart from the double-decker buses. They always catch the 6 a.m. workers' bus from home—the village of Radnage—to High Wycombe. Jan sits with Elf and looks out the window. If his father, Colin, takes him, they sit upstairs where smoking is allowed; the fumes of Woodbines always make Jan's eyes smart. He follows Elf out of the bus and onto the platform, past the poster of a ship sinking under the words 'Walls Have Ears', past the old red machine on the railway platform that reminds Jan of a tomb standing in mute testimony to those golden days of pre-war Rowntrees Chocolate Bar sixpence, then into the 7:15 train from High Wycombe to Marylebone: 'Please shew your ticket'.

Then they arrive in London and search for breakfast. Jan always makes a game of seeing which café in the district cooks the best dried [powdered] egg. Lyons Corner House is the preferred eatery with their scrambled egg on toast. Once the cashier is paid, Elf and Jan continue on the journey, passing the Royal Academy of Music and turning down Nottingham Place.

Now after Baker Street's gaps and shards of glass, this street is untouched—the same dreary row of townhouses, except the metal railings which used to guide you to their black front doors have been removed to be turned into guns. Jan knocks on 34—the London Cello School.

It's a typical London house—built around a stairway. Jan and Elf take seats in the waiting room, which resembles a doctor's surgery. The narrow hallway reaches well into the back, where somewhere Jan imagines Herbert Walenn—head of the school, renowned cello teacher, who's taught at the Royal Academy—sitting in majestic isolation, smoking cigars at a baize table. He has a dotty sister with dyed red hair who lives below stairs. Jan waits to see if today she'll emerge as she does periodically, cackling and clutching a teapot.

Jan peers past the large grandfather clock at the foot of the stairs to where the hall divides—either to the back, or up and up and up, up the landings to the skylight at the top, covered in grimy green moss. It always seems to be raining up there. The farther up a London house you go, the more private it becomes. Jan doesn't remember ever getting beyond the second floor, which is given over to the recital room. He remembers today is recital day just as the clock chimes the quarter hour in minor sixths, a most depressing sound that ushers him into the large front room where Jan's teacher, Alison Dalrymple, known to everyone, except herself, as Dilly Dally, is in residence. Jan studies the huge oil painting of an airman, his plane in flight behind him, that hangs on her wall, then the shelves of cello music low to the floor and albums of 78s featuring Casals's 1939 recording of the Bach suites.

Sometime past his sixth birthday, Jan happened to meet Dilly Dally, then in her seventies. She'd taught the cello to everybody, including John Barbirolli and Jan's father. Her indomitable spirit cowed everyone. She cruised through the Blitz on a cup of tea and a sandwich, never dropping a lesson from her schedule. 'And when is this little chap going to learn the cello, eh?' she said, her wattles shaking. Dilly Dally's character never accommodated opposition; Jan's fate was sealed.

The cello is balanced diagonally from the floor, its scroll lying against the seat of the chair Jan is about to sit on. There is only one instrument; Jan has never actually seen Dilly Dally with a cello in her hand.

(Dilly Dally had a cello once. Colin told Jan he remembered her leaving it in the same diagonal position against a chair. Colin as a teenager had knocked it over, damaging the edging. Dilly Dally made him take it over to Hills' to be fixed. When Colin went to collect it, Paul Hill said to him, 'Now, be sure to tell your teacher *never* to leave a cello like that; always place it with its ribs on the floor with the spike in.')

'Take your coat off, it's not too cold in here, is it?' she says, still standing with her coat on. She points to the music. 'Now, let's hear E-flat.'

After his lesson, Jan climbs the stairs and enters the recital room, which contains a modest dais with a grand piano behind it and open racks on two walls on which hang cellos of various sizes and colours.

Jan, because of the difficulties of transportation, never brings his own cello to his lesson. Today Mr Walenn picks out a suitably sized cello for Jan and tunes it. The cello is strung with gut. Mr Walenn mumbles in Jan's ear, 'Do you play on the C string?' Jan shakes his head. Actually, he doesn't know and, taken by surprise, hasn't the time to figure it out. There's a war on, gut is precious and all the cellos around the room are kept with strings well below pitch to save them. No need to tune an unused string!

Three woman cello teachers, including Dilly Dally, hover at the back of the room. They work in mild rivalry to one another. The dreaded student recital has hardly changed in format or content in generations. It is the opportunity to feel out the competition. Jan nervously awaits his turn, listening to the same warhorses that keep showing up, no matter which decade. This is hardly surprising; the cello repertoire isn't that huge. He waits through a Beethoven sonata, a few movements from the Bach suites, a concerto movement by Boccherini, then David Popper's 'Gavotte'—as famous a piece as Saint-Saëns's 'The Swan'—preferred today over Fauré's 'Elégie', which is often played less, as its musical graces will only be appreciated by the more mature musician.

Among the crowd of cellists who wrote music for cello, David Popper is the uncrowned king of composers. He wrote a lot of stuff, much of it difficult; while his 'Gavotte' will be played by any kid who sticks at playing the cello through his high school years, 'Elfentanz' will be programmed only by a very confident professional soloist. Photographs show Popper with piercing dark eyes under a thatch of hair. He must have been a vital personality; like Strauss, he was married to an opera singer, who probably brought elements of the melodramatic as well as the lyrical to their marriage.

Oh no, not this again, thinks Jan, wiggling in his chair, anxiously fingering Popper's 'Arlequin' on his leg while he listens to another student perform it. There's not a recital at the London Cello School that doesn't include at least one, if not two or three performances of 'Arlequin'. It's finally Jan's turn; he is the third to listen to the piano's chattering introduction. He then moves purposefully up the fingerboard to the high B, repeating this several times before—gulp—the high C. The stretch for the fingers playing the cello is invariably larger than the hand that plays it. The passagework abounds with inconveniences. The higher reaches on the cello are dangerous territory; the leaps to the thumb position at the southern end of the fingerboard always carry a degree of uncertainty. The risk factor is low today and Jan negotiates the jumps without a wince. The melody is varied when it returns at the end into quick turns of five notes, like pygmy hippopotami.

So close to the end, a moment's inattention finds Jan's hand playing the notes in the wrong order. Embarrassed, he gives a perfunctory bow, forgets to acknowledge the pianist and flees the platform.

Jan's ordeal is not over; he has to take part in a cello trio two items farther down on the program. A few weeks previously, Dilly Dally summoned two other youngsters into Jan's lesson and produced a manuscript arrangement of 'Barbara Allen'. Jan was given the bass line. The children played it through and Jan felt a tingle of pleasure, entranced. He had no idea that three cellos together could sound so beautiful.

The recital is over. Bridge rolls with cress are served, inevitable as the 'Arlequin'. Dilly Dally claps her hands—somebody terribly important has arrived and all the kids have to play again, 'So don't eat too much so that you forget your music.' Such is the power of suggestion that Jan does and leaves for home in tears of humiliation.

Outside once again, Jan reflects that if there hadn't been a recital, he would have been out of the cello school by midmorning and he and Elf could have taken in a news flick before heading home. There are several news cinemas close by. The game is to find the program with the most cartoons and the least news. The program takes an hour; you just walk out where you walked in. To quote Danny Kaye, 'This is a movie that begins in the middle for those who came in the middle!'

The train home always seems the slow one, stopping at stations where nobody gets in and nobody gets out. It's important to leave London before the light fades; the bombing will continue at nightfall. Jan looks out his window into the darkening afternoon and listens to the warning sirens sounding early, the minor thirds rising and falling chromatically and striking a note of fear. On the 'All Clear' the thirds hold steady—then the sirens are turned off, moaning down the chromatic scale, getting ever lower and quieter. Above the clack of the train, Jan strains to hear the last dying note.

∗ ∗ ∗

In 1940, Jan's family evacuated from London to the village of Radnage (Saxon: Red Oak) in Buckinghamshire, the Thames Valley, to escape the Blitz. Jan's first impression of Radnage is of the Higgins children, all seven of them, sitting on the curb, watching them arrive. Later, Jan plays army games with the Higgins family, '8th Army' scrawled on an elastoplast on his sleeve. He brings his troops up to a ravine. 'We have to pee in it so the soldiers can swim across.' Dutifully, each boy lifts the leg of his short pants and pees. 'That's a funny one,' observes the worldly Shirley Higgins. Quickly, Jan drops his pants leg and finds another boy peeing on his ankles.

(In thirty years, Jan will undergo a vasectomy:

'I see,' says the Jewish doctor, 'that you are circumcised, but you are not a Jew. How come?'

Jan tries to marshal his thoughts. 'Well,' he begins by way of explanation, 'I was a wartime child.'

'Oh,' interrupts the doctor. 'We'll fight 'em in the trenches and on the landing fields …' Jan, supine, feels he isn't in much of a position for a witty response.)

Jan and his parents, Colin and Elf, take the only room available, a large one above the saloon and public bar at the Crown. It has no plumbing so eating becomes an extended picnic, and Colin takes the chamber pot—full to the brim—downstairs and empties it each morning. Rodney, Jan's cousin, moves with his parents, Isolda and Frank, behind a

Chiltern hill into Wellground, a valley which has resisted the passage of time, near a village called Ibstone. Bar and Guv, Jan's paternal grandparents, also settle in this area.

Jan's entire family is connected to music. The Griller Quartet is making a name for itself across Europe and Colin is its cellist. Jan plays outside, sitting on the bench that Guv has built around the cherry tree. Tiny red spiders run around it while through the back door comes Colin's voice describing all the munitions trains he's seen on his quartet's recent tour to the Midlands. Rodney's father, Frank, is a violinist about town, working at Frascarti's Restaurant. Both dads are often away playing in the Royal Air Force (RAF) Central Band. Both moms are singers, Isolda is a pianist and Elf has studied violin at the Royal Academy.

And then there is Jan's grandfather, Guv. A former member of London's theatre world, Guv has become a peripatetic organist for several Norman churches in the villages hard by. Every Sunday he cuts a commanding figure on his bicycle—beret, black bow tie, jacket and pin-striped trousers gathered at the ankles with bicycle clips. The church organs he plays are modest. They have to be hand-pumped and Jan is sometimes pressed into service wearing a surplice and sharing the bench with Guv, with strict instructions to work the bellows so that the wire in the 'thermometer' slot never falls to less than halfway. Jan anxiously keeps his eye on the slot for fear of the organ making the sound of a pig being turned to bacon. Coming down from the organ loft at the end of the service, Guv, a cheerful disbeliever, greets the vicar, 'That was a silly sermon you gave this morning.'

The family settles down to life in the country. From Jan's limited perspective it provides an idyllic boyhood, usually spent on a clunky bicycle riding the lanes, which have no traffic. Part of the early war effort was to turn all the signposts around to confuse the enemy, should they invade. Jan knows the network of lanes: Radnage 2 miles (which has been turned from midday to 12:15), Stokenchurch 4, Ibstone 7, High Wycombe 8, West Wycombe 7.

At the intersection near the pub, a wooden cart, along with shafts for a horse, has been placed near the hedge. This is to be pulled out to block the junction if enemy tanks threaten. Jan, along with the village children, plays cowboys on this. As the theatre of war escalates, bits fall off the cart. Grass, then brambles begin to grow through the shafts. A wheel goes missing. Colin, when he performs for Churchill and Stalin and Truman as a member of the RAF Central Band for the Potsdam Conference at the end of the war, picks up a detailed German map of Buckinghamshire; incredulously, the intersection is clear for the invader to assess his next move, though he wouldn't have known about the cart.

The next village, Stokenchurch (Saxon: just guess) is where Elf rides her bicycle—shopping bag astride each handlebar—to buy supplies. Mr Anstead, the grocer, carefully cuts out the coupons of the family's ration books and puts the sugar, butter, meat, etc. into small blue bags. (The colour blue, Jan will find out later, is an insect deterrent.)

Radnage is a modest little Buckinghamshire village but it has its moments of reflected glory, not the least because of its proximity to West Wycombe whose prominent church stands over the caves built by Sir Francis Dashwood for his Hellfire Club in the eighteenth century. Through the Second World War, various luminaries pass through—Arnold Van Wyk, the South African composer ('Jan Hampton lives in Radnage, has his nose tied in a badnage') and Howard Ferguson, who, running a stick against Jan's bicycle spokes, observes that it sounds like Alban Berg. Stanley Holloway, noted entertainer, opens the village fair and tries to catch the greased pig. He must be very well off, as he wears two-toned shoes. Roy Boulting of the Boulting Brothers—cameramen for Ealing Film Studios—lives in the village when he isn't making the movies *Whisky Galore!* and *Passport to Pimlico.*

In the high summer of 1941, Jan is sent over to Ibstone to stay with his cousin Rodney, in the valley of Wellground where history stopped five hundred years previously. The asphalt of the road turns to gravel as it descends—punctuated with horse or cow droppings—into the valley. There, it is flanked by fields and leads to the squire's home. (Rodney, with an obeisant sign, calls it in undertones, 'The Parkers'.) The valley is surrounded by beech woods resonant with the sound of doves and cuckoos.

The reason for the move, it turns out, is the birth of Jan's brother, Andy. Jan spends a happy summer holiday with his grandparents. Guv harvests shallots on his hillside garden and Rodney tries to avoid learning Vivaldi's A Minor Violin Concerto. Rodney practises the violin in the garden, sticking his music in the branches of a tree and going at it. Rodney, being three years older than Jan, is always so much better at everything. He can run faster, throw farther, eat a boiled egg faster and fart louder than Jan. The summer is hot. They play French cricket and throw dried horse dung at one another.

Portrait: Guv

'C'mon, Old Iron, let's go to the shed,' says Guv, and Jan follows him out of the cottage to Guv's workshop in the back. It smells of varnish. On the windowsills are bottles filled with the amber sticky stuff. A long bench runs along the windows with a vise at each end. Upon it lies every conceivable tool for woodworking. Those too big for the bench hang from hooks on the wall.

Jan stands among the shavings and watches Guv fashion wide bamboo pieces into shoehorns, appropriate Christmas gifts for the war years. Jan sometimes thinks Guv comes here to escape the wireless with its regular newscasts blaring in the sitting room; they shut the door earlier on Vera Lynn, the Forces' sweetheart, singing 'We'll meet again, don't know where, don't know when,' for the umpteenth time. Dislike of Vera Lynn's voice is the one thing Guv and Elf see eye to eye on. (Years later, Dame Vera Lynn will visit Vancouver to perform a concert with the CBC, Jan and Phil playing in the orchestra. The performance will be delayed because of technical failure. Jan is surprised at Dame Vera's inability to deal with the situation. She stands about, mute. Phil: 'Funny thing, my mother couldn't stand her voice.' Jan: 'Neither could mine.')

Guv takes a bamboo shaft from the vise. 'There are three great composers, Old Iron,' Guv pronounces, 'Bach, Wagner and Glazunov. Bach is the greatest of all. Hand me that sandpaper. No, the fine sheet.' Jan shuffles through the shavings. 'I remember the Bach choir at the Albert Hall singing the B Minor Mass,' Guv resumes. 'It begins with a grand B minor chord with the choir. No introduction. The singers have to find their note from the orchestra tuning up. When that conductor came in, he got the strings to play the chord first.' Guv, a Londoner down to his toes, pauses. 'Old Iron, there's a right and a wrong way of doing everything.'

Jan wonders what a B Minor Mass is, kicks at the shavings, listens to 'The White Cliffs of Dover' through the open window.

INTERLUDE: SNOW

The rehearsal at Phil's house begins late. Most Quartet rehearsals begin late. Each colleague receives a tough cup of coffee prepared by Phil or Margarita and before they leave at the end of the morning, drinks a pint of bitter. Phil is into beer-making and whatever yeast is leftover in the present batch makes for pungent farts driving home. Phil is old world European, his father was the head chef at the Piccadilly Hotel, and his mother collected and sold antiques. Of Swiss extraction, Phil has trouble with his Rs. He also takes after his father and is an excellent cook; the house smells of garlic and food sautéed in butter. Walking into Phil's house is like walking into the past—floral china, antique corkscrews, rooms crammed with antique coffee tables, unexplained drawings on the walls. Invariably, Margarita's coffee or Phil's beer is anchored down with an unusual cheese, or a newly discovered salami with homemade bread.

This morning begins with snow. Vancouver winters rarely deliver snow, maybe one weekend. It usually arrives as temperatures are rising and rain is to follow. However little snow falls, it is wet and slippery and causes immediate chaos. Fred, who has the farthest to drive and the steepest slope to negotiate, is the first to arrive. His wife is from Edmonton; Fred knows how to drive in snow. Fred is into his second cup of coffee before Jan arrives. Fred makes a point of getting his violin out and appearing to practise as Jan enters the front door.

'You're late,' Fred crows.

'Well, I had to dig out the drive. How come you made it?'

'Oh, I took Chance for a walk.' (Chance is Fred's highly strung Irish setter, the only creature in the world to ignore Fred's admonishments. Chance has the incurable habit of leaning into his walking companions, pushing them off the sidewalk into the ditch.)

'After I took Chance in, I just drove the car down the hill, mostly sideways, leaning on the horn to warn the school kids out of the way.'

A little while later, Normsk arrives.

'You're late,' Fred cries. 'What are we rehearsing today?'

'Debussy. Sorry, I had to take the kids to school.'

'I remember,' says Phil, handing Normsk a mug of coffee, 'there was a terrible snowstorm when I was in the City of Birmingham Orchestra. Snowed all day. There was a concert scheduled that night. Of course, all the orchestra figured there couldn't possibly be an audience, so everybody stayed at home. Except for one elderly viola player who took the bus as far as he could and walked the rest. He found the theatre in darkness so turned around to go home. He never made it. Had a heart attack and died. Poor sod. Such a sense of duty.'

'Okay. Debussy,' says Normsk. 'Can we begin at the 15/8 in the Scherzo?'

Playing pizzicato in five time creates a scurrying effect which, to Jan as he is playing, seems a musical description of the snowflakes blown against the window pane.

NN

Brahms Piano Quintet

* 1940 *

Jan is five, listening to Brahms's Quintet for the first time, sitting beside his mother. They have sneaked seats in the gods so that Jan can see the platform. To him the seats seem steeply raked. The familiar figure of his father playing the cello looks miniature. The Griller Quartet is playing a series of concerts for a festival in Bournemouth.

Sitting in the gloom of the hall, Jan remembers their arrival that afternoon, seeing the sea for the first time. There it was at the end of the road, glittering and blue. There it had to remain; the beach was barbed-wired and mined against possible invasion.

Jan doesn't quite understand the connection between the large lady playing the piano and Brahms's powerful melody, but she is a figure of considerable authority and her playing is very lively. The piano is played by Myra Hess, famous for organizing the lunchtime concerts throughout the war at the National Gallery in Trafalgar Square. She and her colleagues provide spiritual solace for a weary populace.

(When the fortunes of war turn, Jan will be taken to a few of them. No pictures then—they were spirited away before the Blitz. Jan remembers that newscast of men taking an oversized painting down into the underground, and wondering if it would have been safer leaving them on the walls. On each corner of the atrium, tall slender columns of marble will lead his eyes to the ornate ceiling. Since Jan can hardly see the musicians, he'll listen to them while looking at the top of these columns. It will seem to him that music occupies a rarified place, a recurring idea in his future life.)

But Jan is still five, listening to Brahms. During the slow movement, his attention begins to wander—the music doesn't seem to go anywhere. The sea seems so infinite—Jan imagines sailing on a boat forever. Pretty soon, he feels a gentle nudge in his ribs from his mother's elbow; back to Brahms.

✷ ✷ ✷

The Quintet is among a number of chamber works which, due to the constraints of wartime, Jan doesn't hear again until he plays them himself as a young adult. They are immediately familiar to him. As Jan acquires opportunities to perform, he recognizes quartets of Haydn, Mozart, Schubert and Beethoven. In his twenties, playing in the London Symphony Orchestra (LSO), Jan accompanies Dame Myra Hess, a figure of granite as soloist in Beethoven's 'Emperor' Concerto, and remembers her playing Brahms in Bournemouth in those far off days. She etched in his brain the opening melody played two octaves apart, her shoulders signalling the arrival of the pause.

The Piano Quintet is the jewel of Brahms's chamber music. Mindful of the irrevocability of going to print, Brahms took his time, honing his scores, making corrections, blue-pencilling in afterthoughts on dynamics after hearing private performances, invariably turning to his friends Clara Schumann and Joseph Joachim for their impressions. Despite his proverbial gruffness, Brahms might have been a wee bit insecure. The magnetism of his music, however it pulled for those who had any possible connection with his world, was considerably weakened by the advent of the twentieth century (Stravinsky and those boys); the battles between the Brahmsians and the Wagnerites has become the stuff of musical history books.

For the longest time, as he becomes reacquainted with Brahms, Jan doesn't really understand Brahms's music. His four symphonies are the staples of the orchestral repertoire. They are challenging to play and Jan can never appraise the music without drowning in the intricacies of the passagework. Eventually he realizes that Brahms writes by the eighth note, seldom in cut time, and that some conductors think he is a latter-day Beethoven and take Brahms too fast to gain theatrical effect. After the tumultuous opening of the Piano Quintet, the slow movement that follows seems initially inadequate. Each measure begins with a snap rhythm ('Donald'), suggesting that the melody is merely one bar long, but with familiarity, Jan comes to realize that with Brahms's masterly guidance, the tune is capable of infinite expansion.

As a student in 1952, browsing through the Reid Library at Edinburgh University, Jan comes across a score of the Piano Quintet in which an adoring student has written under the opening theme of the slow movement, 'Donald Francis Tovey'.

Donald Francis Tovey, the previous dean of the Music Department at

Edinburgh, retains a ghostly presence; his personal library, with all its marginalia—every work in the Bach *Gesellschaft* has received annotations—is housed in the Reid Library. His disciple, Molly Grierson, teaches Jan harmony, as well as the tradition of playing Brahms at a leisurely pace. This is maintained and sometimes enhanced by visiting artists who have been taught by somebody who knew somebody else who knew Brahms. Tovey hobnobbed with the likes of Thibaud, Cortot and Casals, and his successor, Sidney Newman, valiantly, amidst tightening budgets, endeavours to maintain these performing traditions.

At a student Christmas party, Sidney describes his interview when applying for a vacancy. Tovey was in the bath. 'Come in. Sit there,' said Tovey, motioning to the toilet. Thus it came to pass. Sidney says that Tovey had two party tricks. He could climb over and under the width of the piano without touching the ground, as if being keelhauled, and he could lie on top of the piano facing down to the keyboard and play a Bach fugue. Tovey was a large man in every sense. Jan never had the opportunity to meet him, but Tovey's potent observations on music will continue to be an influence.

Despite its commanding presence, the Brahms Piano Quintet does not suffer overexposure. For one, the piano part is difficult; for another, there are ensemble, tempo and balance problems that are unlikely to be solved in one rehearsal. Thus, down the years whenever a distinguished pianist passes by and says, 'I'd love to play with you boys,' the Quartet always groans inwardly because the follow-up is inevitably, 'I'd love to play the Schumann.' It's always the Schumann. The Schumann is a joyful piece but the Finale always requires much bloodletting by the strings.

There is a famous portrait, much-reproduced, of Brahms playing the piano, cigar in mouth. For proprietary reasons, the artist has perhaps omitted the glass of brandy on the piano. The picture suggests Brahms entertaining his hosts after dinner. The mood is of repletion, satiation. Relaxed, Brahms is prepared to make his musical points with rubato. A wiser Jan knows that this is the mood of the Quintet's slow movement—a wonderfully sustained piece of music-making that reaches an emotional fulfillment far beyond the musical cell that fuels it. The very first note is a challenge—the cellist, Jan, has to pluck in sync with the pianist whose antennae are not necessarily attuned to ensemble playing. Colin told Jan that he always left it out.

Years after his student days and still plucking away, Jan opens the

Scherzo with a foreboding low pitch, very softly. Judgment for the appropriate tempo is critical because the movement ends in imitative rhythms like machine-gun fire, straining at the musicians' tendons and nerve ends. At a CBC studio recording, Jan begins, then stops after two bars, says he is sorry, and restarts at a slightly faster tempo. It is soft enough but not foreboding enough evidently for the producer to notice in his control box. So the Brahms Piano Quintet is thus broadcast, with Jan's apologies, unspliced, across the nation.

* * *

Back in Bournemouth, Jan watches and listens to his father in the Griller with Myra Hess playing furiously towards the Quintet's end. He knows it will be over soon, and he'll walk outside with the final notes still in his head and watch the sea going on without measure and, years later, during his father's final days, Jan will be surprised by one of the last comments on music by Colin, a man who had revered Bach and Beethoven through his life. 'You know, son, in the end I think it is Brahms who is the greatest of them all.'

INTERLUDE: VICTOR DE SABATA

'The most terrifying conductor I knew,' says Normsk, 'was Victor de Sabata. His reputation arrived ahead of time when he returned to concertizing in England after the war. Somebody told me that if he looks at you, never take your eyes off him. The BBC Symphony was set up in Walthamstow Town Hall facing the stage, their backs to the front door. The rehearsal began at 2 p.m. Just for once, everybody was in their seat ten minutes ahead of time. At two o'clock, a miraculous silence descended. The door opened at the back of the hall; everybody kept staring ahead. We heard these footsteps get closer and louder like the executioner. He spent a long time tuning the orchestra, getting the basses tuned first and then everybody took the A from the basses. Then he began rehearsing. Pretty soon he began to look around the orchestra and his eyes settled on the first violins. Then his burning eyes settled on me! I remembered what I'd been told, so I fixed my eyes on him. His eyes didn't flicker; he was demanding passionate playing. I didn't take my eyes off him. I played passionately—any old notes.'

'Sounds familiar,' Fred says into his music stand.

THREE

Pacific 231

'This is an old-fashioned record player,' says Jan to William, his youngest student. 'You put on this vinyl LP and press this lever.' Magically, the arm picks itself up, moves to the edge of the now revolving record, and gently lowers the needle to the beginning of the track. 'When it's crossed the record, the arm will lift itself up and return to its cradle and the record will slow to a halt.' ('Show me …').

'There's a slightly bigger needle on the other side. That one plays the old 78s, the records I used to play when I was your age.'

William's fingers dart for the levers. Reactivated, the arm lowers onto the record, turning Isolde's 'Liebestod' into chipmunk chirps.

* 1943 *

The suitcase-type gramophone that Jan loves is a result of a lucky day early in his parents' marriage. Elf tells a story about the time when she and Colin were first married and they had absolutely no money. Colin opened his cello case and found a crisp five-pound note. Found money was silly money. Jan assumes it went to purchase the gramophone. Daily, he opens the lid, unclips the handle by the turntable and inserts it into the side of the case where he winds it up. In the corner is a box of steel needles.

Along with the gramophone came a mixed bag of 78s, small and large. The young couple must have bought them at Foyles second-hand bookshop. There is Mozart's G Minor Symphony, the overture to *Idomeneo*, plus a selection of music hall records, including a very plummy English, 'I'm hard-hearted Hannah, the vamp from Savannah.' Jan, beginning a voyage of discovery, gives them all equal time and does so without prejudice, but he particularly prefers the sound of metal mixed with the steam from Arthur Honegger's *Pacific 231*, to the train from his soundtrack of the movie *Dumbo* ('I think I can, I think I can …').

Unlike Disney's cute creation, Pacific 231, Honegger's inspiration, is a monster engine of 300 tons. The numbers 2-3-1 refer to the axle configuration that makes this steam locomotive distinct from other engines in the Pacific Class. Before the advent of diesel, these engines were used around the world.

Jan puts his ear to the gramophone lid and listens carefully as the train begins its journey from slow snuffling to faster thumping to clanking and grinding to cogs and pistons whirling as the train reaches its optimum speed, the landscape hurtling away behind it. Jan wildly imagines the train racing through the Thames Valley, the sheep-flecked Chiltern Hills giving way at the moment of deceleration to London's urban sprawl. He waits for this moment, and listens for the motif that earlier presaged increasing speed now slowing the train toward its destination. Multiple rhythms suggest the numerous points the train traverses as railway lines join the queue for a platform at Marylebone Station. The train shudders past ugly row houses with their tiny, charmless gardens, each with its Anderson bomb shelter.

Pacific 231 is a landmark piece. It is not the cinder-covered carriage without corridors that takes Jan to his cello lesson each week, nor is it the overstuffed compartment that Brahms missed when travelling to Clara's funeral. Nor is it the buffet carriage where Berlioz enjoyed a repast on the *Chemin de Fer*, his trunks in the luggage van heavy with the orchestral parts of the *Symphonie fantastique* awaiting a luckless porter. Nor is it the Royal Scot on its journey from London to Edinburgh, the restaurant car trying to emulate French cuisine by including a fish course after the brown Windsor soup.

It is subtitled a 'symphonic movement'—a study in contrapuntal rhythms and blocks of sound that suggest the gathering of powerful forces. Urban sounds inevitably enter the musical vocabulary—sirens, factory whistles and automobile horns share the notoriety of *Pacific 231*. Honegger loved machines, and probably contributed generously to the sonic background of Paris when driving his red Bugatti. In occupied Paris, Honegger taught, wrote critical articles and composed in his overcoat in unheated studios. His musical language, frequently tough, bears witness to wartime France; the music of those years exposes moments of sadness, danger and vulnerability. *Pacific 231* sets out on a track to take Jan at his gramophone into the world of serious twentieth-century music.

* * *

It seems that Jan's boyhood is spent between his gramophone and his bicycle, but that discounts the radio, a very powerful influence over a population threatened. There is the news of course and the horrors of war can be diluted by the comedy of *It's That Man Again* (*ITMA*) with England's favourite humorist, Tommy Handley. It's the era of the big band; records of Artie Shaw, Glenn Miller and Benny Goodman have invaded England more successfully than the Nazis. Protecting the home front are Vera Lynn, Joe Loss, George Formby, Gracie Fields, Noël Coward and many others more courageous.

Years later, Jan will speculate that the popular music of one's childhood defines who one is—play a Joe Loss record and you're back in short pants. Jan's grandfather harrumphs quite a bit about Jan's idol, Danny Kaye. Guv, whose own idols are Wagner and Bach, nevertheless has been chorus master of *Chu Chin Chow*, the hit of the First World War, as *Oklahoma* would be after the Second. Guv is a wonderful pianist; he accompanies various local luminaries at village concerts during the Second World War. 'That man doesn't know how to swing,' a starlet says of Guv, stumping off after a concert.

Colin, who during the First World War was a similar age to Jan during the Second, remembers that musical entertainment was frivolous—it morphed into the flappers of the Jazz Age—in contrast to the seriousness of music during the Second World War. Culture is at stake. The most profiled musicians in England are scooped up and placed into the RAF Central Band. Wing Commander O'Donnell, its conductor, suddenly is directing an orchestra the calibre of the future Philharmonia.

(Stories abound: Denis Matthews, a prominent piano soloist also in the band is once apprehended by the wing commander.

'Oh, Matthews, could Beethoven's 'Emperor' Concerto for piano and brass band be reorchestrated so you can play it with us?'

'Yes sir.' A pause. 'You know, sir, I do believe that Beethoven did an orchestration himself.'

'Excellent, Matthews, see to it.')

* * *

Each morning as Jan sleeps, Colin leaves the house at 5 a.m. to rehearse with the Central Band in Denham. The members of the Griller Quartet are allowed considerable autonomy and, playing concerts as a quartet dressed in RAF uniforms, they become as iconic in their classical way as

Tommy Handley is in his comedic role. Sidney Griller, as leader of the group, is elevated to a sergeant.

'You boys are wonderful,' exclaims an elderly lady after a concert. 'Bombing Berlin one night and playing Beethoven the next.'

However heroic the evenings, the 5 a.m. bus looms large for Colin, even after the family moves out of their room at the Crown. Before moving comes the only dramatic moment of the war for Radnage. There is an air raid warning—at the sound of sirens everyone runs downstairs and sits under the billiards table. A single bomb drops in a field nearby. Little does anyone know that Bomber Command, the nerve centre for all the aerial missions over Europe, is just seven miles away near High Wycombe.

The family moves into a portioned flint cottage rented out by Miss Bowden. Miss Bowden is a diminutive octogenarian with a face like a well-stored crabapple. She cuts her tiny lawn at the front steps with a pair of scissors. The house has no plumbing. Bar, a nurse, inspects the offerings of the outhouse and pronounces one or other medications for the evacuee. She empties the lavatory bucket weekly, filling a trench that snakes up to the back of the garden. Late in the war, Bar falls over the lavatory bucket and into its contents. Shortly after that, the house gets plumbing. (Besides, the well from which they were drawing their water became full of slugs.)

The house rejoices in two things—an anthracite stove which heats the whole house; if you open its doors, you can toast bread on a fork; and an AGA cooker, Bar's pride and joy, on which she heats kettles for hot water bottles and mash for the chickens out in the yard. Their eggs are kept under isinglass in a large bowl in the cupboard under the stairs. There is no refrigerator. Perishable food is kept in a perforated metal cupboard outside the front door where a breeze might keep it cool.

Milk is delivered every day—real milk with half a cup of cream rising to the top. Failure to bring in the bottle promptly loses the cream to the birds that can peck off the cardboard seals. Bar makes scones out of sour milk. Food is not plentiful, but every Sunday the local farmer delivers to the door a cornucopia of vegetables—still earthy carrots, Brussels sprouts, cabbage, broccoli and potatoes. From time to time there are treats. Government decrees that anyone who can keep pigs can raise three and keep one. Less choice cuts of the pig world circulate the village; Elf makes pig's brawn. One time, some lemons appear in the store. Bar hogs the family rations of butter and sugar for a month and with the eggs makes lemon curd. This she jars, then drops the lot—a tragedy worse than Dunkirk. She puts it all through a fine sieve and nobody's innards are perforated.

Guv, whose hobby is carpentry, makes frames for the window to which blackout material is affixed. The windows aren't square and Guv curses a lot. After the job is done, he seeks solace in a pint of bitter, however watery, at the Crown. Through the war, through the blackout, people feel their way to the pub. Old Art presides in the saloon bar. Bent, gnarled and deaf, he is the village patrician. He sits in the corner. 'Oi, slit me dog's tongue.'

'Art. For God's sake! Why?'

'So 'e can lick his balls both sides.'

Cycling home from the pub one dark night, Guv is stopped by a policeman: 'Your bike light's shining too bright.' Guv gets a fine and a half-inch column in the newspaper—'Local Organist Apprehended'.

Spring in Radnage and it's whispered that something tremendous is about to happen—even Jan catches it on the wind. D-day arrives and soon Jan is caught up with the BBC news as the Allies advance across Europe. Then there is the excitement of VE day with American convoys throwing cans of bully beef into gardens and soldiers inflating condoms in lieu of balloons.

INTERLUDE: TOURING BC

The Quartet and their families gather every summer at Naramata on the shores of Okanagan Lake. They are housed, along with some of the adult students, at the Naramata Hotel, ramshackle huts that stand at the top of the road leading down to the village. Behind the huts is a substantial area of cherry trees, grass and grasshoppers. The rest of Okanagan's wildlife seems to live within the walls of the huts; the nocturnal slithers, scrabbling, buzzing and whining suggest a Darwinian succession. Each hut is divided into two apartments, for lack of a more modest term, each with a kitchenette. It is possible to speak down your basin and your voice sounds, sepulchrally, in your neighbour's basin. To a student practising for tomorrow morning's session: 'F-sharp. This is Beethoven speaking. F-shaarrp! The key is G major!'

Phil and Margarita don't stay in the hut. Phil has recently bought a small school bus and converted the interior to living quarters. His father-in-law panelled the walls and Phil has attached a number of his mother's antiques. He parks the bus among the cherry trees and draws up one of several available picnic tables. The musical schedule finishes at 3 p.m., and everyone heads for the beach. The sun is fierce, the Okanagan Lake cold. Refreshed, families barbecue outside their huts. Jugs of sangria are produced. Finally the Quartet children, tired of trying to catch grasshoppers, are put to bed. The sun fades and in the twilight large moths appear, eluding capture by the children who are also intent on eluding capture by their parents for bed. In the perfumed night the adults gather around Phil's bus and talk of cabbages and kings accompanied by a recording of a Hungarian band that Phil and eventually the whole neighbourhood come to love.

Phil's bus had done yeoman service before it fell into his hands. Sixteen years later, as Phil is driving up to Naramata late in the evening, the bus headlights go out every time he turns a corner. On the return trip, the stick shift comes away in his hands. A tow truck takes him in his crippled vehicle back to Penticton and dumps it into a works yard. Abandoned in his bus, Phil is miles from anywhere. Armed with some brandy, he goes to bed hungry to wait for the dawn.

FOUR

The Rite of Spring

'Was the radio invented when you were a boy?' asks Eujune, Jan's student.

'When I was a boy we listened to the radio a lot—there was no TV. I was crazy about the music of Stravinsky. I tried to listen to everything he'd written—he was still writing—and I read all about him. He liked cats. He had one called Sasha.'

Eujune looks at Jan blankly. 'Did Stravinsky come before or after Brahms?'

∗ 1946 ∗

Jan is banging out the fractured rhythms of the 'Sacrificial Dance' from *The Rite of Spring* on his bicycle handlebars, which may explain why he falls off his bike in front of a funeral procession. The driver of the hearse halts, and men in black suits and hats descend on Jan with concerned expressions, dust him down with their handkerchiefs, and send him on his way. Jan has acquired the grace to be embarrassed.

For Jan, *The Rite* is love at first listen. The unearthly sound of a single wind instrument ushers him into a world both ancient and new. He plays and replays the records endlessly. He loves the tortuous introduction with the gurgling of the bass clarinet somehow complimenting the straining opening bassoon. He stomps to the 'Dance of the Adolescents' that mirrors his own developing pubescence. He loves the sadness and emptiness of the world in the 'Mystic Circles', and responds to the ejaculatory rhythms of the 'Sacrificial Dance'.

Stravinsky becomes a superhero. Jan gets another present, a stack of 78 records called *Petroushka*. Though born thirty years too late, Jan is drawn into the golden age of Diaghilev, and Stravinsky's music never fails to excite him. With global interest in every premiere and his controversial declarations about music, Stravinsky is seldom out of the news.

∗ ∗ ∗

The Rite's pagan Russia is uncomfortable subject matter, involving the fear and superstition and violent rituals of primitive man. Stravinsky's jagged rhythms, couched in an uncompromising harmonic language, was unleashed on an unsuspecting audience on May 29, 1913. Within twenty bars, the music began to create disturbance in the theatre, developing into the most famous riot in musical history. Even during fiftieth anniversary celebrations of this event in 1963, audiences still left the hall.

The wit and intelligence of his music propelled Stravinsky to remain the foremost composer of his age until the last decade of his life. *The Rite* is required listening for any student interested in twentieth-century culture. In fact, that same student could read Stravinsky's diaries (even though his amanuensis, Robert Craft, has come in for some criticism for his perceived manipulative editing), as it is a veritable who's who in cultural events.

As a cellist in the LSO, Jan takes part in a complete recording of Stravinsky's *Firebird*, conducted by Pierre Monteux, who was the original conductor of *The Rite's* premiere, and who also conducted the LSO for the fiftieth anniversary of that premiere. As a conductor in the employ of the Diaghilev Ballet, he conducted premieres of *Petroushka*, Ravel's *Daphnis and Chloe* and Debussy's *Jeux*.

At a rehearsal of the Quartet, Normsk, who also played under Monteux, imitates the conductor by moistening his fingers to turn the pages of the score and murmuring, 'Comm ahne, comm ahne.' Normsk rosins his bow. 'Everyone loved Monteux,' he says. 'Doráti was another matter.'

Unlike Monteux, Antal Doráti was a Hungarian conductor with a short fuse. Normsk imitates Doráti's cry: 'Zat is not a 'uman sound.'

'But he did rehearse well,' says Jan.

'Sure,' says Normsk. 'It was the performances that fell apart. The worst was our first concert of an American tour—Carnegie Hall and televised. The second half of the concert was *The Rite*. To our horror, after the intermission, the stagehands had removed his music stand. He was going to conduct it from memory! It started out okay, but then somewhere in the middle, Doráti threw a curve.'

'Where exactly?' asks Fred.

'I don't know, we were all lost,' says Normsk. 'But we were coming up to the famous 11/4 bar and little Hughie Maguire, the concertmaster, jumped up and signalled the first of those thumps. By the fourth thump everybody was back on track, including the conductor.'

'After my time,' says Jan, 'but I do remember Eugene Goossens conducting it with the LSO. You know—he made his reputation originally conducting that piece.'

'Ah yes,' says Normsk. 'Sir Eugene slunk back into town after dirty pictures were found in his suitcase at customs.'

'Yes. Everybody was talking about it, and as Sir Eugene lifted his enormous baton, Gervase cried out, "Dirty pictures!"'

'People said the only good thing coming out of Gervase's mouth was when he stuck his clarinet in it.'

'Goossens took no notice. Such a sang-froid Englishman, he always sported a blazer and had a head as if sculpted of wax.'

'You remember,' Normsk continues, 'with his baton as long as a broomstick he changed all the beatings for the final "Sacrificial Dance": "Gentlemen, I beat this in 4/4." There he was, majestically beating a slow four while the orchestra frantically played um CHA CHA-cha cha cha, cha cha cha-um CHA cha.'

* * *

However complicated the rhythms of Stravinsky, there is something visceral about the music. The performer can cope with the fractured rhythms with relative ease because the metabolism of the music reflects our physical condition. Jan in middle age is no longer stomping to the 'Dance of the Adolescents', but his students are. Returning to *The Rite* after a lapse of many years, he finds that Stravinsky's harmonies have darkened and mellowed with age. After decades of listening to twentieth-century music, Jan finds that Stravinsky doesn't sound radical anymore. *The Rite* and 'Eroica' don't seem so far apart, which they aren't chronologically—110 years. Stravinsky's 11/4 bar and Beethoven's giant hemiolas seem curiously related.

Jan regrets that he didn't get to play under Stravinsky's direction but he did see him live. The British film star Dirk Bogarde had been invited to Hollywood to play the part of Liszt in the movie *Song Without End.* Jan accompanied his father to the boat train leaving Waterloo for the liner *Queen Elizabeth* at Portsmouth. Colin's seat was in the next carriage beyond Dirk Bogarde, who was posing in the carriage doorway, legs and arms outstretched and an army of photographers snapping away.

Unnoticed by any of them, a diminutive Stravinsky with a woman on each arm walked by. Colin had previously phoned Stravinsky in New York to enquire whether the Griller Quartet could commission a work, and had been turned down by Stravinsky. 'My dear, I am two years behind on my commissions.' Colin recollected that the *Queen Elizabeth* crossing had been rough. One stormy day, he came across Stravinsky at the gift shop. He helped him up the stairs.

'Mr Stravinsky, you won't remember me. I'm Colin Hampton ...'

'I most certainly do. You are cellist of the Griller. We met.'

The occasion had been a dinner, the first course of which had been herring. Nobody knew how to handle the bones. There was an embarrassed pause, broken by Stravinsky spitting out the bones and then everyone relaxed, spitting also.

Jan hopes to meet Stravinsky at a reception in the composer's honour after a concert with Robert Craft and the San Francisco Symphony. An elaborate Russian buffet has been prepared, which is to be preceded by a house concert that features, among other inappropriate items, a Schubert piano sonata and chamber music by Ralph Vaughan Williams. Perhaps the distinguished entourage got wind of the concert; they send their regrets at about the same moment they should be walking through the door. Jan sighs and settles into his seat.

There is another encounter. At last, Jan and Sue visit Venice. The city has figured large in the musical history books and Jan's anticipation intensifies as they drive towards the Veneto. Across the water, the skyline appears, so familiar from paintings by Canaletto and Turner.

As a gesture of homage, they take the vaporetto over to the cemetery at San Michele to visit Stravinsky's grave. The vaporetto follows the route of that day in 1971 when Stravinsky's body in a coffin bedecked with flowers was taken by gondola—with a flotilla of boats following it—to his last resting place. Stravinsky had close associations with Venice—*The Rake's Progress* was premiered there, as was *Monumentum Pro Gesualdo di Venosa, Canticum Sacrum* and *Threni*. While his ballet *Agon* was not premiered in Venice, its masterly blend of Renaissance processionals and atonal procedures seems to Jan to evoke the city.

Alighting from the vaporetto, Sue and Jan are confronted by necropolis sprawl—every inch of the island is taken with tombs and every grave has fresh flowers on it. How to find Stravinsky's. They wander about until they see a wrought-iron hand pointing the way. In a corner, they come across the austere slab saying, merely, *Igor Stravinsky.* It is flanked by his wife, Vera, and Sergei Diaghilev. A pair of ballet shoes lie on Diaghilev—a program from a recent performance of *Mavra* lies on Stravinsky.

Those who have passed on remain among us.

IS

INTERLUDE: LITTLE TITCH

After lunch, the Quartet returns to the studio to rehearse Stravinsky's *Three Pieces.* They open the music reluctantly. Its inclusion on the program is a token gesture to the twentieth century, though 1914 was not a particularly vintage year for chamber music. The work is almost the antithesis of the spirit of the string quartet. The first piece has the virtue of brevity—the Quartet scampers through it in less than thirty seconds.

'Well, there it is,' observes Normsk, quoting an oft-used phrase that members of the LSO used when visiting the washroom in intermission.

'There you are,' echoes Jan.

They turn to the next piece. This is a very different proposition—the music stops and starts, it changes speed, and involves tricky ensemble movements. The music supposedly describes the antics of Little Titch. At one point, Fred is supposed to hold his violin down like a cello to pluck a chord over four strings.

'What's the point of that, when I can just pluck it backwards? Who was Little Titch anyway?'

'Comedian, or I suppose more like a clown,' says Jan. 'He wore very long shoes, which probably allowed him to be a bit of a contortionist. My grandmother loved the music hall. She followed her favourite comedians as they began to appear on the radio.'

'Before my time,' says Normsk. 'But I did meet Charlie Chaplin.'

'Where?' asks Jan, amazed.

'Elstree,' says Normsk. 'We were recording a soundtrack and Chaplin asked for my violin. He played it, but the wrong way round. The bow was in his left hand.'

Fred laughs. 'Perhaps he played it for Stravinsky.'

'Humour has changed,' pronounces Phil. 'Anything went on the music hall. There was that guy Le Pétomane, who, like Mozart, could fart up the scale of C. He actually gave a command performance for Queen Victoria.'

'How did Her Majesty command it?' murmurs Normsk. 'Perhaps it was a Royal Misunderstanding—We are not amused.'

'Still, the line was drawn in curious places,' says Jan. 'Marie Lloyd had her wrists slapped by the Lord Chamberlain for singing "I sits amongst the cabbages and peas" so instead sang "I sits amongst the cabbages and leeks".'

Normsk picks up his violin purposefully. 'We'd better put in time on Little Titch.'

The Quartet returns to the second piece, which Stravinsky titled 'Eccentric', their lurching triplets suggestive of oversized shoes—the choice of clowns.

FIVE

The Magic Flute

A small classical orchestra comprised of faculty and students is assembled in front of the platform in the recital hall of the Langley Community Music School (LCMS) for the final performance of *The Magic Flute*. Jan divides his time between following the conductor and keeping his eleven-year-old desk partner in the right measure. The stage has been raised in the middle to enhance sightlines, and giant cardboard cut-outs of mythological creatures loom over the performers. Preschoolers disguised with long tails, ears and whiskers play smaller animals while students ranging from elementary to college-age sing Mozart's refulgent music.

The inevitable crisis always waiting for opera struck with perfect timing two hours before the performance. Tamino fell sick; the understudy, surprised at Starbucks, must now sing from the score. But as the performance unfolds, Jan soon stops worrying about the new Tamino, realizing that the charm of the child actors and singers carries the day. Preschool mammals follow Tamino as he plays his magic flute, 'Oh voice of magic melody.'

* 1945 *

Jan sits in the dark, enveloped in his plush seat at London's Sadler's Wells Theatre, listening to the portentous brass chords of the overture to *The Magic Flute*. The Grillers have received some freebies for a matinee and Guv has dutifully prepared Jan for this with an afternoon at the piano pointing out significant moments of the score, and explaining what a fugue is. Jan settles into his seat, thinking this might be another long elbow-in-the-ribs experience, but, at the last scurry of the fugue, is elated when the curtain rises—three ladies are chasing a monster with spears. The war effort has precluded the creature; the ladies are spearing the wings while Tamino runs in unmanly flight—no monster in sight.

Although he can only imagine a monster, Jan is transported. The dialogue is in English, the plot easy to follow and the music a joy. Papageno's aria 'Ein Mädchen oder Weibchen' is etched into his brain as a recurring *motif fixe* for life. (The jaunty tune will pop up at times of great happiness in Jan's life, just as the opening of Schubert's G Major-Minor Quartet will appear unbidden at times of stress.)

As a boy of ten, Jan instinctively understands the desolate abandonment expressed in Pamina's G-minor aria when she thinks Tamino has forsaken her. He understands the anticipation of love in the perfect coming together—pa-pa-papa—of the birdlike creatures Papageno and Papagena. Afterwards, the Grillers share a taxi and Jan listens to everyone enthusing about the performance. 'The Queen of the Night hit her top F,' says Colin, while Griller quips that Sarastro descended to his low F. Jan listens to the four men talking about the opera, and has a sense of the locked-in relationship of a string quartet that feeds on itself rather than relating to the real world as Jan has so far experienced it.

Mozart's opera is a unique miracle—it is the only opera that is suitable for children, can be performed by children, is magically childlike and not about children at all. Unlike *Figaro* with its conventions, politics and contentious libretto, *The Magic Flute* was written by a childlike Mozart in 1791 in German for his friend Schikaneder, who was running a low-life theatre. Maybe Mozart's inherent impishness coincides with that of his two sons, Carl and Franz Xavier. Recollection has it that at the height of *The Magic Flute*'s successful run, Mozart had to hire a series of carriages to collect his kids from school, pick up his deaf mother-in-law, drive to the theatre and then play the magic celeste parts while Papageno played his muted bells on stage. Sounds like our own diaries of modern life.

* * *

In Edinburgh there is a small opera company whose annual production is notorious. Cost-saving measures require hiring a student orchestra, and Jan in the 1950s is among them for a couple of gleeful years. The cast is taught to sing, but not *when* to sing, with dire results in the orchestra pit. On one of these occasions, Jan is down in the pit amidst prolonged orchestral chaos because an overhead stage light has caught fire during the scene where Tamino and Papageno are forbidden to speak. This makes ad-libbing a bit tricky. The curtain is rung down. When it is rung up again, the same situation prevails. Nobody is talking. The orchestra is in the dark, so to speak; they can't see the stage. They look to the conductor for guidance, but he has his baton clenched between his teeth and is frowning at the stage. There is some thumping and scuffling before the next music cue.

There are probably fewer than twenty operas whose popularity insures any operatic company from impending financial disaster. These are recycled endlessly. *The Magic Flute* is probably the last opera audiences will ever tire of and productions pop up at least once a decade in every musician's life. The dialogue, spoken not sung, seems to us stilted, and worse, politically incorrect. Schikaneder's words, two hundred years on, invite rewrites with every production, but the music remains enticingly fresh.

At the opening of Ingmar Bergman's marvellous movie of *The Magic Flute,* the camera pans across the rapt faces of the audience as they listen to the overture, suggesting the worldwide appeal of Mozart's music that bridges many ethnic groups. The three spirits commenting on the action from their air balloon (an invention first launched in Mozart's time), is a transcending image for Jan. In fact they are three spirits urging Tamino on his quest for virtue as well as for the girl—'Be silent, patient, persevering.' It doesn't really matter what the plot is about, thinks Jan, somewhere deep in the nonsense lies truth—always a difficult commodity to find.

He glances at the cut-outs and frames painted by parent volunteers, thinks about others who worked kitchen duty to keep the troops happy after long rehearsals, of the student and faculty orchestra drills which began separately two weeks earlier. He hopes that in this dim light his tears will not be noticed as the three spirits disappear, leaving Tamino, encouraged and resolute, at the entrance of the temple. The music has accompanied Jan for more than fifty years. He hopes that for all those taking part, from the smallest mammal to the largest horn player, Mozart's music will also become a lifelong companion.

Portrait: The Mozart Quintets

Leaving the sunlit world of childlike Mozart, mention must be made of those other great works from a lamentably short life—the four late viola quintets. Offered to subscribers who were indifferent to the music's stature, these quintets show Mozart the philosopher. He has known love and loss, triumph and failure, tasted the fruits of fickle fortune. The G Minor Quintet is the most frequently played, perhaps because it is the darkest and most deeply personal. But the C Major occupies an enormous landscape; the D Major is a biting comedy; the E-flat Major an irresistible drive of energy. All the late quintets have at their heart the slow movement, the inner Mozart, great dialogues about the soul of music.

The Quartet, with violist Simon Streatfeild, recorded all the Mozart viola quintets with the CBC on vinyl in 1972. Thirty years later, these recordings are transcribed to CD. In the process, it's discovered that one of the records is slightly below the pitch of the others, so the group heads over to a small recording space where a whiz kid recording engineer has reconciled the pitch.

'You wouldn't hear this on your machines,' he says, turning up the volume, 'but listen to this.' Sure enough, Jan hears behind the music the very faint sound of a truck starting up.

Years later, Jan will recall a similar story from Arnold Griller, reminiscing about the Griller Quartet's recording of Mozart's Horn Quintet with Dennis Brain in 1944. Always in demand, Dennis once ran into Colin and Jan in the crowded street outside Covent Garden. 'Can't stop and chat,' said Dennis. 'I'm double booked. I've just played the horn solo in *Tristan* and am on my way to play the quonium solo in the B Minor Mass at Festival Hall.' Dennis was known for never fluffing anything. 'But,' said Arnold, 'in that recording, if you listen very carefully to the third movement, the horn has a trill at the end of which is a very faint fluff. My father told me a bomb had just gone off at the other end of the street.'

INTERLUDE: AUDITIONS

Phil is unfolding his music stand. 'The opening of *The Magic Flute* last night was a mess. The brass was just anyhow. Embarrassing. Black tie audience.'

'I know.' Jan is unfolding his. 'Things got better. But right up top, left hand edge, let's hope the punters were still fiddling with their Black Magic chocolates.'

'I don't understand,' Phil continues, 'why conductors think it's beneath their dignity to give a clear upbeat or two if necessary. It's like they've forgotten why they're there. It's not a career move; they're there to help the orchestra. Give seven … eight for God's sake!'

'Krips solved the problem by making the brass play the upbeat on his down beat. There's such a long silence between events it actually doesn't make a difference.'

'Ah,' Normsk says, 'Krips mastered the art of 4/4, even 3/4, but give him 5/8 or 7/8 and his eyes were likely to bulge out of their sockets.'

'It's funny how the overture to *The Magic Flute* remains a perennial favourite for auditions.'

'Well you know,' Normsk replies, 'it reveals if you have control—to keep your rhythm, spicatto bowing and play the gruppetti loud and all the rest soft. There was a guy who came for an audition. Instead of playing six eighth notes, he played seven. You try it. That's difficult. Mind you, he had begun with his party piece—the Mendelssohn fiddle concerto. He was one of those guys who played his violin up here when he was high on the E string'—Normsk stretches his left arm to the ceiling—'and down there when he played low on the G string.' Normsk hunches his right shoulder to the carpet. 'And he played with his eyes shut. He kind of wandered as he played, moving gradually up the hall until he crashed into the auditioners' table.'

'Did he get the job?'

SIX

Die Meistersinger

'My youth orchestra is learning the *Meistersinger* Overture and I can't play these scales,' says Jessica, Jan's last student of the afternoon. 'They're too fast.' She tentatively plays the opening bars. Jan points to where his studio wall meets the ceiling. 'Imagine, that's where the balcony is. There are 500 people up there. You're playing to the very back row where they've paid the least amount for their ticket. You have to project your sound. This is the grandest of grand operas.'

* 1946 *

The war is over. Jan is in Covent Garden with a pressing need for the washroom during the first intermission of *Die Meistersinger*. After a long Act One, relief is never so sweet. Euphoria is cut short, however, when he finds that his zip refuses to ascend. Jan spends the rest of the evening—the next several hours—in sartorial subterfuge.

The offending long pants are Jan's first pair. Up to this point—age twelve—he, like other English schoolboys, had worn short pants. Jan felt very grown-up in his long pants as he rode in the taxi limousine Guv had hired to take the whole family up to London for the first staging of *Die Meistersinger* since before the war.

Guv had seen every production of *Die Meistersinger* in London during his lifetime. Whereas, for instance, Myra Hess had played German music—Beethoven, Brahms, Bach—as the apex of musical culture at the National Gallery concerts, and the BBC before every news broadcast had a timpani beating out the opening rhythm of Beethoven's Fifth Symphony, Wagner's music had been banned in England, as it had been hijacked by the Nazis for its anti-Semitic ideology.

Tonight in Covent Garden, Guv—who managed to make his final cigar last the whole war by smoking a few puffs on it after every lunch—is in Wagner heaven. Jan sits next to him reflecting on his broken zipper as Hans Sachs reflects on the innovative quality of Walther's prize song.

Guv had again gone through Wagner's score earlier with Jan at the keyboard. He explained the prize song scene, described Beckmesser as a thinly disguised music critic, Hans Sachs the cobbler who bangs his mallet after Beckmesser's every mistake, the triple counterpoint at the end of the Overture, the 'Dance of the Apprentices' constructed in seven-bar phrases. Despite his preoccupations, Jan manages to follow all of this through the performance.

In Jan's family, Hans Sachs and Sixtus Beckmesser are household names; they often enter into conversations with Guv. In *Die Meistersinger*, Hans Sachs is the humble artistic spirit whose altruism in renouncing personal desires for the greater good is a role model Jan is encouraged to emulate. Beckmesser (who, it is explained to Jan, was modelled after the severe music critic Eduard Hanslick, whom Wagner hated) is the epitome of a mean-spirited, negative attitude. According to Guv, most bureaucrats are Beckmessers.

The goodness of Hans Sachs is a model to strive for but Hitler, who also presumably shared Guv's love of Wagner's music and was influenced by his ideologies, used them to support his idea of the supremacy of the Aryan race. One could not be left without an opinion about Wagner but Guv, always a musician first, concentrated on the operas and not on the millions who died to prove the wrong of the Third Reich. Wagner's final moments came as he overlooked the Grand Canal in Venice, a stone's throw from St. Mark's Basilica, scene of those preceding glorious and joyful occasions provided by Monteverdi, Gabrieli and Vivaldi.

Wagner's music suffered a body blow from which it did not recover during Jan's career. Jan is glad of this; he doesn't have to learn all those notes. All he has to play is *Die Meistersinger* Overture and the 'Siegfried Idyll'. True, twice in Jan's time, the Vancouver Opera stages *The Flying Dutchman*, a wonderful opera about the sea, but not as wonderful as Britten's *Peter Grimes*. Wagner captures the turbulence of the ocean but Britten captures the tang of the sea.

Jan has a photograph of Wagner's wife, Cosima, Liszt's daughter, crossing the Platz at Bayreuth. A sensitive, noble profile topped by fine white hair. Her time and that of her husband's will come around.

Portrait: Guv

Guv, a very busy musician in the London theatre scene before the war, didn't ever return to his London house because wartime tenancy laws decreed that tenants had to leave of their own volition and couldn't be evicted. When the tenants finally left his house in Hammersmith, Guv and Bar's daughter Isolda moved back to London. Guv died an itinerant village church organist. Perhaps a more permanent legacy was the furniture he made, including two pieces for Colin—a Welsh dresser and an Elizabethan dining table with seven legs. They were copied from examples in the Victoria and Albert Museum and eventually shipped to Colin in California. He had them appraised when they arrived. Beautiful antiques! Priceless!

INTERLUDE: H-H-HUH

'Why the hell are you dragging the rhythm here?' Fred asks Normsk.

'It's marked *Beklemmt*,' says Normsk of the famous passage from the Cavatina of Beethoven's op. 130 Quartet. 'It means sobbing, like a child catching its breath between sobs. You just keep steady with the triplets, lead Phil and Jan, and don't listen to me.'

'Ha!' chorus the lower strings triumphantly.

'Actually,' says Jan. 'The passage reminds me of my mother-in-law. She has a lovely stutter, especially when she enthuses over something— h-h-how gorgeous.'

'There were these two guys walking along the street.' Normsk is talking into the music stand. 'One turns to the other—"H-h-h-h-h-did you see that?" "No. What?" "H-h-h-h-h lovely girl. Sorry y-you m-missed her." They continue walking. "H-h-h—did you see that?" "Yes!" "Then w-why did you t-tread in it?"'

Normsk raises his violin. 'Back to the *Beklemmt.*' They return unscathed to the opening Cavatina playing *sotto voce* and ending with a long sigh from the first violin. The final chord dies in tied eighth notes, the Quartet playing precisely the dynamic gradations that Beethoven wanted. The following silence is eventually broken by Normsk: 'Well, the sun's over the yardarm. Time for a little h-h-huh, then lunch.'

SEVEN

Stardust

* 1947 *

Jan, thirteen, sits in the recently renovated cinema of the RMS *Queen Elizabeth* on his way to California, his first ocean voyage. The theatre—in fact the whole ship—smells of new varnish. As he waits for the lights to dim, the speakers softly play 'Stardust', Hoagy Carmichael's evocative tune. For each day of the voyage, the movie changes but the music remains. Nobody else ever bothers with the movies; 'Stardust' plays for Jan alone.

With ears recently attuned to the harmonies of *The Rite of Spring*, Jan nevertheless is seduced by the suave chromatics of the strings and the angularity of the melody—*High up in the sky the little stars climb/always reminding me that we're apart.* To Jan, 'Stardust' comes to symbolize England's romantic notion of the USA and of California as its paradise—sunshine, Hollywood and wartime parcels with Hormel hams—a notion that has since faded but was very potent after the war. The Griller Quartet introduced themselves at Carnegie Hall in 1939; they continued wooing North America as soon as they were demobilized after the war. The Academy of the West in Santa Barbara has invited them to teach. The two married members, Sidney and Colin, are bringing their wives and children—Honor Griller with Arnold and Catherine, Elf with Jan and Andy.

For one glorious summer, Jan is catapulted from the grey landscape of wartime Britain to the perfumed colours of California and into adolescence. The change is instantaneous—from gruel to gruyère. One moment on the quay at Southampton Jan is looking up at the prow of this enormous boat, the next, he's sitting in the lounge among the Quartet party with pretzels and unfamiliar drink in hand, overlooking the quay that appears to be receding as the *Queen Elizabeth* begins its journey to New York.

The air of modernity pervades the ship because it's recently been converted into a passenger liner from a troopship. (The Grillers sailed on her during the war when the RAF central band toured the USA as part of a bond drive.) As well as daily movies, there are movie stars on board. Jan asks John Mills for his autograph; a familiar face, smiling, acquiesces. 'Did you ask for his wife's?' Elspeth asks. 'You should have done. She's famous too.' There is a seventeen-year-old making a stir above decks—Elizabeth Taylor is on her way to reconquer Hollywood. The child actress who made her mark in *National Velvet* has more adult roles in mind. Jan's mother 'harrumphs' a lot about her. 'That girl is no better than she ought to be.' Elf gazes starboard and adds, less indignantly, 'Nor can she act.'

From sticky New York to crisp San Francisco, the Griller party crosses the continent by train. Arriving unwashed on a blue morning, they take the ferryboat *Eureka* across the bay to Mill Valley. 'After five days in a Pullman, eureka says it all,' observes Colin. (*Eureka*, later decommissioned, will become a floating museum in San Francisco.)

Before taking the train down the coast to Santa Barbara, the Griller party has lunch with Lillian Hodgehead and Ada Clement, the founders of the San Francisco Conservatory. After coffee, the conversation turns to musical business. Elf, noticing the children fidgeting, suggests they take a turn round the garden. The colours are intense in the afternoon sun. The redwoods glow, the creeper up the stone wall spatters purple blooms. The cactus seems gigantic. The smells are pungent in the heat, and Jan recognizes the aroma of eucalyptus amid the unfamiliar parfumerie.

The elderly ladies live in a spacious redwood house with a sprawling hillside garden. Here they have entertained Pablo Casals, and Ernest Bloch lived here for a while. (Years later, they will try to bequeath the house to Mill Valley as a Bloch museum but the city officials decline the offer. As a curious sideline to history, the ladies in 1928 responded to a general call by the Soviet government to invest in their first five-year plan. Five years went by and they heard nothing. After ten years, they received their money back with interest.)

The Music Academy of the West is held in ranch-style buildings in the hills overlooking Carpinteria. Every afternoon, a school bus carrying students and faculty wends its way down through the orange groves to the beach. The beach, spacious and well-used, has concession stands dotted along it. Under the striped umbrella is a boy's wonderland—chewing gum in a wide variety of shapes, packaging and flavours like cinnamon and spearmint, rolls of caps for toy guns, comic books that outshine Jan's previous favourite, *Radio Fun*. Above all, there is Coca-Cola, new to Jan, antithesis of the artificial fruity cordials he's been used to and darkly fascinating. (Twenty years later, Jan will revisit the beach and will be shocked to find it deserted. Crabgrass grows where concessions once stood. Oil derricks offshore have claimed the view to the sea and rows of bungalows have claimed the orange groves.)

Back up the hill at the Academy, Ernest Bloch is composer-in-residence. The Grillers will have a long association with him, premiering four out of his five string quartets. Bloch, a granite-faced man, warm, passionate and with strongly held opinions, dominates any crowd. Colin has been collecting autographs of the famous music teachers at the Academy for Jan. After a rehearsal, the Grillers stand about with Bloch before lunch. Colin hands him the autograph book. 'Who is this for?' he roars. Colin explains, and Bloch's leathery face looks down on Jan. It's an unforgettable face. 'Your father's quartet plays my music superbly.' He hands the book to Jan, signed 'Uncle Ernie'.

(Decades later, Jan will remember Colin telling him that Bloch had the humility to write hundreds of exercises before starting his Second String Quartet. At a ceremony at the end of one of his residencies, Bloch lambasted the Americans as being thirty feet of entrails with a mouth at each end, then received a gift of the Bach *Gesellschaft*, the complete collection of Bach's work. Colin told the story of the New York critic who panned Bloch's Second Piano Quintet. Bloch was dining in a restaurant when he spied the critic at a table on the other side of the room. Bloch strode across the floor, threw his napkin down and said, 'YOU! You, if you ever write another review like that on a work of mine again, I'll pull out your eyeballs and shit in the sockets.' Ironically, Bloch died of rectal cancer. He refused a colonoscopy: 'I couldn't live like that.')

Towards the end of the summer school, one of the voice students, a meatpacker's daughter, has her father send out crates of steaks for a farewell barbecue. Elspeth is aghast at the amount of meat eaten: 'One steak would feed a family of four and then some, back in England.' The student groups are coming up for their final performances. Colin's group is playing Borodin's Second Quartet. They have been working at it through the summer.

Colin has talked a lot about Marie Manahan—the young cellist—and her playing of the opening theme. A freckled Californian with bangs, she draws some personal harrumphing from Elf. Jan doesn't quite see why, even though he somehow expects it. Borodin's music is fresh to Jan's ear—he basks in its rich harmonies—but he is aware of Elf sitting beside him, listening to the coaching, crossing and recrossing her legs—a sign, Jan has learnt, of rising irritation.

All good things come to an end (and so, Colin would say, do bad ones), and the wives and children return to England on the RMS *Mauretania*, leaving the Grillers to tour North America. No 'Stardust' on the way home. At their leave-taking, Colin whispers reassurances to Jan. On subsequent leave-takings, Jan will begin to feel these promises turning into platitudes. Saying goodbye becomes a dreaded finality as the Grillers leave on longer and longer tours.

The autumn mists are rising in London. Jan says goodbye to his mother at Waterloo Station and, apprehensive and homesick, takes the train to his first taste of boarding school. Back to the cello, to piano lessons, back to the land of rationing. Each student at Bedales School brings their own pot of jam. For elevenses, they may spread it on several slices of bread—no butter—for as long as the jar lasts.

The following spring—1948—at Wigmore Hall, the Grillers celebrate their twentieth anniversary with an all-Beethoven concert. Jan, as well as Sidney's son, Arnold Griller, attend the concert, Arnold sporting a brilliant pink school cap with black piping. In the green room afterwards, Elf stands close to Colin. 'Any mistakes?'

'Oh, just a couple of small ones.' An odd exchange, thinks Jan.

A party is held at the Grillers' house in Marloes Road. At the genial leave-taking, somebody remarks to Colin on the maturity of the quartet playing late Beethoven. Colin's reply: 'You know, I found a white hair on my balls yesterday. I plucked it out.' Jan, standing next to his father and feeling pleasantly tiddly after his first glass of wine, feels very grown-up to be included in this exchange.

The response, casting pretence aside: 'Well, you know, two will grow in its place.'

* * *

On this irreverent note, it might be well to close the curtains on the Griller Quartet while it is at the top of its game. The residency at the University of California at Berkeley (1949–1961) ensures that their pre-eminence on the European concert scene begins to wane. Eventually, they feel obliged to break their contract with Decca Records; they are never in Europe long enough to make recordings, whereas there are recording studios in the Bay area at the university's doorstep. (Decca eventually relegated their records to the archives, which the Dutton label is opening now that all the quartet members have taken the second ending.)

The Griller Quartet was coached and encouraged by Lionel Tertis, the famous viola player, to be uniquely and singularly a string quartet. None of the players earn a living in any other capacity in the profession. Once launched, they embarked on a pattern of concertizing that other famous ensembles had followed for decades: endless tours, trains, trans-Atlantic liners, modest hotels, desperation for cash advances from management.

Playing quartets is no way to grow rich. After management has taken its percentage, the fee is divided into four. In the days before credit cards, long tours can become a problem. Concerts punctuate a day's Greyhound ride as you progress across the continent. There is always a reception after the concert. (Colin: 'The end of the tour was wonderful. You'd hole up in a Pullman and sleep your way back to New York for three days.')

The money problem is just as acute touring in Europe:

Colin arrives back in London in the early 1950s. He and Jan are sharing the empty family house in Hammersmith. Colin has in his pocket the pay dirt of a European tour—a disparate coinage of guilden, francs, marks and lira—and wants to borrow ten shillings from Jan for a can of soup and the tube fare to the Victoria and Albert Museum where the quartet is to play that evening. Jan can just squeeze the amount together. Later, Colin returns after a reception. Jan has waited up. Colin empties his pockets of sandwiches and cigarettes. They survey the booty on the kitchen table. Colin bites into a sandwich. 'It's quite nice but I'm reminded of a famous pianist—was it Solomon?—who, at a reception after a gruelling recital was offered a sandwich and said, "I don't want that, I want a steak."'

A taxi picks up Colin the next morning and takes him to the boat train. Jan is left in the empty house with chest-constricting sorrow, playing 'Stardust' on his grandfather's old piano.

INTERLUDE: CONCERT IN THE BOONIES

The president of the Kaslo Concert Society, a portly lady sporting a large corsage, bustles in. The corsage seems a mite overdressed for the school locker room that is serving as the Quartet's green room.

'If you boys are ready, I'll welcome the audience. I have a couple of notes about our subscription series. Somebody's left his lights on in the parking lot. I'll introduce you and then you'll walk straight on?' She glances at the musicians anxiously.

'We'll tune first,' says Fred. 'Could I have your A, Normsk?' The president is already welcoming the audience. The Quartet tunes loudly.

'Shhh.' Jan is holding his ear to the gymnasium door. 'I can't hear when she introduces us.' The tuning dies down for a moment. Normsk as usual wanders out of the locker room, down the corridor, inspecting the photographs of school teams lining the walls. Jan hears a stir in the audience as the president reads out the license number of the offending car.

'And now I would like to welcome the Quartet.'

'Psst. Phil, Fred; we're on. Where's Normsk? Normsk, for fuck's sake!'

'Where's my Haydn? Come on. They're still clapping, poor sods.'

After the concert, the locker room door opens. 'I'm Dr Clarke. There's a reception at my house after the concert.' Jan's heart sinks. There is a bottle of Irish back in his room. How much nicer to go back to the hotel. They have an early plane in the morning.

Normsk does his British ambassador accent. 'That's terribly sweet of you.'

'Not at all. You have a car? Good. We'll go in convoy. Country roads. Dark! I live about fifteen clicks out of town.'

The parking lot is chaotic and the convoy slow to line up and move off. It soon becomes apparent that the good doctor underestimated or downright lied about the length of the trip; it seems about 350 clicks. They drive ever onwards through the night. Since the Quartet's car is last in the convoy, the boys pass the paper bag around. 'Would you like another drop of h-h-huh?'

The doctor's house is a huge, state-of-the-art log cabin in the bush. Clearly, the other guests, unhindered by convoys, know a short cut to the liquor cabinet and are well ahead. Conversation is loud and people jostle by the buffet table. Pretty soon, people are shouting to make themselves heard.

These are the perfect conditions to raise the Irishman in Normsk. He loves a party. Things are getting progressively boisterous and Jan despairs of getting back to the hotel. The car was rented in Normsk's name. There is no sign of the doctor. Nobody seems inclined to leave or offer to give him a ride back. The night drags on. Jan decides to try a taxi. He looks for a phone book. No such thing in the probable places. He opens a door and turns on the light. There is a groan from the bed. It's the good doctor, who has relinquished his role as host and turned in, leaving the festivities to their ultimate conclusion. Jan retreats hurriedly. Nothing to do but wait it out.

The party dies at 2 a.m. Normsk is persuaded into the car and they begin an uncertain journey though dark countryside until at last the glow of the town lights up distant treetops. Back at the hotel, they find the door locked. They ring the doorbell fruitlessly. Fred sniffs, says, 'Hang on, guys, I left my window open.' They go to the back. Sure enough. Fred is given a leg up and eventually reappears at the front door.

'What time should we set the alarm?'

'Plane leaves at 7 a.m.—5:30 I should think.'

'Geez!'

EIGHT

Of Hymns to St. Cecilia

Jan lies in bed listening to Benjamin Britten's 'Hymn to St. Cecilia' with earphones. Recently he bought the CD on a whim, not having heard this piece for fifty-five years. There in the dark, half a century falls away and the past becomes intensely present. Jan is back in the school library at Bedales again, moving across the dark, varnished wooden floors to the light of the whitewashed stairwell on which small frames housing mysterious objects loom into view.

* 1947 *

Jan sits in his wicker chair in the music bay and opens his homework. He begins, listens, hesitates. He puts down his pen, listens to the choir in the adjoining hall rehearsing Britten's 'Hymn to St. Cecilia'. All through his first winter term at boarding school, Jan has been listening to this lovely music complementing the warm, timbered interior of the library. Through two windows, across the lawn, Jan catches snippets of Auden's text. Britten only composed the piece some five years before. (Years later, Jan will reflect that it was adventurous of the choir to be learning it; although the production in 1945 of Britten's opera *Peter Grimes*—it's one of the few twentieth-century operas to be regularly performed—solidified his reputation, his cleverness was generally disliked by critics and he was compared unfavourably to established composers of the day such as Ralph Vaughan Williams and Arnold Bax.)

Back at his homework, Jan, a reluctant scholar distracted by books on music, tries to complete his assignments in Latin and Mathematics as he listens to the falling cadences of Britten's hymn. The choir disperses. He closes his books. The autumn is chilly, especially early the next morning when Jan takes his place in the line of naked boys waiting for their *douches écossaises*—six baths with cold water taps running constantly. The game is to crouch at the tap end, then push your legs forward and swoosh as much water out of the bath as possible. It doesn't occur to Jan to temper his behaviour in the presence of the school master, who is there in solidarity with his charges, standing naked next in line. The boys farther behind eye the master speculatively, wondering whether he slept with his wife the night before. After the bath is the run around the school estate, followed by a no-frills breakfast. Although Bedales, a co-educational school, is considered progressive, its daily routine still subscribes nominally to the severe English public school image—'Spare the rod and spoil the child'.

In the aftermath of the Second World War, Bedales is a pioneer school—its educational program endeavours to draw out the potential of each child. It specializes in the arts literary, visual and musical. Jan has a fellow cellist in his class—Christopher Finzi, son of the composer Gerald Finzi. Kiffer, as he is called, has a younger brother, Nigel, who plays the violin. A cloud of curls envelops the head of each brother. How they inherited this is difficult to discern; their father is a small man with close black hair, their mother a tall, statuesque English Rose with fine blond hair.

One weekend in the early summer, Jan is invited down to Ashmansworth, the Finzi home, to help out the cello section of Gerald Finzi's group, the Newbury Strings, in a concert that Gerald is conducting. The concert—*en plein air*—is very English: Warlock's *Capriol Suite*, Elgar's *Serenade*, Holst's *St. Paul's Suite*. During the weekend, Gerald drives Jan in his convertible sports car through the Berkshire Downs that shimmer with ripening wheat, and for the first time in his life, Jan begins to feel that playing music might have added compensations. This is a thought reinforced after the concert when he is plied with egg sandwiches and sponge cakes by pleasant elderly ladies.

At the beginning of the summer vacation, Jan is invited to stay again with the Finzis at Ashmansworth. Their house is a gorgeous modern building of brick with an extensive wooden interior. On this occasion, the schoolboys from Bedales—Jan, Kiffer and Nigel—mostly have the house to themselves. There is a big, well-kept garden, the berry patch protected by a fence of netting. The boys are allowed to eat strawberries while Kiffer's mother, Joy Finzi, shells peas. She sits on a stool outside the kitchen door, holding the bowl between her knees. She drops the pods into a large saucepan by her side on the patio.

'Why are you saving those?' Jan asks.

'I'll make pea soup of them.'

The boys whoop with glee—'Pee soup!'

Beyond the kitchen door, there are grafted fruit trees around a brick patio in the middle of which is a very deep, empty well. The Finzis have cats and any litters are dropped down the well. 'It's not cruel,' Gerald explains. 'The kittens are already dead before they hit bottom.'

Inside the house are several framed drawings of Joy's hung on walls about the house. She specializes in drawing elderly people—fine, pencilled portraits, sometimes highlighted in silverpoint.

The music room runs the length of the house with a wall of glass overlooking the Berkshire Downs. Here, the composers of the day might variously gather—Edmund Rubbra, Lennox Berkeley, Elizabeth Poston and maybe even Gordon Jacob, Howard Ferguson, Herbert Murrill and, most notably, Ralph Vaughan Williams. (Uncle Ralph to the Finzis, RVW to the cognoscenti. Many years later when he is in the LSO, Jan from the cello section will eye RVW, very visible in a box near to the stage in the Royal Festival Hall. A hulk of a man, his shoulders so bowed it seems his chin rests on his belly button. It will seem amazing to Jan that a man so immersed in composition manages to be such an indefatigable concert-goer.)

Gerald has a small studio behind the stairs that barely accommodates his grand piano. Descending the stairs, Jan is drawn into the small room at the sound of the piano. Gerald is playing a new song by Lennox Berkeley and stops to discuss it with Jan. 'A lot of people don't like this song—they object to this measure'—he plays the offending passage on the piano—'but I think they haven't understood why he wrote it. To me, that measure absolutely makes the piece. Lennox writes with grace and great facility. I'm a very slow composer myself. I'm lucky if I write more than twelve bars in a day.'

* * *

Finzi and the composers he staunchly defends defy the German musician's pronouncement that England is *das Land ohne Musik*, an opinion that is both unfair and untrue. Ironically, it was the German public who first recognized the stature of Delius and of Elgar, whose reputation has grown through the twentieth century. Cecil Sharp, a contemporary of Elgar, collected a treasury of English folk songs and dances, which profoundly influenced the generation of composers who followed—Finzi and his generation.

Despite his Italianate name, Gerald Finzi is the epitome of an English composer whose music is lyric and pastoral. (Later in his career, Jan will play Finzi's Cello Concerto with Kenneth Leighton conducting. Leighton is a composer as well, with Bartókian inclinations. When Jan and Leighton play through the concerto, Leighton's dog, an Irish setter, sleeps under the piano. 'He's always asleep except when I play a particular passage from Hindemith's *The Four Temperaments*,' says Leighton. 'Here, I'll show you.' He plays and at once the dog springs up and howls.) Finzi's Concerto has gained performances in recent years. Its slow movement in particular is beautiful but it lacks the scope of Elgar's Cello Concerto that so poignantly paints his despair of the crumbling Empire in the aftermath of the slaughter of the First World War.

Finzi, as well as Britten, wrote an ode to St. Cecilia, setting words by Edmund Blunden. Unlike Britten's spare hymn, Finzi's ode to the patroness of music, *For St. Cecilia*, is given a ceremonial setting with full orchestral palette. The music hearkens back to England's glory days which by 1947—the year it was composed and also given its first performance at the Albert Hall—were becoming a memory.

Henry Purcell also wrote three odes to St. Cecilia. As the last universally accepted 'great composer' to spring from English soil, he is the first musician to whom English composers refer. Britten honed his craft of word-setting by studying the music of Purcell, and acknowledged Purcell's influence with the *Young Person's Guide to the Orchestra*.

* * *

In 1955, less than ten years after Jan's visit to Ashmansworth, Jan is a student in London and Kiffer rings up. 'Would you like to come to the premiere of Tippett's new opera, *The Midsummer Marriage*? My father has chicken pox and can't use his tickets. They say it's going to be incredible. Tippett wrote so much music for it, the opera was going to be too long—he's had to cull it. Everybody's talking about it even though they haven't heard the music.'

As Jan sits with Kiffer in the theatre at Covent Garden, he feels the air electric with anticipation of the new opera. At the opening bars as the curtain goes up, Jan is moved to another plane; from that moment, Tippett becomes a new hero. While for Jan *The Midsummer Marriage* will have a huge impact, the reception of the opera is controversial; like *The Magic Flute*, it is a concoction of mythological, animal and spiritual elements that is either confusing, incomprehensible or inspiring to the listener. As a humanist, intellectual and musician, Tippett doesn't take the easy way out—his language is contrapuntal, rhythmically flexible and harmonically luminous. The ritual dances from the opera can—like the sea interludes in *Peter Grimes*—be performed separately. After the grand climax, the music subsides in a leisurely way, the flute notes gyrating—slowly, singly, randomly—like fluffs of cottonwood floating through the June air, a lovely effect.

* * *

When Gerald Finzi dies in 1956—he suffered from Hodgkin's disease, the chicken pox dealt him a last mortal blow—Jan is incredulous at the news. All those school years—visits on Parents Day, Jan's visits to Ashmansworth—Gerald probably knew that he had a terminal disease. He was so engaged with life, with enthusiasms—his eyes sparkled, his hand gesticulated. His was a vibrant presence.

More happily perhaps, Finzi's compositions, which were not numerous and stood in the shadow of RVW (at the time of Finzi's demise, RVW was the grand old man of music), have since received their due respect. Credit is due to recordings made by Kiffer as well as to the singer Wilfred Brown.

At the end of the old century, Jan receives an invitation from Bedales for a reunion of its former students who attended the school fifty or more years before. It is now considered an educational phenomenon, enhanced by the fact that it is a destination of choice for children of the prominent and the well-born, from Sir Laurence Olivier to Princess Margaret. A group of well-manicured Brits fills the Laurence Olivier Theatre: long faces, long noses, protruding teeth, well-modulated voices, among them, Kiffer and Hilary du Pré—but that story belongs elsewhere. Jan finds the place transformed, hardly recognizing a thing except when he visits his old haunt, the library, where he finds himself in the music bay at his homework again, in the warmer months when the sun sets behind the entrance a floor below, illuminating through their skirts the legs of the girls who enter.

Are all life's memories lying in wait to be unlocked? Jan doubts it; the really boring bits have little or no shelf life. For instance, when Jan returned to school after each vacation, how did he get from Petersfield Station up the lane three miles to the school carrying a cello and a suitcase? Maybe the luggage was sent in advance? Jan has no idea.

But 'Hymn to St. Cecilia' lives for Jan in the library, in the creak of his wicker chair and in shelves of books, light warming the timbered wood as he listens to Britten's phrases exquisitely descending with Auden's text: 'Blessed Cecilia, appear in visions/To all musicians, appear and inspire...'

Portrait: Death in Venice

Like Mozart, Britten's image in the public memory is of the composer as a young man. The composer of *Peter Grimes* sits at the rehearsal piano and appears to be still in his teens. In modern terms, Britten's death at sixty-five cuts a creative life as short as that of Schubert, who died at thirty-one, or Mozart, who died at thirty-five. Schubert, aware that he was a doomed man, wrote furiously for his life in his last great works. Likewise, Britten, who loved Schubert—aware of his own mortality after heart surgery, strove to express the ineffable. His last opera, *Death in Venice*, was finished against doctor's orders. It is unique, an opera which is entirely interior, focussing on the longing of the character Aschenbach for a young boy who is forever out of reach.

With the story set in the largely empty city of Venice in the grip of cholera, Britten pulls off the impossible—to make theatre out of all those themes that haunt us and that we generally leave unspoken. Occasionally, the backdrop is revealed—the putter of the vaporetto, the bells of St. Mark's Basilica, the tarantella of the hotel musicians—but largely the voice of Aschenbach and the language and colours of the orchestra tell the story, Britten's story.

INTERLUDE: BRITTEN'S SECOND QUARTET

'Our Es are a bit high,' says Normsk, ever diplomatic.

'I don't hear that.' Fred's trying to readjust.

'Listen to the bottom C, we can't argue with that.' Normsk points to the cello's fine tuners.

'Should we retune?' Phil plays an A.

'No, we can't rely on a perfect tuning at a concert, this movement is *so* C major. Also,' Normsk continues, 'don't play your tenths too rhythmically, this movement ends languidly, like the opening.'

Normsk is good at languid, thinks Jan. So good that we don't always know where he is. He makes poetry, though, as he sends the music to another place.

Normsk loves the music of Benjamin Britten. One evening after dinner at Jan's place, Jan had put on a record of Britten's arrangements of folk songs sung by Peter Pears. 'Oh, don't,' moaned Normsk, 'I can't bear it,' and spilled his cup of coffee right across Jan's LP rack. Jan, wiping down LP covers, thought that Normsk's reaction revealed his intense affinity for Britten's music.

The Quartet gave the Canadian premiere of Britten's First Quartet, and, at Normsk's insistence, Britten's Second Quartet became a cornerstone of their repertoire. Now the Quartet is resuscitating it yet again for a concert in Victoria. Like so many great quartets, it contains knotty problems. In quartet life, these problems are never quite solved but lurk to be fought over yet again in another season.

'Let's go on to the Scherzo.' Normsk sets off at a cracking pace. Halfway down the first page, they arrive at the passage where the cello stabs the strong beats. Jan is eternally happy about this—the viola and second violin have to bounce their offbeats from his. They break down.

'It's too friggin' fast.' Fred's exasperated.

'Look at the metronome mark.' Normsk points with his bow.

'It's impossible. Britten doesn't understand strings.'

'Oh, yes, he does. He played the viola, for one thing. You three practise it slowly.' They do, getting a little faster every time they repeat the passage.

'As you get fast,' Normsk observes, 'it's easy to distort the rhythm. You come in late, and then play the two offbeats too fast.'

'Yup,' Fred agrees. They play some more.

Eventually, Phil puts down his viola. 'I'm going bananas, let's go on to the Chaconne.'

'The meat and potatoes.' Normsk turns the page.

Fred turns to Phil. 'And we're the two vegetables.'

NINE

Sibelius Second Symphony

As Jan was growing up, he became accustomed to a certain postage-stamp-sized photograph of Jean Sibelius, regularly featured in the BBC schedules printed by *The Radio Times*. There it was, year after year beside the announcement for the upcoming BBC Symphony concert—Sibelius in his retirement years, unsmiling, a hairless skull over the furrowed brow of a career of concentrated musical thought.

So it comes as a surprise to Jan, now almost as bald but not as furrowed, to come across a large-format photograph of Sibelius standing in a doorway dressed in a white suit, smoking a cigar and laughing, the glee on his face strongly suggesting a penchant for banana-peel humour. Who is standing beyond the doorway? It almost seems as if Sibelius is laughing at the unseen someone's hilarious discomfiture.

* 1 9 4 8 *

The Scherzo is going faster than Jan practised. His fingers leap at the notes like a dog running after rabbits. Checking that he's in the right bar, he looks ahead to Rowena, the principal cellist, whose tight skirt seems inappropriate for cello-playing; the zipper seems to be stuck at the halfway mark. 'Keep your eye on the music, laddie,' says Douglas Cameron, the cello instructor, standing close by. Jan blushes. His fingers catch up with the rabbits.

Jan is playing in a symphony orchestra for the first time—the Second Symphony of Sibelius is exhilarating. This is also Jan's introduction to the music of Sibelius.

'Sibelius's music doesn't look like anybody else's,' Elf had once said to him. Nor does it sound like anybody else's. The National Youth Orchestra (NYO) is large, with copious string sections and a full complement of winds and brass. Jan has never been confronted before with such a legion of trumpets, French horns and trombones. In the second and last movements, Sibelius provides columns of brass sound entirely new to Jan, accustomed to the modest school orchestra at Bedales.

Sibelius's music is of a different place. The language is post-Tchaikovskian but the ingredients are shaken up. Jan loves the warmth of the first movement with its consummating melody opening with five repeated notes, and the second movement's suggestion of a slow walk through Finnish forests with its hint of bad weather. In the NYO, Jan does finally learn to scamper through the Scherzo. (Later, in the LSO, Jan will listen to the conductor, Sir Malcolm Sargent, putting the words, 'Oh what a long and beautiful summer we've had' to the repeated notes of the Scherzo's middle section that echo the opening theme.) He revels in the glorious brass sound of the Finale when Sibelius inverts the symphony's opening notes to a motif of increasing intensity.

Jan's deep experience with the NYO is such that he remembers the hall in Liverpool instantly every time he encounters the Second Symphony. On one such occasion, as principal cellist of the Vancouver Symphony Orchestra, he'll play it in Seattle and the local critic will observe that the conductor, Meredith Davies, 'has fine horns'. Listening to these fine horns in the Finale on the car radio, the mother of one of Jan's students is pulled over for speeding: 'Oh, officer, listen to this. How could I possibly keep within the limit?'

✳ ✳ ✳

It is in the Second Symphony that Sibelius finds his individual voice. In this symphony, cementing his style, Sibelius writes large structures containing ideas which he reveals gradually rather than presenting at the opening. Sibelius shakes up the staples of a symphonist and produces a tonal landscape that is uniquely northern.

The First Symphony, while regularly played, is memorable for its opening movement but seems a pale relation to its younger brother. Jan is a student in the Reid Orchestra under the direction of Sidney Newman at Edinburgh University when he catches up to the slighter Third Symphony. Sidney is also conducting the inscrutable Fourth when Jan, still running after rabbits, comes in with his cello solo a bar early at the beginning of the Finale and they have to start over. Such is the dubious quality of the orchestra that it doesn't seem to be embarrassing.

Jan discovers the Fifth in the LSO. His partner, Harry Dugarde, is infuriated at the conductor. There is a moment in the opening movement where the strings slide into extreme syncopation over a languid bassoon solo. 'Conductors always get glassy-eyed in this passage,' says Harry. 'They never bother to beat for the strings.' In the performance, Harry beats his bow loudly against the music stand. (Normsk remembers: 'We were finishing Sibelius's Fifth at an open air concert in Holland Park. As we got to those short chords at the end with their lengthening silences, a steam train started up, accelerating gradually—chuff-chuff-chuff-chuff—in conflict with the chords. The orchestra had to cling desperately to the conductor.')

Sibelius had a fascination with amalgamating two contrasting movements—a scherzo with a finale for instance. This juxtaposition creates an exciting tension for the unwary listener, suddenly swept into the fast lane. Thus, his last symphony, the Seventh, is one long movement. The key of the opening is enigmatic until the noble chorale—introduced by divided lower strings—culminates in an assured C major with the first of three fine trombone moments, the third of which is the triumphant climax to the symphony. The glory of playing this solo must be worth a lifetime of delivering pizzas.

Sibelius's last major orchestral work is *Tapiola*. Despite being described as a tone poem about Tapio, god of the northern forest, *Tapiola* is possibly the eighth symphony that the public was anticipating in vain. The harmony is static, implying a vast landscape—ranks of pines shaking a little, snow, biting cold, the brooding winds in the middle perhaps Tapio himself, sullen and unpredictable. Near the end, a storm howls through the trees. As it calms, the primeval feel of the landscape returns and the tone poem ends with a major chord—a smiling utterance—Sibelius's last contribution to the orchestral world.

Rumours persisted that an eighth was in gestation. Sir Malcolm Sargent, a friend of Sibelius's, was sent to Finland by the BBC to get proof positive from the great man himself. Story has it that Sir Malcolm couldn't bring himself to ask the crucial question. At last, at the train station as they said their goodbyes, Sir Malcolm asked, 'Have you any news that I can take back to our listeners in England?'

'Tell them I still have the biggest prick in Finland.'

Inexplicably, the physiology of great musicians' ears have not been investigated. A photograph of Sibelius in his last years dramatizes a large, pendulous ear with an unusually generous entrance to the auricle, but his ears have not excited the interest of doctors as Beethoven's did.

While deafness was the issue that spurred Beethoven's greatness, Sibelius's interest in Norse mythology drove his musical language. A listener who has heard the symphonies and the tone poems will probably intuit that this music springs from a northern landscape.

When the Grillers were to record Sibelius's quartet *Voces Intimae*, Colin rang up Sibelius to ask whether he had any advice for them. 'Just observe the dynamics,' came the answer. Tapiola, back to the woods.

INTERLUDE: INTIMATE VOICES

The rain, pounding on the studio roof, provides an aural wallpaper to the Quartet's rehearsal of the slow movement of Sibelius's *Voces Intimae*.

'You'll have to play louder there,' complains Phil to Fred. 'I can't hear you.'

'It's *pianissimo*, for Chrissake,' retorts Fred. 'And, Normsk, you're always coming in late after the Più Adagio.'

'No,' says Normsk. 'I enter after a sixteenth rest.'

Fred leans over to peer at the offending bar. 'Oh!!!' he says, melodramatic. 'Well then, your entry is not on the first beat.' He pencils in a cue with exaggerated gestures. 'Geez!'

He picks up his bow and, thinking that he has lost this round, says, 'Actually, one of the nicest pieces by Sibelius I know is the middle movement of *Rakastava*—straight ahead triplets played *pianissimo*. It's titled 'The Lover' but to me it describes the grey drizzle of a Vancouver spring.'

Phil adjusts his shoulder rest. 'Finland too, perhaps. Maybe they changed the name to Helsinki from Hellsinkole.'

TEN

Music for Strings, Percussion and Celesta

Jan is fourteen, in the summer term at Bedales.

'Come and listen to this,' says Jan's classmate Peter, handing him an LP cover. 'It's Bartók's *Music for Strings, Percussion and Celesta.*'

'The whole piece on one record?' Jan is astounded.

'Yes, and it's got the *Divertimento for Strings* on the other side.'

Peter places the record on the turntable and flicks the switch so that—another surprise—the arm with the needle swings over automatically and begins playing. Two violas lead a bleak procession of strings across a lunar landscape. This is Jan's introduction to Bartók. The two friends become so drawn into the music that it becomes an obsession for the entire term.

Once, at the subsiding of the strings into the eerie entrance of the celesta, Jan turns to Peter and confides, 'I think my parents might be getting a divorce.'

'Aren't everybody's?' comes the world-weary reply.

* 1 9 4 9 *

After the summer term, Jan says goodbye to Peter and his Bartók LP but the music is ever with him as he travels with Elf and Andy, not home to the Thames Valley but to Edinburgh and the house belonging to Dorothy, Elf's great-aunt. Great-Aunt Dorothy's house has a faded bourgeois elegance she finds hard to maintain. She was married to a bank manager who worked in both the Shetland and Orkney Islands. Widowed, she lives within her pension and cheerfully accepts her privations. She suggests vacationing on Orkney with Jan's family for the summer while she rents her house to Vittorio Gui, who is conducting at the Edinburgh Festival. Colin, away as usual, has promised a visit later in the summer.

On Orkney, Jan cycles alone in the gentle rain. He notices a cottage with cheeses drying on its roof and pays it a visit. The lady picks a cheese off the roof and goes inside to wrap it. From the door, Jan sees a half-naked child standing on the dirt floor, gnawing on a slice of raw potato. Leaving Stromness, he spies a footpath sign—'Ring of Brodgar'. On a whim, he turns up the lane, which leads to a heather-covered plateau on which rises a circle of Neolithic standing stones. Beyond the plateau is a mountainous backdrop. There is no sign of life near or far. The area seems so bleak it is difficult to imagine the human activity that placed the stones there. Jan's feeling of foreboding about this monochrome landscape matches the chromatic lines of Bartók running through his head.

Jan turns reluctantly with his bike and thinks to return soon as he heads back to Birsay. Bartók's music, still in his ear, opens, wending its way without a tonal centre or a strong feeling of pulse. Bartók calls for two groups of strings. From a brace of violas, the first movement gradually gathers players, adding percussion towards the climax, joined by the celesta, a drizzly ostinato with the ghostly presence of Orcadian ancients as the music subsides.

It rains every day on Orkney. Near Birsay where the family is staying, Jan climbs the island—Orcadians call it a brough—a triangular lump that can only be reached at low tide, while the younger children hunt for 'groatie buckies', small cowrie shells. He crosses the rocks that run like long knives into the sea, and walks up the cropped grass where a thousand chickens run silently toward him hoping to be fed. During winter storms their coops are blown out to sea, and years later under that cropped grass, a Viking settlement will be discovered. At the top of the hill, Jan stares down a sheer cliff to the sea churning hundreds of feet below. High above him wheel gannets. They fold their wings and dive-bomb the fish they spy below the water's surface. The waves roil into the *geos*—crevices sending up white foam as they narrow. Jan speculates that the razor-like rocks could turn unwary gannets into forcemeat.

Colin appears for a few days, a break from recording sessions in London, and he and Jan ride bicycles back to the Ring of Brodgar. They stand in silence, except for the wind blowing across the circle. Colin's visit to Orkney is as a stranger, not as family. Jan, standing in the ring with its ancient ghosts, sees clearly the reality of divorce—the sweet Thames will run softly no more in his life, replaced by the icy waters of the Firth of Forth. For Jan, the rancour and reproach of separation is muted; Colin has never been at home.

Musicians lead difficult lives because music has to come first. It offers little room for compromise; at the hour when other husbands are putting on slippers and heading for the armchair, Colin is putting on his tails in a cold green room. There are tours, travels, concerts, broadcasts, interviews and recordings.

* * *

In the 1980s, Jan records the *Music for Strings, Percussion and Celesta* with the CBC Vancouver Orchestra. John Eliot Gardiner—'Jiggy' to his colleagues—is the newly appointed music director. Jiggy initially built his reputation with his Monteverdi Choir, but his acute ear, high musical standards and strong sense of style reach far beyond the Baroque. Jiggy re-examines the role of the CBC Orchestra and its personnel. With magisterial authority but only a tourist's knowledge of the Vancouver music scene, he shuffles musicians around.

His introduction to the Vancouver public is a program devoted to Bartók, performing the *Divertimento* and the *Music for Strings, Percussion and Celesta*. The concert is a casebook study of poor management strategy. Rehearsals are held in the sound studio of the newly built CBC building prior to the concert being held in the Orpheum Theatre. Due to prior bookings, the theatre isn't available for a dress rehearsal. Musicians have to walk in off the street and battle Bartók—a recipe for disaster.

The *Divertimento* receives safe if turbulent passage but the *Music for Strings, Percussion and Celesta*, with its reconfigured seating and larger forces, escapes control. There is a whiff of danger early on in the first movement with an early entry. The opening movement is slow, a tonal moonscape with craters ready for everybody, in ever-changing eighth note meter. The only way to conduct it is in eighths. John Eliot beats steadily, like a chef chopping short ribs. Looking for the strong beats, uncertain of an entry, a musician looks in vain for clarity in a ballet of karate chops. Undermined by a bad start, the following fast movements with their loud rhythmic interjections are a rout. After the concert, John Eliot meets his musicians as they flee the stage. 'What happened?' he keeps asking. But the musicians, smarting over recent dismissals, offer no answers.

With Jiggy's arrival, the CBC Orchestra's mandate is expanded from classics and Canadian music to include early music. Bartók is to take a back seat. (In his seventies, Jan will reflect that Bartók, like Sibelius, seems under-represented in the concert world. This is odd, because his music is finely crafted. Jan's grandparents hated the novelty of Bartók, but contemporary audiences should have caught up by now. Jan's early initiation to Bartók's music was strange but exciting. Returning to listen again, he thinks some moments are dated to his post-minimalist ears. The world moves on. It's probably a phase most composers suffer—J. S. Bach lived long enough to see his music trashed by the new style led by his son C. P. E. Bach.)

Bartók, evidently anxious that interpreters would remain faithful to his musical intentions, placed metronome marks along the way. Such instructions may be ideal but they don't take into account performance conditions. Stuart Thyne, the pianist who accompanied Jan in his student days, remembers attending a choral concert in St. Andrew's Hall in Glasgow before it burnt down. The hall, with a wooden interior, was very resonant. Bartók was there for the rehearsal of a choral piece of his. The acoustics didn't allow for clarity. Bartók's companion suggested to him that the choir was perhaps singing it too fast. Bartók pulled out a pocket metronome, which swung, yo-yo-like, from the end of a tape. Bartók suspended it—no, the choir was singing exactly the tempo.

Stuart also remembers that at a recital in Edinburgh, the solo pianist misread the metronome mark for one of Bartók's *Mikrokosmos*—eighth equals 60, instead of quarter equals 60. The performance was agonizingly slow.

* * *

In the Orkneys, fog doesn't last long—it's blown away by the incessant wind. It blows in Jan's face as he labours on his bicycle, visiting prehistoric, Neolithic sites. While the first movement of the *Music for Strings, Percussion and Celesta* evokes these sites, the last movement with its obsessive, thrusting rhythms and Lydian-flavoured harmonies matches the physical effort of getting there against the wind. On rough days, early man could hardly be a match for his environment. Looking down the cliffs to the foaming sea, Jan is partly frightened but also exhilarated. Down the centuries, things haven't changed. Hidden beneath the water is Earl Kitchener's boat, the HMS *Hampshire*, which was hit by a German mine. The heaving seas threw the sailors onto the rocks. The islanders looked down helpless. The storm was too furious for them to descend the cliff.

Autumn appears early in the north. It is time for Jan's family to leave Orkney. Jan's parents are separating. His mother stays in Edinburgh, the place of her antecedents, where Andy is young enough to acquire a Scottish brogue worthy of Sean Connery. Colin returns to Berkeley, where the Grillers are in residence. Returning to Edinburgh, Aunt Dorothy discovers that the Vittorio Gui family has used her kitchen wallpaper as a dartboard. Jan returns to Bedales, trying to make his pot of jam last until exam time.

INTERLUDE: FOG

The Quartet is on tour; they are to play Bartók's Fifth Quartet in St. John's, Newfoundland, then fly to New York for a series of concerts down the East Coast. There is fog and the plane has to land in Gander, which is equipped to deal with all kinds of flying conditions. The fog is so dense that Jan can't see the terminal until the plane has stopped. The Quartet waits at the carousel for their luggage. The rest of the passengers, locals used to such situations, line up at the car rental. The Quartet, once alert to the problem, hires the last car. Jan has a fever and is running a temperature. For hours, they inch their way down the highway to St. John's. At this rate, they'll have time to book into their hotel, change and go straight to the concert.

But what if the fog persists overnight? They have to get to New York. Bartók Five has not been in their repertoire long. It has rhythmic traps and nightmarish rapid passagework. Somehow Jan, flushed and ill, manages to get through the concert with mental radar. Afterwards, they decide to snatch an hour's sleep in St. John's, then drive the hours back to Gander in order to intercept their flight. Whenever he hears the 'Alla Bulgarese' with its lopsided rhythms—trying to make an entrance in the middle of a bar that has no middle which calls for the finesse of a cosmonaut—those awful twelve hours come back to haunt him.

ELEVEN

St. Matthew Passion

Jan is conducting an eleventh-hour run-through of the chorales of Bach's *St. Matthew Passion* with a parent volunteer choir before the doors open for a performance at Langley Community Music School. There is a bang at the door. Jan gestures for a student to open it, hoping it's the volunteer taking tickets at the greeting table. His heart sinks. It's the first audience member.

These concerts need at least two volunteers—one to take money and another to prepare the reception for the intermission. It doesn't matter who volunteers, Jan reflects, none seem to understand show biz. The reception volunteer arrives with the audience and disappears into the kitchen, which lies behind a serving hatch beside the performers. Well into the performance, the coffee urn begins its inevitable rhythmic gurgling and wheezing, a prelude to the last supper—'... and he took the cup ...'—there is a rattling of teaspoons, Jan sighs again— '... and said drink ye all of it.'

* 1950 *

Jan tries to rescue the remains of a messy egg sandwich from his wrists as he walks with his friends along the perimeter of Hyde Park. Lunch was below Prince Albert at his memorial among the daffodils and now the class is being summoned across the road into the hands of the High Priest Caiaphas as they make for the second half of the *St. Matthew Passion*. After the cold bath and run around the Bedales school grounds, the class boarded the train to London and arrived at Albert Hall midmorning to watch the assembling of instrumentalists—the Jacques String Orchestra—leading the singers onto the stage.

As Jan began to listen, it seemed to him that the size of the Albert Hall—it holds in excess of 5,000—matched the music. Bach's conception is on a vast scale—the story of Christ's agony in the garden from the last supper to the rending of the veil is interspersed with commentaries.

These take the form of arias with instrumental obligati, choruses and chorales, which are Bach's invitation for the congregation to sing along. The work calls for a double orchestra, a double choir, a children's ripieno (the paternal Bach doesn't ask the children to sing in the second half—he knows it'll be after their bedtime) and most important of all, an evangelist (narrator) who, accompanied by the continuo, tells the story through recitative. Jan's foreign language teacher, Wilfred Brown, who has a beautiful tenor voice and regularly gives German and French art song recitals at Bedales, has prepared the group for this occasion. Since Christmas he has helped the students to become familiar with the oratorio. They've examined the music and had opportunity to hear excerpts at the school's musical functions.

Back in his seat after his egg sandwich, Jan settles in for another two hours. He is familiar with Bach's language, having learned in his piano lessons several preludes and fugues from the '48' (*The Well-Tempered Clavier*). The sheer length of the oratorio takes on a ritualistic involvement. At each turn of the story there are richly varied musical meditations—obligatos from flutes, oboe d'amore, violins, viola da gamba and theorbo accompanying a wide range of voices so that Jan feels himself walking every step of the way to Golgotha. Jan is not particularly God-fearing, but is familiar with the Sunday service; the Church of England is never far away. Bach's devotion has provided a catalyst for the ordinary listener to reach God. After the rending of the veil, when Bach captures in two bars the amazement of the onlookers at Golgotha—'Surely this was the son of God'—heaven beckons to us all. Jan files out with his class from the hall into the late afternoon; back to Bedales.

In his early twenties, Jan enters the Albert Hall again for the *St. Matthew Passion*, this time through the stage door as a cellist in the Jacques Orchestra. As tradition has it, the performance in the Albert Hall begins midmorning. There is also a sartorial ritual that underlies the *St. Matthew Passion* for the performers—once a year the pinstripe trousers and frock coat are taken from the wardrobe along with the silver-grey waistcoat and the matching cravat. In the giant opening chorus, Reginald Jacques, a diminutive man, turns from the podium to bring in the ripieno—small boys singing from the balcony. 'Poor dears, they always sing so sharp,' Jan hears Jacques whisper to the cellos as he turns back to the orchestra.

Peter Bevan, perennially the solo cellist, must continually think quickly as he accompanies the Evangelist telling the story in recitative, especially if it's sung in German. Quickly turning the page, he plunges into the following orchestral numbers without a break. Further, he must play two obligati to accompany the arias, such as the one describing Christ carrying the cross. The obligato stumbles under the weight of the cross with complicated chords, jagged rhythms, the cellist playing across the instrument's wide tessitura.

* * *

The length of the oratorio, not to mention its solemnity, requires that all the participants empty their bladders before walking out on stage. Indeed, if the performance is in a church, the performers may feel like prisoners surrounded by ecclesiastical furniture. In Aberdeen Cathedral, Jan is crammed with the orchestra in against the altar rails just launching into the first chorus when one of the violinists, jammed as in a Tokyo subway, is sick. The poor violinist spends the next hour and a half hunched over while the vomit oozes down the runnels to the nave. Fellow violinists nervously shuffle their feet while their fingers deal with Bach's tortuous lines.

Sometimes, thanks to Bach's singular use of an obligato instrument, the player can be excused one or other half of this grand liturgical setting. Thus, in the Orpheum Theatre, in Vancouver, Eric Wilson appears in the second half to play the gamba solo. He comes out on stage with a rickety folding music stand and three unattached, Xeroxed pages of music. The page with the elaborate recitative that introduces the aria has to be turned. As Eric is doing so, the third page falls off the stand and wafts towards the audience. He quickly spikes it with the point of his Baroque bow as it teeters on the edge of the stage. Had it floated into the hall, it would have been the perfect showstopper, as the gambist alone starts the aria.

A novice cellist, raised on the 'Air on the G String' or later, the *Brandenburg* Concerto no. 3, can be forgiven if he thinks that Bach is pretty much manageable, but some of the gamba solos will provide nasty shocks. An older, wiser cellist, pondering over the intricacies of the Cello Suites, realizes that within the scope of a single line, Bach develops melody, harmony and counterpoint that transcend the limitations of a single cello.

Bach's original manuscript of the suites is lost, leaving cellists poring over the fair copy Anna Magdalena made for her husband after their last child was tucked up in bed. Her script contains inaccuracies, but is very expressive. The rhythmic complications of the D Major Allemande are such that the cellist has to count sixteen to a bar. Anna Magdalena joined torrents of sixty-fourth notes with wavy lines that resemble the skies of a late Van Gogh painting.

The music provides a lifetime's fascination that Jan has difficulty explaining to a young student. What's the difference between Bach and the pedagogical studies the student endures? Beyond counterpoint, chromatic harmony and melodic line, Bach's music is essentially noble. 'Bach lived his life in church or by a church,' Jan tells his students. 'He goes at his own pace.' Like Gaudí on the progress of his cathedral in Barcelona: 'My client is in no hurry.'

The church, however, had a tighter itinerary. Bach wrote a cantata for every week of the Christian calendar. His collaborator, frequently providing the text, used the name Picander and, curiously in a double life, wrote erotic verse. Perhaps this shouldn't surprise us; to some extent we all live public-private lives. Think of Mozart's scatological letters. For all we know, Bach made advances cancrizans to Anna Magdalena after the candles were blown out.

∗ ∗ ∗

A confirmed bachelor, Chalmers Burns is Elf's cousin but always known to Jan as Uncle Willy. During the 1950s he is the head of music at Newcastle University. Moustached, hair parted in the middle, he suggests an Oscar Wildean figure. He also has a wicked sense of humour, describing a train ride to Edinburgh during which a lady next to him was breastfeeding a baby: 'Take titty or I'll give it to this gentleman here.'

He buys a car even though the rudimentary principles of driving seem to him unclear. (Jan, in his teens, listened to him describing to Elf how he took his graduate students out to dinner at the end of the university year. They celebrated liberally, and the police apprehended Uncle Willy on his way home. He tried the circular breathing technique favoured by wind players while taking the Breathalyzer and was sent on his way.)

Uncle Willy invites himself to stay in Elf's tiny apartment each Edinburgh Festival. A proud Jaguar owner, he takes his cousin out for a spin. He takes a right-hand corner too fast and the car ends up on its side in the ditch. Silence settles in. 'You're lying on me,' Elf complains. Whatever response Uncle Willy has in mind never passes his moustache; the glass in the back window suddenly shatters.

As befitting his position at Newcastle, Uncle Willy undertakes an ambitious concert each spring. Visiting again in Edinburgh, he vents his annoyance over a recent fiasco:

The student choir is to sing the *St. Matthew Passion*. Uncle Willy books soloists and the English Chamber Orchestra (ECO) to rehearse in the afternoon and perform in the evening. He books hotel rooms for the orchestra; the last train from Newcastle to London leaves at 11:15 p.m. At the end of the rehearsal, Quin Ballardie, manager of the ECO and violist, comes up to the podium to tell Uncle Willy that the performance better begin promptly as some members of the orchestra have to return to London that night. They have a recording in the morning.

By intermission, it becomes apparent that the rending of the veil won't arrive before the last train does. Cuts are arranged and passed out surreptitiously as the orchestra returns to the stage. Bach's magisterial drama can only proceed at its own pace, despite prodding. By the time Pilate is washing his hands, Uncle Willy is shouting across the stage, 'Omit the next number,' and finally, 'Cut to Golgotha!' After the last monumental chorus with its clashes of minor against major, Uncle Willy bows to the audience, acknowledges the soloists, invites the chorus to stand, indicates to the orchestra, but they've all disappeared, save one double bass player trying to get through the door. Behind the stage is a melee of panicking players putting their instruments away in the dark. Musicians are running for the train. Uncle Willy drives the bass player down to the station. The train is late—everyone makes it. Three days later he receives a bill from the ECO for hotel overnight accommodation. *Consumatum est.*

INTERLUDE: PUBLICITY PHOTOGRAPH

The Quartet in their tails arrives late at the photographer's studio—an old warehouse, bare brick and timber partly hidden by lighting umbrellas and a large roll of white paper slung from the ceiling. The photographer is unsympathetic. 'Unpack in the kitchen, then come in here.' The Quartet returns with instruments, music stands and music. 'We need chairs,' Normsk says.

The photographer eyes them dubiously. 'What do you do?'

'Play string quartets.'

The photographer rummages round the back and collects four ill-matching chairs. 'This one's got arms,' says Phil.

'So?'

'You can't play strings in armchairs.' Phil demonstrates.

'Sit on the edge—diagonally.' The photographer pulls down the paper sheet, hiding the floor and the wall behind. 'Sit down like you usually do.' The Quartet sits down in a square, a music stand in front of each of them.

'That's much too far apart. Move in.' The Quartet edges in. The photographer rearranges the music stands into a tangle of metal. 'Do you really need all these stands?'

Fred: 'Usually do.'

'We need to get rid of two. You'll have to move in closer. Knees touching. Phil, it is Phil? Right. Remember to keep sitting diagonally. The arm won't show. Cellist, do you have to have your bow across the cello?'

Jan: 'I could pizz.'

'I beg your pardon?'

Jan: 'Like this.' Jan plucks.

'Good, only keep your bow low. Violinists, play at the pointy end of your sticks so they don't intrude into the portrait. Now sit tight.' The photographer goes up a ladder to adjust the lights. He clicks something, then looks at the set-up through a small lens. Normsk begins to play Dvořák's 'Humoresque' with tiny bows. Jan attempts a plucked accompaniment.

'No moving. Stay tight. We're ready for the camera. Wet your lips.'

This is too much for the Quartet. Fred's shoulders begin to heave. Since everybody is touching everybody else, it's catching.

'Stay still!' The photographer is snapping away. Tears are running down Fred's cheeks. Normsk tries to egg him on. There's a stifled snort from Phil.

'Okay. That's it. Relax,' says the photographer. 'The contacts should be ready on Wednesday.'

Back in the sunlight, Normsk turns to his colleagues. 'How about a beer?'

'Yes, I could wet my lips!'

Cara Mia Mine

It is the Sabbath in the Grenadier Guards barracks at Caterham, a bus ride from London, and Jan with his squadron is confined to sitting astride his bed to spit and polish his boots for the whole morning. Someone has flicked the switch on the Tannoy, and David Whitfield singing 'Cara Mia' takes over from the Sunday sermon. The Tannoy offers to a captive audience the choice between the Sunday church service or the Top of the Hit Parade. The Sunday service usually wins out—it offers a half-hearted consolation to the young soldiers who feel abandoned to their fate. But sooner or later some atheist inevitably reaches for the knob, and Jan, after listening to an hour of proselytizing, is relieved.

'Cara Mia' is the song of the moment. Its hook—'Cara Mia mine'—is everywhere. Nobody notices the dislocation of two languages if indeed anybody knows what it means, but the rising phrase with its rapid fall somehow embodies the soldiers' hopes as well as their loneliness. They sing it in the canteen, they sing it in the latrines as they scratch off the days of their confinement. 'Pissed fourth week inspection,' the walls read, a pivotal moment in a recruit's life.

∗ ∗ ∗

England retained conscription and a reservist list for some fifteen years after the Second World War, so Jan, after graduating from Bedales and attending university for two years, was plucked from his music and dumped into the military. On the advice of his cousin Rodney, who bowed his way through the military on the double bass, Jan decided to join the Grenadier Guards Brass Band, which has under its wing a small salon orchestra. But first he must endure eight weeks of basic training in Caterham. The Grenadier Guards, those red-coated, bearskin-capped soldiers in the sentry boxes at Buckingham Palace, are supposedly at least six feet tall, preferably anything up to seven feet. Jan, entering the gates of

Caterham, clocks in at five feet eight, the smallest recruit around and the only musician in camp.

This is the era of the Teddy Boys—young guys with long hair, tight jackets and drainpipe trousers, sauntering off the bus and into the barracks. Jan is jostled with them into the barber and seconds later they emerge wide-eyed and shorn like sheep. They are quick-marched to the quartermaster who throws at them uniforms, coveralls, green underwear, rough towels and boots. Staggering under the weight of their kit bags, Jan and his squadron are hounded up three flights of stairs to their sleeping quarters. Twenty beds stand in two rows and at the far wall is a very large mirror.

A recruit's day usually ends with a body inspection but there is none that first night. Instead, the soldiers line up, bare-torsoed, to receive their jabs. In the days before AIDS, little heed is given to hygiene. The men are lined up in tens and jabbed with a melange of stuff from the same needle. The soldiers are told to 'bump' the floor to get this soup of serum through their bodies, so Jan pushes and pulls the handle of a large wax polisher across the floor. The largest man in the squad, nearly seven feet and built like a Churchill tank, goes berserk on the insertion of the needle. The soldiers try to hold him down while he thrashes about. Eventually he's subdued and never seen again. Jan is encouraged.

During the first weeks of basic training, Jan begins to understand that though he is the smallest man in the camp, he isn't as disadvantaged as he first thought. This is confirmed when they're led outside to the sports field. First up is the long jump. First up to try it breaks his ankle. Next up is to scale a tall wall. Everyone scrambles up the webbing. Once on top of the wall, Jan looks down to the ground falling away. He regards the drop dubiously. 'Jump!' booms the sergeant. The soldier next to Jan falls to his knees and prays. Jan is further encouraged.

That long-awaited day finally arrives when one of their number scratches 'pissed eighth week inspection' on the latrine wall and the squad must go on to learn how to handle firearms. As a musician, Jan is excused from this. He'll soon be called to Birdcage Walk, the home of the Grenadier Guards Band. The authorities seem to have forgotten about him. Jan spends his last days in Caterham helping the second lieutenant iron the squad's best Battle Dress—BDs—for their final inspection.

Jan checks the notice board every day, but there's nothing for him.

Eventually he asks the second lieutenant to check for him. 'Sure enough, they forgot about you. You have to leave tomorrow morning.'

At Birdcage Walk, Jan is told to report to the conductor of the Guards Band. Major Harris has silver hair, clear blue eyes and a closely clipped white moustache. 'Glad you've arrived. We need a cellist. Report to Sergeant Goodwin. He's in charge of the Salon Orchestra. He'll look after you.'

Sergeant Goodwin's office is right by the back gate of Birdcage Walk, where the string players in their street clothes may slip in and report every morning without having to salute anyone. Sergeant Bill Goodwin looks like a benign version of Punch. He speaks through a stump of a cigarette, the doofa ('do for later') hanging from his lips, his words lost in a halo of smoke. 'The boys have gone home. We rehearse at 10 a.m. Report here tomorrow. You've got digs?' Jan indeed has digs—a bedsitter off Bayswater Road. Jan is elated. He glides in his civvy shoes out of the back gates and makes for the Underground at Victoria Station. Someone is whistling 'Cara Mia'.

* * *

Although his physique doesn't suggest that he was once the man wearing the leopard skin going boom-boom, Bill Goodwin was a drummer in the Military Band. The story goes that Bill's fall from grace was over a BBC broadcast, which in those days of course, went live to air. There was a dead spot in the broadcasting day preceding 'Children's Hour', an alternating spot reserved for cinema organists or brass bands. The routine was that after the title—'Marching with the Band'—had been announced, there would be a cymbal crash followed by details of the band, its director and the music to be played. On this particular afternoon, Bill, in charge of the suspended cymbal, swiped and missed. 'Goodwin,' threatened Major Harris, 'if that ever happens again, you'll be demoted to the library.' A few weeks later the band was back at Broadcasting House. The band was set on a dais with several rising steps. Bill sat in state at its apex surrounded by his kitchenware. 'Marching with the Band' was announced. Bill grabbed his stick and took the biggest swipe of his life. The cymbal snarled and rocked off the suspending rod. It rolled through the band, hissing and crashing down each step, to the feet of the announcer.

Down in the library, Bill accesses a seemingly inexhaustible supply of light music. It's his job to rehearse the Salon Orchestra for two hours every weekday morning. Musicians in civvies are required to be there and, if necessary, to be available for any occasion requiring their services. It is in their best interest to maintain this fiction at all times. Every morning, Bill turns up with a fresh pile of folders for everyone to read through. Rehearsals begin late and finish early. Coffee breaks get longer and after payday, which is Thursday, the musicians consider the week finished. Nobody is expected to turn up on Friday.

Disliked as a bunch of skivers by the rest of the Guards, the Salon Orchestra consists of a bunch of violinists and a brace of violists and cellists, although they sometimes acquire a couple of wind players from the band proper for grand occasions in London when royalty or city dignitaries are in attendance. Two or three times a month a chosen few play for old comrade dinners, mostly in the Midlands. Usually they are paid, in addition to getting a free dinner. Jan relies upon these perks, as his rent takes most of his army pay and the hot plate in his bedsitter can only cope with eggs and sausages.

Bill is chaperone and keyboard player for these dinners. If no piano is available, he takes a portable harmonium, in the form of a suitcase, which he unpacks on a table; two pedals attached to the bellows drop to the floor. (Once, Bill discovered some joker had punched a couple of holes into the bellows. He pedalled furiously all evening to get any sound out of it. For once his lips held no doofa. He was too exhausted.)

Bill isn't exactly Mr Showman, but he announces the numbers if he thinks anybody's listening. Nor is he a linguist: 'We will now play a selection from the opera *La Boheemee*.' Nor is his sense of location very exact: 'We will now play a South American number called "Mexican Nights".' The dinner that follows starts with an announcement from the head table: 'Gentlemen, I sent today a telegram to the Queen—"Your Majesty, the old comrades of the Grenadier Guards dining tonight at Worcester send you their loyal greetings." I have received the following reply—"To the old comrades dining tonight at Worcester, the Queen thanks you for your loyal greetings."'

Once the clapping dies down, Bill launches his musicians into a series of galops, the theory being that dining in quick two time should speed up the eating. Likewise, if the musicians are required to play after the speeches, they perform soothing melodies like Borodin's 'Nocturne' or Tchaikovsky's 'Andante Cantabile'. Before the speeches, the emcee toasts the Queen (God bless her) and the other members of the royal family (all the other mumble-mumble) and, after the speeches, there is a chance for the diners to mingle. Inevitably, old officers in an advanced state of decrepitude with a chest of medals ask one of the musicians his age. The musicians learn to be miserly: 'Seventy, sir.' 'I'm eighty-eight,' comes the triumphant reply, as though he's just won at bingo.

There are moments when the importance of the occasion requires the presence of Major Harris rather than Sergeant Goodwin. Dinners at the Mansion House and the Guildhall are often attended by esteemed dignitaries and other persons so illustrious that the musicians have no idea who they are. In deference, Major Harris appears in his finery, down to the white gloves, looking the very model of a modern major general. These banquets feature the loving cup—a thousand guests individually rise in pairs to offer each other a sip from a large golden chalice—a ceremony that might, in the light of modern hygiene, be discontinued. The grotesque figures of Gog and Magog look down from the corner as the cup bobs its way around the tables. The band plays on.

No free dinners here. Jan cares little for these protracted evenings, and for similar reasons, cares little for the the Royal Investiture. Musicians march over from Birdcage Walk to Buckingham Palace and are shown upstairs into an organ loft. The organ turns out to be fake; the musicians creep through the spaces that should be holding pipes, and into a small musicians' gallery at the head of the ceremonial hall. Rows of chairs are laid out. However softly the musicians play, it never seems soft enough. There is a little buzzer by Major Harris's elbow. If the musicians wander into *mezzopiano*, as they do periodically throughout the afternoon, a reminding buzz causes the major to jump nervously.

There is another occasion that calls for perpetual *pianissimo*—the graduating ceremony of London University which takes place annually at the Albert Hall. The Queen Mother, their president—invariably looking radiant in powder blue—takes centre stage. The small band of musicians discreetly placed in the corner plays *pianissimo* throughout the afternoon, a very tiring thing to do. After the speech of welcome, the graduates are invited to stand up and in single file, come down to the stage to shake hands with the Queen Mother and receive their folios. The entire audience stands. Between numbers, Jan looks out at the huge arena. For the first hour, the density of bodies seems about the same. By the third hour, significant gaps have appeared in the higher rows of chairs, and by the fourth hour, only the last row files up to the lectern to receive their parchment and shake hands with the Queen Mother, who's still smiling. The band plays on, *pianissimo*.

INTERLUDE: BEDSITTERS

'Every house on the street was a bedsitter,' says Normsk. 'Every person a different person living a different life.'

'That's right,' says Jan. 'I would look across the street and see people in the windows typing, working out, going to bed, getting up. In my house we had bachelors, mysterious spinsters, young nurses, Australians, Dutch. It's where I first met some Canadians—four girls sharing the front suite. There were two sisters, Alice and Veronica, whose father had helped shore up the foundations of Salisbury Cathedral.'

'I met my first Canadian girl in a bedsitter,' muses Normsk. 'We looked out of the window in the morning and across the street there was a naked guy in the window drying himself off after a bath. He had a huge erection right at the window. Rather embarrassing at the time. But didn't you know Andy Babinchuck? He's Canadian.'

'Sort of. Viola player.'

'There's a lovely story about him,' says Phil. 'The Royal Philharmonic Orchestra were working with Stokowski who, although he was born and raised in London, affected to know little English. Andy offered to take him back to his hotel in his little car. They were driving past the Houses of Parliament when Stokowski peers out of the passenger window and says "What name big clock?" "Hell," says Andy, "I dunno. I've only been here six months."'

Phil pulls on his pipe. 'When I was single, I was in a succession of bedsits and boarding houses while on tour with Sadler's Wells.'

'Mrs Davies was the name of the lady who ran our bedsitter,' says Jan. 'Ex-actress. She kept reminiscing about her glory days. Always talking about Esme Percy. When you came home there was mail on the table in the hallway along with a quarter pint milk bottle, each bottle with a wooden collar bearing your room number, which you replaced with an empty. I don't know what the deal was but that bedsitter in Inverness Terrace was actually illegal. Once a year the house was inspected—the cooking hot plates dismantled, the milk bottles hidden and the chairs drawn over the greasy areas of the carpet. Could have fooled no one except by backhanding them a crisp five-pound note.

'Inverness Terrace was the boundary line between the boroughs of Paddington and Notting Hill. It bordered Hyde Park and was a popular road for the tarts to solicit. When the Bayswater municipality decided to haul them in, the tarts moved across the street to the Notting Hill side. Sometimes, crossing Hyde Park from the Albert Hall, I scuttled past them and they eyed my cello case and said, "Can I help you carry that home, dearie?"

'It was a soft case in those days and I did a lot of walking. One evening, walking to Hampstead Tube Station, I passed two policemen having a smoke in a brick archway to a well-appointed house. One of them nodded in the direction of my cello case. "If that had the word swag on it I'd nab you."'

'Ah, Hyde Park,' says Normsk. 'One evening Diana and I went for a picnic. We took wineglasses and a blanket and hired two deck chairs from the attendant. We set out the blanket under a chestnut tree and, having eaten and drunk the wine, were pretty soon under the blanket. After a while, in the encircling twilight, I saw the attendant walking across the grass towards us. We frantically pulled at our clothes and tried to hide the bottles and glasses and ourselves under the blanket as he arrived: "I thought I should tell you that the chairs have to be back in ten minutes. The park is closing."'

THIRTEEN

Große Fuge

Jan opens a newly arrived BBC music magazine. His interest is quickened by news of an auction at Sotheby's of the manuscript of Beethoven's *Große Fuge* (*Great Fugue*), which Beethoven arranged for two pianos from the string quartet original, as was the fashion. The story goes that Beethoven, infuriated by another's arrangement, decided to go one better. Embedded in the article is a small photograph of the manuscript. Beethoven gave the world an eternal musical mystery by writing the principal theme not as quarter notes but as tied eighth notes. Whereas a string quartet can hint at the subtle difference by the way they bow it, the hammers of a piano can make no such distinction. Jan gets out the magnifying glass to study the photograph—Beethoven has left in the ligatures. Later, Jan phones Normsk to discuss the article.

'Funny you should phone,' Normsk replies. 'Hughie Maguire told me that his son works for Sotheby's and arranged for Hughie to have a private viewing. Personally, I could never stand the piece, neither for string quartet or a brace of pianos.'

* 1 9 5 6 *

In the barracks near Windsor Castle, Jan, with a pickup string quartet of fellow soldiers, battles the giant leaps of the opening of the *Große Fuge* for the first time. In the fury of the fight, Mike Casey, the second violinist, shouts, 'Whoa!' and everyone puts down their instruments, relieved. 'How are you supposed to play this motif?' he asks. 'Like this?' He plays a jabbed quarter note. 'Or like this?' he asks, bowing two tied eighth notes, leaning on the second.

'No,' interrupts Arwyn Jones, 'Beethoven keeps writing *forte* on the first note.'

The quartet begins again. The battle with late Beethoven will last all morning, if not a lifetime. At noon, they emerge from the heights of the *Große Fuge* to find a café that serves up the cheapest meal.

Each spring, the royal family escapes the tedium of its obligations for a month's seclusion at Windsor Castle. Bill Goodwin's Salon Orchestra of the Grenadier Guards is dutifully deployed here also. The barracks sit below the castle and seem almost devoid of life. Nobody seems to be in charge. Here, the string musicians moulder.

On rare warm afternoons, the boys of the quartet rent a large rowing boat. Since they are musician soldiers, not sailors, they struggle to get the craft pointed upstream. Suddenly, there's a flotilla of Eton scullers racing towards them, a master with a megaphone and bicycle riding down the towpath shouting advice: 'Get that bloody rowboat out of the way!' There is a frantic slapping of oars on the water. Eventually, the musicians steer the craft upstream to the first lock. The lockhouse advertises afternoon tea. In a moment of gentility, the soldiers have tea on the grass enjoying the warm sun and looking at the manicured banks of the river.

Duty sometimes intervenes with the exploration of chamber music. One morning the Military Band is required to play in the inner quadrangle of Windsor Castle. Three members are poached from the string quartet—two to take a handle on each side of the wicker hamper that holds the music, and one to carry, like a standard bearer, the director's music stand. Once inside the castle, they become music stands themselves, holding the cards for the players whose instruments are too short for accurate reading of the cards normally clipped to their bells. Jan draws the E-flat clarinet. As he stands there in the midmorning sun, sweating inside his red uniform, the leather banding of the bearskin shrinking around his damp forehead in the full frontal assault of the clarinet, he thinks, 'This noise must rival that of the bagpipes to frighten off the enemy.' Returning to barracks, Jan has a huge headache.

The Salon Orchestra is ordered to the castle only once more to play during the three springs of Jan's duty at Windsor. They have to provide background music for a royal banquet. A truck drives them through the gates; they lug their equipment across a lawn and down some steps leading to a spacious basement. No official welcomes them; they are greeted by suits of armour—visored figures leaning on swords pointed between their feet, amongst which are strewn small children's tricycles and bright plastic toys, playthings of Prince Charles and his siblings. The heirs apparent are hardly out of diapers.

The musicians climb a narrow stairway which leads to a small room, three flights up, which has a dumb waiter shaft but no windows. This room, the size of an average kitchen, barely accommodates the dozen musicians who, in full uniform (the director doesn't even remove his white gloves) play *fortissimo* for two hours until the air runs out. The sound has to be relayed down the shaft two floors and through the serving corridor into the banqueting hall. Whether 'The Pajama Game' actually reaches the ears of the diners is beyond surmise. After they finish playing, an official brings in thickly cut corned beef sandwiches with a crate of beer: 'You've got ten minutes to get this down and get out.'

Sometimes, if the afternoons are fine, the musicians rent a couple of punts to explore the Thames. The punts are narrow and flat-bottomed and are usually poled or paddled from the raised stern. These are ideal craft for exploring the secret backwaters that flow into the main channel. One sunny afternoon, a crew splashes the crew of a rival punt and races away up a backwater to escape reprisals. British naval heritage wells up in the soaked chests of the other crew who quickly give chase. In a series of manoeuvres that would have made Admiral Nelson proud, the craft closes in and engages the enemy between overhanging willows. Jan, furiously paddling, fails to notice the limb of a tree as the boat races underneath it and is swept into the river.

The willows belong to somebody's garden. Jan clambers up the bank onto the lawn. Nobody appears to be at home in the cottage. Jan takes off his clothes, wrings them out and lays them to dry on the grass. He lies in the sun for an hour before getting dressed and then walks, wearing soaked clothes, back to the barracks.

Since laundry is a problem at Windsor, Jan decides to wash his already wet clothes and have a warming bath at the same time. The bathroom sports four oversized baths designed for seven-foot guardsmen. Each bath has an oversized hole underneath the taps and none has a plug. The drain, visible through a metal grate, connects the baths and runs the length of the bathroom. Jan stuffs his clothes in the plug hole and runs the bath, soaping himself and hoping he won't drown.

He then does a silly thing. Propping himself on an elbow, instead of pulling all of his clothes out of the hole to wash them, he whimsically pulls out a single sock. Instantly, all his clothes are sucked into the drain. Jan scrambles out of the bath—he can see his clothes bobbing along under the metal grate, but there is no way to lift the grate. Jan follows his clothes the length of the bathroom until they disappear. He only has one spare set of clothes until he returns to London at the end of the week.

The days settle back to inactivity. Being out of town for a month is highly inconvenient for the strings. Most of them are serious students trying to continue their studies concurrently with their national service, all of them trying to eke out their army pay with whatever modest gigs fall their way. A third violinist, excluded from the quartet sessions, builds a canoe in the army shop and, at the end of the spring sojourn, phones for an army truck to take it back up to London. The quartet resumes their exploration of late Beethoven.

* * *

Beethoven chose at the heart of the *Große Fuge* to notate the principal motif not in quarters, as any other composer would have done, but in tied eighths. In the musicians' lexicon, tied eighths and a quarter should amount to the same thing, but the fact that Beethoven uses this notation throughout has to make the performer pause. It is possible that Beethoven, after years of chronic deafness, imagined double images, as a swimmer might experience when the ears are blocked with water. A simpler explanation is likely—Beethoven philosophically wanted to contrast his assertive counterpoint with an uncertain, vulnerable motif. Whereas the bowing of a string instrument can suggest the tied eighths, the piano, as we understand it today, cannot. Jan remembers Colin saying that the mechanism of Beethoven's piano could be influenced by the pianist's touch, as could the mechanism of Bach's clavichord.

It's tempting, nevertheless, to attribute Beethoven's eccentricities to encroaching deafness; oddities in notation began to creep in while he was writing his E Minor Quartet. This was a time of crisis when Beethoven struggled to conceive his music as his ability to hear it declined. Musicians fight Beethoven's battle anew each time that quartet is performed, for it is awkward to play. Such is Beethoven's legendary status that his other physical frailties are of little account. He suffered from constipation and complained of flatulence (or was it everybody else who complained?) and attributed his deafness to his gastric problems. He could roar with convivial laughter, but as that world grew ever more silent, his music took on inward, spiritual dimensions that will never be replicated because of his unique position in musical history.

Beethoven pricks out vanity, pokes at complacency, takes the scruffs of our necks and drags us to places we don't recognize. His sense of structure is ever-enquiring, his use of unexpected accents would make

Stravinsky blush, his idiosyncratic dynamics set traps for the unwary. His banana-peel humour lurks in every score; Beethoven never tired of telling instrumentalists to crescendo to *subito piano*. Does Beethoven in heaven laugh daily at musicians on earth falling for his unexpected jokes? His critics were alternately baffled and irritated: 'We know Beethoven is a master but he's certainly screwed up this time.'

* * *

The demands of playing Beethoven create considerable tension in performing his works. He has a predilection for choosing an awkward tessitura to make his effects. Back in the barracks at Windsor, playing the *Große Fuge*, the quartet has stormed the heights of the first fugue and are now set on a search and destroy mission, groping for notes in the key of G-flat major, surrounded by a swarm of flats. Jan is stranded at the end of the fingerboard trying to play *pianissimo* when the members of the Military Band burst in. There are giggles and a sound like fingers tapping the side drum in Elgar's *Enigma Variations*. Jan had left his raincoat on the floor. The tuba player is pissing on it.

The Military Band were playing earlier at the parade celebrating the tercentenary of the Grenadier Guards, where the Queen inspected her guardsmen at Windsor Castle—not only those presently serving, but all former guardsmen who could still stand to attention. The ranks, lined up under a sunny sky on an unusually warm day, awaited Her Majesty who was royally late. Several proud old comrades keeled over under the weight of their medals and were ambulanced off to obscurity.

At the end of the parade, the band was allowed into the refreshment marquee where they found bottles of champagne and scoffed the lot. Now the quartet puts away thoughts of any more Beethoven. The tuba player is about to pass out, so he's led to his bed, which is unfortunate because he's also the double bass player and his presence is required for the dance band that is to play for the evening festivities. Clearly, he isn't going to make it. Jan offers to sub for him: 'No, I don't know anything about a bass, but I can thump out a bass line. Nobody will know the difference.'

Nobody does. Nobody cares. Jan, uniformed, plucks at the bass all night until his first two fingers are covered in blisters. Someone hands round restorative beers to the band at the end of the show: 'Here's to the next 300 years.'

Portrait: Normsk

One of Normsk's more embarrassing moments came when he was in the Royal Horse Guards, serving duty at Windsor Castle. His horse suddenly ran amok. There was nothing he could do except hang on to its neck as it raced through the castle grounds. It threw up turf in the lawns, ripped through bushes and flung gravel off the paths. The gardeners waved their rakes behind him. Says Normsk, 'I was deep in the Windsor soup for that!'

INTERLUDE: PRINCE GALITZIN

The Quartet tends to linger over coffee breaks. The boys know that, back on their chairs, they will have to tackle the slow movement of op. 127, Beethoven's Quartet in E-flat Major.

'Why did we ever agree to play this at Carnegie Hall?' moans Fred.

They reach the E major section. The music is very slow and Jan struggles to play the first bar in one bow.

Normsk stops. 'Why do you play it in one bow? Can't you split it?'

'That's what I was doing, until I read that Beethoven sent the music to Prince Galitzin in St. Petersburg and followed up with a letter,' says Jan.

'Saying what?' asks Fred.

'That he'd left out a slur in this bar of the cello part and could it be added to the manuscript,' says Jan. 'He went to all that trouble.'

'I once played squash with Prince Galitzin,' says Normsk. The others look at him in disbelief.

'No, really. Simon and I used to play squash at a club in Berkeley Square. Not too posh but it had amenities other than squash courts. Anyway, I was practising one Saturday morning when the squash coach came by and asked if I would give the prince a game. I asked the coach his name—Galesteen. Sounded Pakistani—all the world champions at squash are Pakistanis. Turned out this boy was fourteen years old and I beat him. He was the direct descendant of Prince Galitzin who commissioned Beethoven. There are various lines of the Galitzin family—some in England and Ireland. I played with another fourteen-year-old boy named Khan who would become a world champion in a few years' time. This time he really was a Pakistani. I beat him, too.'

FOURTEEN

Schelomo

In the hall of the Vancouver Academy of Music, Jan watches young cellists wait their turn to play for Zara Nelsova, who is conducting a masterclass. In the middle of the morning, there is a ten-minute break. A tray with coffee and biscuits is set down beside Zara.

An elderly man with wild white hair suddenly appears. 'Zara, my dear,' cries Jan Cherniavsky, a long-time friend of Zara's whose attachment probably stems from them both having family piano trios made up of siblings. Cherniavsky has contributed much to the Vancouver music scene, not least because he helped to develop the VSO. (Jan has regarded him as an eccentric ever since he pinned Jan down at a post-VSO cocktail party. Cherniavsky, pipe in hand, standing too close, kept poking Jan in the chest with its stem: 'It must come from the heart'—[poke, poke]—'and not from the head'—[poke]—'You understand, yes?'—[poke]—'Of course, it has to come from the heart and not the head.')

Cherniavsky now brandishes his pipe over the coffee tray, talking excitedly to Zara. Hardly stopping for breath, he pulls out his tobacco pouch and begins to fill his pipe. Flakes fall into her coffee. He tamps down the tobacco into the bowl; more flakes fall into the milk jug. The inconvenience of folding the pouch and putting it back into his pocket produces a further shower of tobacco over the sugar and Zara's plate, which holds a digestive biscuit.

'Zara, we must continue,' comes a voice from the back. She resumes her place on stage, coffee and biscuit abandoned.

* 1958 *

Jan in his bedsitter listens to Zara Nelsova's recording of Ernest Bloch's *Schelomo*. Even on his small LP turntable, Jan finds her sound sumptuous. The memory of Bloch's powerful, physical presence has stayed with Jan since his summer in California, but it's only now that he's fallen under the spell of Bloch's voluptuous music, and daily listens for every nuance of Zara's playing of it.

Jan's military days are coming to an end. After three years, Bill Goodwin has exhausted the Guards' music library, and is reduced to bringing up old silent movie scores, written in pale blue ink on silver paper. Thinking about the necessity of earning a living in a few months, Jan has applied to the LSO for an audition and is preparing *Schelomo*. He tries to copy Zara's tonal extravagance. A recording exaggerates sound production and Jan, putting all those studies—Klengel, Grützmacher, Romberg et al.—behind him, puts an intensity into his playing that has not occurred to him before.

Like Normsk, Jansk and many other musicians including Leopold Stokowski, Zara didn't always have a Russian name. Originally Sara Katznelson from Winnipeg, she attended the Royal Academy of Music where she met Colin. They remained lifelong friends. Colin introduced Zara to Bloch while working with the Griller on his quartets at Agate Beach in California, where Bloch lived. Colin recommended that Bloch consider her for a proposed recording of *Schelomo*, and Bloch agreed. The circumstances surrounding the recording were not propitious. Postwar London's electrical grid was not yet stable, and so sessions were held at night while most Britons were in bed in order to avoid the fluctuations of current that occurred during the day when the system couldn't cope. It was very cold in the studio. However, Bloch, at the control booth, kept the musicians' fingers nimble through his insistence on strict adherence to his surprisingly fast metronome markings. Despite these obstacles, the result was a magnificent recording with the Royal Philharmonic Orchestra (RPO), which now entertains Jan's bedsitter neighbours for weeks on end.

Months after the recording session in London, Zara performed *Schelomo* again at a concert in the USA, this time with Bloch conducting. The cellist opens the piece with a solo A under a fermata before the orchestra enters. Jan heard from Colin that Zara, mindful of Bloch's metronome and with the length of her bow already half spent, wondered if Bloch would ever bring in the orchestra.

Bloch wrote *Schelomo* in 1916. It was a compositional period when Bloch, a late starter, found his unique voice through his Jewish background. *Schelomo* is a triumphant masterpiece blending the solo cello's warm and sometimes plaintive sound with a rich orchestration. By listening to Zara's recording and trying to replicate everything she does,

Jan begins to understand what is possible, if not achievable. Zara's recording lifts him to a new level of performance. But fine as it is, Zara's isn't the defining interpretation. Public opinion awards it to Emanuel Feuermann's 1940 performance with Leopold Stokowski and the Philadelphia Orchestra. Soloist, conductor and orchestra were equally heroic. Incidentally, Bloch disliked this recording. He thought it too schmaltzy, preferring *Schelomo* to be more direct and universal. But even so, the passion, loquacity and enlarged orchestral sound are all evident, expressing the burning sincerity of Bloch—Swiss-born, American citizen, but *primus inter pares*, a citizen of the musical world.

At the bedsitter in Bayswater, Jan is striving for a colourisitic effect as he swoops down the fingerboard to the high point of the melody. A large shift is a matter of faith for a cellist but for Jan it's the right fingering to express the melody's plaintive quality in contrast to the astringent harmony that supports it.

A tread on the stair—his neighbour returning from work—reminds Jan that it's his turn to go to work, and he packs up his cello and takes the Underground to Piccadilly and Lyons Corner House, where he is subbing for musicians taking summer holidays. With *Schelomo*'s sorrowful melody still in his ears, he sits down next to the leader of the band and his gaze falls on the numbers tattooed on her forearm. Lily Mathé is a Hungarian woman who played violin in the camp orchestra, serenading the prisoners filing to the gas chambers at Auschwitz. Playing, she had watched her parents file past. 'They never looked up,' she said.

Jan reflects that Bloch's celebration of Jewish melodies in *Schelomo*, written forty years earlier, takes on a new and frightful perspective when played in the aftermath of the Second World War. (One Saturday during the war, on his way to his cello lesson, Jan and Elf walked past the cinema where they usually took in the cartoons and newsreels. That Saturday, and for several Saturdays afterwards, there were life-size cut-outs of emaciated prisoners in striped garb. Jan saw, in graphic detail, the horrors of Belsen. Jan's mother avoided the cinema for over a month. The world was forever, for Jan, a changed place.) Jan has always felt a haunting guilt for what was perpetrated and allowed to happen. He glimpses Lily's tattooed numbers catching the light as her hand travels up the fingerboard of her violin.

Lily now announces to her band, who are wearing—a nod to the Gypsy element—yellow boleros stored in smelly lockers back of the spacious kitchen, 'Now, "Dance of the Icicles". Somebody's written under the title, "Dance of the Testicles". What's that?'

'It's a medical term,' the pianist explains.

The band launches in.

As much as national service is a constant distraction, life in the army enables Jan to continue studying. In London after basic training in Caterham, Jan enrolled part time at the Guildhall School of Music, and now studies cello with William Pleeth at his house, plays chamber music with student colleagues and plays gigs as all students do—weddings, low budget musicals, enterprises that never pay up and events where everybody involved shares the gate. Jan and his fellow musicians are gaining experience in the field—between gigs, comrade dinners and daily rehearsals, they play a lot of music.

On Sunday afternoons, Jan is frequently invited to play quartets with three doctors at the Hampstead home of the first violinist who owns several Italian instruments. Jan's afternoons with the doctors usually begin with Haydn, bound in leather volumes. A tray of tea, complete with sponge cake, bisects the session. Following tea is something more demanding like Beethoven or Brahms. As Jan leaves, the leader thanks him and presses a ten-shilling note into his hand. The leader is a well-known heart specialist who, Jan hears years later, was consulted by Rostropovich. Perhaps Rostropovich had been prevailed upon to play quartets with the worthy doctors of an afternoon, probably without the ten-shilling note. In England, where music education has been universally strong, there have been orchestras comprised entirely of members of the medical profession. Doctors make good musicians—generally it doesn't work the other way around.

* * *

Audition day finally arrives. Jan plays *Schelomo* for all he is worth to a group of men sitting at a table under a haze of cigarette smoke. He is not playing for them. He is reaching out to the musical heavens. He is not nervous. He starts his bow at the point, giving the opening A a slight ping, developing the note from *piano* to *mezzo voce*, where, underneath, the imagined orchestra releases him to play the first aching phrases. He plays phrase after phrase; the orchestra is still there. A voice in the distance says, 'Thank you.' Jan continues. 'Thank you,' the faraway voice insists. 'That's enough.'

Afterwards, he is given the cello solo from the slow movement of Brahms's Second Symphony to sight-read. Jan launches into it without a second glance—allegro. Harry Dugarde, the chairman of the orchestra, approaches Jan afterwards. 'That was fine. We'll use you. By the way,' he says, pointing to the Brahms, 'Adagio.'

Portrait: Rodney

Jan's cousin Rodney swigs his pint of bitter. 'Are you glad you're out?'

'Of course, civvy street has never seemed so sweet,' replies Jan. 'One thing I was always anxious about was the trooping of the colour. As Bill Goodwin explained it, in case of rain, we were to hide in the truck parked round the side of Buckingham Palace. Then if it began to rain, we were to rush the capes out to the band, giving one to the music director first. It had the potential to look totally idiotic. Thank God it never rained.'

'But it did this year,' says Rodney.

'I know. Luckily I was back on civvy street. I went to the News Theatre to see the Gaumont British News and there they were, the string players running around in circles with those capes like a disturbed ants' nest.'

Rodney takes another swig. 'The soldiers used to stand behind those trucks, having an illicit cigarette. They would hide one in the palm of the hand and blow the smoke up their sleeves. Sometimes they'd have to stand to attention and wisps of smoke would appear to be coming out their ears. You know that story, how one warm spring morning the band was playing in front of the palace and King George suggested they take off their greatcoats? Beautiful coats—they buttoned tight at the collar right down to the ankles so the band didn't bother to wear their red jackets underneath. The men, very reluctantly, began unbuttoning until the music director began to see white singlets. Then he barked the order to adjust their dress.'

'There was that other nice story about King George,' says Jan, 'who was concerned about the slovenly playing of the trombones. He complained to the music director: "Why can't all the trombones coordinate their slides so they move together?"'

'Cheers.'

'Why is it?' Phil says, 'that people feel a compulsion to throw a reception after a concert?'

'Well, if it's right there in the hall, that's okay,' says Fred.

'Rarely is,' replies Normsk. 'Inevitably it's miles away.'

'Do you remember that concert in Castlegar,' Phil says, 'we got to this house and there was only one man there. He sidles up to me and nudges me. "Mahler's Eighth," he says. I nod. Then he nudges me again. "*Madame Butterfly.*" I say, "Absolutely." Then he nudges me again. "Razumovsky Quartets." "The best," I reply. Then, thank God, some other people arrived.'

'Then there was the time,' says Fred, 'when the house was so crowded we could only just get in the front door. Trouble was, the food and drinks were in the kitchen by the back door. We had to engage in conversation and try and work our way to the goodies. Everybody was saying goodbye and leaving as we got to the groaning board. We drank and stuffed ourselves frantically as everybody had their backs to us waving goodbye.'

'Then there was that peculiar time in Revelstoke,' says Phil. 'That lady came up to us in intermission to tell us there was a reception at her house in the main street near our hotel. Couldn't miss it. She gave us the street number.'

'Oh, that was odd,' says Jan. 'Talking of groaning boards. Her kitchen shelves were lined with back numbers of *Gourmet* magazines and her dining table was laid out with hors d'oeuvres, savoury dishes, desserts and cheese plates. She'd prepared them all and they were all wonderful. But nobody else came. She kept saying that they would all be there shortly, but the doorbell never rang.'

'It was on the way to Revelstoke,' says Normsk quietly, 'where we all thought we were going to get nabbed. I forget where we were coming from but it took hours of driving cross country without seeing another human being. We were just passing the paper bag around when a police siren made us jump out of our skins. This police car passed us in a hurry and round the next corner we saw a car in the ditch.'

'Close shave, sir!' says Fred.

FIFTEEN

Ein Heldenleben

The adults around the barbecue sip their gin and tonics and keep an eye on the children. Normsk is very good at barbecues. A fine judge of the coals, he turns the steaks to perfection. 'Need the hot mustard?' Normsk asks, passing a plate to Simon Streatfeild, associate conductor of the VSO and a close friend of Normsk's. Normsk then turns to Jan. 'Need a refill?' Needing no answer, he continues, 'Simon has just ruined the rest of the summer for me. He's programmed *Heldenleben* for next season.'

'Better get rosining that bow!' Fred crows, chewing on an ice cube.

* 1958 *

Jan watches from the cello section as sound engineers from Everest Records finalize the position of two microphones the size of index fingers above the LSO, which has been hired by Everest to do three sessions a day for three weeks in Walthamstow. The microphones can hear your beard growing. (The sound is phenomenal and has stood the test of time. Years later, Mercury will buy out Everest and re-release many recordings on CD.) Everest is a technical spinoff from NASA. Space-age recording technology was built into a recreation vehicle, which was shipped over to Walthamstow from the United States and is now parked behind the town hall. Walthamstow, despite its proximity to central London, is a sleepy town. Musicians can pick up a fortifying cup of coffee at George's Tank, a greasy spoon café, to be ready and prepared for the squalls ahead.

Anticipation is running high among the musicians. First up is Richard Strauss's *Ein Heldenleben* (A Hero's Life). Between fighting his enemies, our hero spends thirteen minutes thinking about his wife in the form of a lengthy violin solo. Jan notices the concertmaster, Hugh Maguire, rosining his bow in preparation for his big event—a lone violin just before the battle.

The cacophony of the LSO warming up for *Heldenleben* is suddenly quieted as the conductor appears on the podium. The piece opens with a phalanx of lower strings and French horns thrusting upward in unison, chomping at the bit like nervous racehorses. They're off, braying unaccompanied, Strauss's improbable tune joyously leading the pack as the rest of the orchestra hustles along after them. The piece works on two levels—on one, Strauss is the hero battling his inevitable critics. But there is another level, where a universal hero fights the just cause with sword and shield. Eight French horns, having slain their enemies, empty their spittle while Hugh Maguire muses on the girl that was left behind. Thoughts about her are cast aside. She's left on a bed of G-flat major as the full orchestra charges noisily towards victory.

The hero's final withdrawal from the world coincides with lunch. The orchestra emerges to daylight for one hour's break. Time being of the essence, the musicians have a choice between the pub or the cinema restaurant, the only eating places hard by. Surprised by this sudden influx at the cinema, the single waitress, her black doily unruffled, toils at the brown Windsor soup, labours under the liver and onions and triumphs over the Bakewell tart and custard. No time for coffee. Musicians late getting their orders in bang spoons on their plates futilely. Back to battle.

They are greeted in the hall by Neville Marriner, the principal second violin, who says to anybody who cares to listen, 'Do you know who I've just seen in the high street? Joseph Szigeti.'

'Go on, Nev, you must be mistaken.' They glance at their music stands. Sure enough, Brahms's Violin Concerto is there. Minutes later, Szigeti walks out, violin and bow in hand, a bath towel draped over his shoulder. Bartók wrote a rhapsody for Szigeti in his proud years. Now Szigeti is an old man and the tremor in his bow, which often dogged the initial moments of his recitals, is not equal to the long phrases Brahms sometimes demands. In an ascending passage where the bow, travelling from point to heel, is about to repeat the melody, Szigeti's bow arm shakes and the sound cracks. Poor man—those two bars are recorded thirty times. He needs that bath towel but he accepts his situation with equanimity. He shows the violinists his spatulated fingers: 'Too much practising as a boy.' He shows them the mutilated base of the scroll on his Guarneri violin. Bronislaw Huberman, its previous owner, had hacked it off with a penknife: 'Got in the way of his thumb.'

The musicians return to the cinema restaurant for the evening meal and figure that their chance of actually finishing is better if they order something cold. Pilchard salad is on the menu. Everybody is served but they've hardly lifted their forks when they notice little hopping things flying from salad to salad, table to table.

It seems that Everest is intent on hopping through the orchestral repertoire as well. At the end of the day, the performance finished ahead of schedule, Max Burwood, the librarian, hands out *Eine Kleine Nachtmusik* to be knocked off in the last half hour of the session. Spare a thought for Max and the rest of the viola section—they've been holding up their instruments for nine hours. It may be 'The Blue Danube' tomorrow night.

✳ ✳ ✳

Heldenleben was Strauss's last great orchestral tone poem. The sweeping brush strokes of the violin solo, where our hero, larger than life, is dreaming of his wife, suggest emotional consummation. Strauss and his wife, Pauline, a singer and fine interpreter of his songs, shared a high-octane marriage. This feeling of fulfillment overtakes the listener with all Strauss's romantic melodies. This, and the brilliance of the music, keeps Strauss a favourite for inclusion in every orchestral season.

He is also a top favourite for orchestral auditions. String players learn early to be wary of Strauss. Even those sitting at the back of a section are not safe. Strauss had a discomfiting habit of directing the last desk to open a passage. (Once, after visiting Colin in Berkeley, Jan found himself sitting next to a violin graduate of the Vancouver Academy of Music on the flight home. 'What have you been learning this year?' he asked conversationally.

'The first violin part of *Don Juan.*'

'The whole year?' Jan was shocked. What a waste of a precious year.)

Strauss, to bring further expression to his music, employed an *al fresco* technique—the sheer number of notes were not there to be played accurately but for effect—the instrumental version of the crowd scene. Thus, in his first masterful tone poem, *Don Juan*, Strauss opens the work with an eruption—the orchestra rapidly ascending from low to top register to introduce a braggadocio tune that strives to climb ever higher. The swaggering character of Don Juan is established right away, which doesn't negate the sincerity of the love music following later.

Strauss had a brilliant career. Once regarded as an *enfant terrible*, his reputation was unhindered by such shockers as *Electra* and *Salome*. Despite its one act, *Salome* is a milestone in operatic excess. The libretto, based on Oscar Wilde's text, is a graphic depiction of sex, violence and decadence set to an orgy of orchestral sound. When it was first produced in New York in 1907, violent protests were the result. It was taken out of the repertoire and not reinstated until much later.

* * *

The LSO in 1959 sets up for a televised performance of *Salome*. Extraordinarily, since there isn't room to accommodate the orchestra, they are housed in the BBC's Maida Vale Studio, while the singers are across town in White City. This arrangement requires an awful lot of wires, with cables running across the studio between music stands. There is an unexplained delay. The musicians sit idle while the engineers gesticulate behind the soundproof glass in the console. Norman Jones, a cellist, glances down at the thickest cable and notices that it isn't plugged in. Problem solved.

Walter Goehr, wearing headphones and watching monitors, has been hired as the studio conductor. The BBC has decided that they can save several minutes' rest for Christa Ludwig, who is singing the role of Salome, by prerecording her 'Dance of the Seven Veils'. Unwisely, perhaps, they decide to save money by filming her dance to a piano accompaniment. This dance ain't no regular two-step; it's a hornet's nest of rubato and changing tempos. Walter Goehr, one headphone on for the pianist and one off to hear the orchestra, has to guide the real sound into the beginning of the recorded piano sound, follow the nuances throughout the dance, then guide the orchestra back to the real singers. By the end of the dance, sweat drips from his face. Unfortunately for him, there's another hour of the opera to run before he can dry off and get to that beer.

This televised version of *Salome*, half a century after its forced removal from the repertoire by the Metropolitan Opera, is viewed by eleven million people. It is a twentieth-century irony that Strauss received the Gold Medal of the Philharmonic Society in London in 1937, and was exonerated by a special court in Munich investigating Nazi collaborators in 1948. Music, not politics, was the lifetime preoccupation of Strauss. His musical characterizations are wide and unerring—from the erotic necrophilia of *Salome* to the wacky elegance of *Don Quixote*, the swagger of *Don Juan*, the medieval humour of *Till Eulenspiegel* and the gorgeous pastiche of a Mozart comedy, *Die Rosenkavalier*. At the end of a stupendous career, Strauss wrote *Metamorphosen*, his great lament for ruined Germany, which dwells upon the opening phrase of the funeral march from Beethoven's 'Eroica' Symphony. It provides a sad coda for the larger than life hero of *Ein Heldenleben*.

Portrait: Sir Neville Marriner

Neville plays principal second violin in the LSO. Known to Jan and his colleagues as 'Nev', he always turns up to rehearsals smartly dressed, with a box containing a lunch that's slightly higher up in the food chain than anyone else's—a globe artichoke, a Belgian endive, kumquats.

While in the LSO, he founds the Academy of St Martin in the Fields, of which Jan is also a founding member. Despite its laborious title, the Academy, as it's shortened, becomes a worldwide success due to Nev's impeccable ear for recorded sound. As he transitions into the world of conducting, Nev doesn't let success and fame set him apart from his instrumental beginnings. Once, on a guest appearance in Vancouver to make a studio recording for the CBC, Nev, unhappy with the acoustics, thinks that the woodwinds should be rearranged and put on risers behind the strings. Most conductors would lean against the rails of the podium and wait for the technician to emerge to do the work. But on making the decision, Nev at once sets about dragging the risers out himself.

Nev will always be Nev to his colleagues—a musician's musician.

NM

Portrait: LSO

In the 1950s, when postwar England is traumatized and deprived, people turn to music for solace. This is fortunate for Jan, who's entering the music profession at a time when London alone boasts five major symphony orchestras and two opera companies. There are chamber orchestras, light orchestras, radio orchestras and theatre orchestras. The BBC inaugurates its third program devoted to high art in addition to its other two channels, continuing its programs of cultural earnestness. The new long-playing record propagates a myriad of performance projects and the film industry still uses a continuum of music to further its plots along. The British musician has a reputation for accurate sight-reading and, thanks to the iron grip the United States Musicians' Union has over recording fees, North American companies prefer to spend their dollars in England where rates are cheaper.

Unlike its North American counterparts, the LSO is self-governing, its directors drawn from its playing membership. When Jan joins the orchestra in 1958, he's required to buy shares, with the expectation that his money will be returned should he decide to leave. The treasurer and chairman of the board is Jan's desk partner, Harry Dugarde. No doubt Harry has seen better days as a player and so has his cello, which has a split down the length of its back. Sometimes, in a careless moment of bowing, this split rumbles like the sound of a departing motorbike. Harry appears not to notice. The cello, when not on stage, lives in a travelling box. The cello and Harry live separate lives.

Harry, however, is the most important person in the orchestra. He pays out the money. Unbelievably, this is paid out in cash during rehearsal intermissions. After waiting for the bank to open, Harry arrives half an hour late for rehearsal with his cello and briefcase. In the thrall of the conductor, Josef Krips, Jan is acutely embarrassed by this routine. Harry, his glasses as thick as Krips's, stumbles to his chair and places his cello noisily on the floor. He tightens his bow, unlocks his briefcase and retrieves his metal box of rosin. The lid of the box, sticky from rosin, resists his attempts to open it until at last it explodes open, spilling several pieces of rosin on the floor. Harry, whose one eye is stronger than the other, looks for the pieces, head cocked to one side like a parrot. He then fits the pieces back in the box and wipes the bow across them with a flourish. Then he reverses the process, trying to ease the lid on the box. He peers at the music and turns to Jan: 'Where are we?' Jan, playing the slow movement of the 'Eroica', points quickly to the place. One day, Harry, fresh from the bank, places his briefcase on the back bumper of his car while in conversation by the stage door. He drives home through central London with the briefcase sitting there. He finds it as he's shutting the garage door. After this, the orchestra is paid by cheque.

The orchestra is male, with the exception of the harpist, Marie Goossens, who, waiting her turn to play in a rehearsal, reads the *Financial Times* while smoking a pipe. Indeed, most rehearsals are attended by a cloud of tobacco smoke. It's at this time when the medical profession first brings forth the correlation between heavy smoking and lung cancer. The newspapers are full of it. (The quip of the day is that the smoker is so alarmed he gives up reading the article.) Jan draws Harry's attention to the articles and is disconcerted by his reply: 'Jan, I was sent to the trenches in 1916 when I was your age. We learned to smoke and it was our one solace against the fear and the miseries we went through. I'm not stopping now.'

In the public eye, humour has to be *sub rosa*. Traditionally, orchestra members shuffle their feet, like applause, when one of their members has dispatched a difficult solo. Musicians vary this practice, for example during the first tableaux of *Petroushka* when the trombones go re papa pom-pom, the shuffling may echo that rhythm. Humour can erupt spontaneously, such as during a particular performance of Ravel's 'Bolero', the beginning of which requires the cellos to pluck beats one and three quietly, endlessly. On the silent beat two, Harry points his right forefinger in the air. This is pretty soon taken up by all eight cellos, getting more elaborate as Ravel thickens his scoring. Managers in North America would reprimand if not fire you for that. In London, you can cross the street to alternative employment—another orchestra, another self-promoting conductor.

Harry can bow the cello, cigarette in hand, or thumb out pound notes and cigarette ash and, if the music requires it, jam the cigarette between the legs of the music stand. One of Harry's cigarettes makes an auspicious appearance once on a quick tour with the LSO to the Netherlands. In Haarlem, in the historic civic hall after a speech of welcome, Harry grinds out his cigarette on the marquetried floor before replying.

There is another cellist in the section, who, like Harry is never without a cigarette. Paul Talagrand has been in the orchestra a long time and keeps well away from his cello. He emerges from the Underground, reading his *roman*, its spine bent back so he can hold it with one hand. He continues reading, walking like an automaton to the escalator, never taking his eye off the page as the escalator carries him up to daylight and so to the green room where he can get reacquainted with his cello. Unlike Harry, he arrives in time for the rehearsal. Just in time. Paul's routine is always the same—he opens the folder and exclaims, 'Oh, not this goddamn thing again,' and positively spitting, 'and this bloody thing, I hate it,' and 'Jesus Christ, we did this last week.' Paul, to his credit, loves Debussy.

The LSO was held together through the Second World War by a number of musicians deemed unfit for armed service. They are now past their prime but the orchestra is reluctant to let them go. The traditions of an orchestra are greater than the sum of its parts. Like the rear gunner, though, the French horn is less likely to survive than, say, the double bass. The double bass section evades the critical ear of many a conductor. To an uncritical ear in the audience, they produce a plausible rumble at the bottom of the orchestral sound, not unlike pushing wardrobes around. (Jan will overhear a bassist, Robert Meyer, produce this gem of a remark at a Vancouver school concert: 'The bigger the instrument, the bigger the fool that plays it.')

The state of things begins to change when Stuart Knussen takes charge of the LSO lower life. A stocky redhead who spices the bass line with plenty of accents, Stuart commands the LSO bass section with regimental discipline. He's on a crusade to clean up or clear out. Stuart at a *Messiah* rehearsal remarks, 'Hand me that rosin, boy. I'll show you who's the King of Glory.'

The LSO directors judiciously rebuilt the orchestra after the war years with young players like Stuart, and placed its artistic hopes in the hands of a series of internationally renowned conductors—Josef Krips, Leopold Stokowski, Pierre Monteux, Antal Doráti and Colin Davis. Jan joins the LSO just before the annual Beethoven cycle conducted by Krips, a batrachian figure—enormous body, wide face and eyes disproportionately magnified by powerful spectacles—who is an interpreter of the German classics.

However awesome his four beats to a bar, his genial humour provides moments of levity. 'It's spring!' he cries, launching into the *Pastoral* Symphony and once, before the slow movement of the Ninth, he says in a sepulchral voice across the heaving shoulders of the strings, 'Beethoven wrote this before he died.' Jan can't figure out Krips's favourite comment, 'ever parade'. It takes him to the next annual Beethoven cycle to realize that Krips is saying, 'evaporate'.

At the end of Jan's first Beethoven cycle, Krips and the soloists walk out for several curtain calls. Krips acknowledges the choir and motions for the orchestra to stand while the vocalists receive bouquets. Then he steps off the podium and strides toward Jan through the cello section. 'Oh my God! What's he going to do?' thinks Jan, his bowels turning to water as Krips reaches his music stand. Krips invites Harry, the chairman, to stand and gives him a bear hug. Relieved, Jan keeps tapping the music stand with his bow.

Antal Doráti, who usually conducts the Everest recording sessions, is an exemplary musician who rehearses his orchestra effectively, but on a very short fuse. His tantrums are renowned. He keeps his eye on his watch, which he places on the music stand by his score. Easily displeased, he's known on occasions to throw his watch onto the floor, stomp on it and walk out. The board of directors, who are also players, immediately walk out, too. Ten minutes later, mollified, Doráti returns with the directors. At hundreds of pounds a minute, they must have done some fast talking.

With an ivory complexion under a halo of thin white hair, Stokowski has the look of a carving lifted from a Baroque sarcophagus. His reputation is huge, as he built the Philadelphia Orchestra into a world-class orchestra, and is the only person ever to shake hands with Mickey Mouse on celluloid. (Stuart Knussen idolizes Stokowski and is in seventh heaven when Stokowski conducts a series of concerts with the LSO. Stuart brings his son, Oliver Knussen, a small boy, to the rehearsals to observe Stokowski's conducting. A few years down the road, Oliver will turn musical heads by conducting his first symphony with the LSO at the age of fifteen, and will in time become a renowned conductor and composer.)

The famous Stokowski sound is immediately achieved by rearranging the orchestra, winds on his right, strings on his left and the basses strung in a line across the back. Free bowing encourages a seamless, romantic sound from the strings. He uses no baton; the minimal gestures of his hands draw forth the sumptuous sound. Insisting on four consecutive mornings of rehearsal, he runs through a program, dismissing the orchestra halfway through the morning. This is repeated each morning except that at the end of the rehearsal, he repeats a couple of isolated passages.

His 'fractured' English, no doubt, contributes to the mystique. He stops the rehearsal in the middle of Debussy's *Images*. 'Trompettes, you have mute?' he asks. 'Nah, nah, not metal. It's *sourdines à la campania*.' He searches for a word. 'He needs an ear trumpet,' murmurs Jan. This remark spreads like an epidemic up the cello section. 'Ah, yes I have,' Stokowski says at last. 'Eet ees leather. Leather mute.'

In Stokowski's eloquent hands, Debussy fares better than Brahms and so the LSO records *La Mer* at Kingsway Hall. The Kingsway Hall is not an ideal recording studio. Originally a church, it stands over the subway. There are moments when recording is suspended while the underground trains pull away from nearby Kingsway Station. (Hugh Maguire is playing the solo violin cadenza from Rimsky-Korsakov's *Schehererzade* when the Central line rumbles below him. 'Don't worry about the train. It's way lower than your violin. We can eradicate it,' says a voice from control.)

Stokowski, who has many distinguished recordings to his name, brings his own engineer, a man called Yonez. Mr Yonez's name is invoked a lot. The studio is bristling with microphones standing like storks in a swamp throughout the orchestra. After every instrumental solo, Stokowski calls for Yonez to place a microphone up close to the soloist and the passage is then rerecorded. Yonez has to do a lot of mixing. No doubt, he's used to it. Jan discovers late in the session that his name is Jones.

Also at the end of a long career, Pierre Monteux is eighty-six in 1961 when he accepts the chief conductorship of the LSO. A benign figure and loved by musicians, he wears technicolor jackets that seem at odds with his French character. Sporting a drooping white moustache and black crinkly hair, he's asked why his moustache is white. 'Because eet has had more experiaance,' replies Monteux.

Monteux is a walking history book. As a violinist, he performed in the premiere of Debussy's opera *Pelléas et Mélisande* and his quartet played to Brahms: 'He was a large shadow in an armchair and didn't say much.' Once a conductor in the employ of the Diaghilev Ballet, he is self-effacing but brilliant, his baton technique unrivalled. He maintains a continued interest in presenting new music and young performers and his conducting students include Neville Marriner and André Previn.

All that upper arm exercise seems to make conductors a long-lived bunch. They have an invincible belief in their own immortality. Monteux, like Toscanini in old age, signed a twenty-five year contract with the LSO.

Eventually Toscanini forgot which Brahms symphony he was conducting. Rumour has it that Stokowski, incontinent, stood his ground on the podium. Monteux put his contract in jeopardy by surviving a fall from the platform. Simon Streatfeild still remembers Monteux's last words to him before his performance as principal viola about to characterize Sancho Panza in Strauss's *Don Quixote*: 'I 'ope you've brought your best viola.'

Portrait: Szeryng

'When I was in the LSO, we did this recording with Henryk Szeryng,' says Normsk. 'Not a happy occasion. At the end, he gave a card to the orchestra: 'Thank you for a fine recording.' The orchestra returned the compliment with a card featuring a photograph of a sheep: 'Thank you for a happy shearing.'

Normsk continues, 'But lost in translation was exemplified when Ricci recorded with Sir Adrian. Boult's British equanimity was tried hard through the sessions when Ricci kept calling him "Sir Boult". For some historic reason, Sir Adrian hated the LSO. He nearly always lost his temper when he worked with the orchestra.'

This reminds Normsk of another conductor. 'Ven I say *poco*, I mean *poco*,' he mutters with a wry smile.

INTERLUDE: JOHN GRAY

The Quartet is eating breakfast in the ferry en route to Victoria for a concert at the university. It's a typical West Coast drizzly day. The ferry noses its way through Active Pass, the narrow passage between the Gulf Islands. Through the raindrops on the window, atop an arbutus, seagulls harass a forlorn eagle.

'How did Stuart Knussen ever end up in Victoria?' asks Jan.

'Didn't he start the youth orchestra there? He certainly conducted it,' answers Normsk.

'He had a big reputation for getting people through professional auditions,' says Phil.

'Yes. Learn a list of orchestral excerpts as long as your arm with all the big violin solos in them—*Scheherazade, Heldenleben, Four Last Songs, Swan Lake, Sleeping Beauty*—all for two hundred a week, thirty-two-week season,' says Fred. 'Aren't you going to eat that sausage?'

'I remember Stuart Knussen and John Gray in the LSO, grunting together on the front desk of the bass section. Lots of accents,' says Normsk. 'We were recording *Alexander Nevsky*—big bass solo—Jan, it was your fellow cellist, Norman Jones, who looked back at Stuart and said of the hefty accents, "There's a difference between picking your arse and making it bleed."'

'John Gray told me this nice story,' says Jan. 'I guess he was in the BBC Symphony then. He had an apartment right across the street from Maida Vale Studios. They'd rehearsed that morning for a live broadcast in the evening. John, having had dinner back home, took off his shoes and was lounging by the fireplace and listening to the nine o'clock news. At the end of the news the announcer said that they would go over to their Maida Vale Studios for a concert by the BBC Symphony. Startled, John leaped out of his chair, put on his shoes, ran out of the door, across the street, down the corridor, tiptoed across the studio and was ready to play as the announcer finished his introduction. Luckily, he hadn't put his bass away; it was just standing in a corner.'

'There was that awful time, just after you arrived in Vancouver, Janski,' says Normsk, 'when the VSO was in the pit for the Winnipeg Ballet. *Swan Lake* I think. As usual, there was not much rehearsal time and I noticed discrepancies in one section between the violins and clarinet. I asked Ron de Kant, the principal clarinetist, if I could take his part home to check. The performance was on the following night. I entered the pit to tune the orchestra and the house lights were dimmed halfway, ready for the entrance of the conductor. As I motioned the winds to tune, I saw Ron beckoning to me. "Can I have my part?" he mouthed. Omigod! I'd left it at home.'

Normsk pauses to wipe bacon fat off his fingers with his handkerchief. 'I ran out of the pit, phoned Simon who luckily was staying at my house and he drove like ninety miles an hour to get to the theatre where the entire house was waiting for the curtain to go up.'

Jan looks anxiously at his watch. 'Shouldn't we be getting down to the car level?'

'Lots of time,' says Normsk. 'I'm going to buy a newspaper.'

SIXTEEN

Warhorses

Jan, in the middle of the Finale of Tchaikovsky's Fifth Symphony, is sight-reading whole paragraphs in a concert with the LSO at the Royal Festival Hall. With some exceptions, London orchestras perform music with inadequate rehearsal time. Warhorses of the repertoire—symphonies of Tchaikovsky, Brahms or Dvořák—are presumed learned from previous performances and are allowed little rehearsal time. In the three-hour rehearsal allotted to a concert—if it includes for instance Myra Hess playing the 'Emperor'—she has, of course, as soloist, to be allowed the courtesy of rehearsing the entire work with cadenzas. No musician will be note-perfect on his first performance—passagework can be rapid, keys elusive and rhythms can trip up the ill-prepared.

Harry Dugarde, playing next to Jan, knows Jan is inexperienced and good-humoredly tries to trip him up. There is a tense moment before the end of the Finale of Tchaikovsky's Fifth where a passage of orchestral busyness suddenly stops and the abyss of silence is stabbed by offbeat chords. This is prime domino country, a moment ripe for public humiliation.

Harry deliberately plays in the rest, a noise like chopping wood. Jan is about to follow, then in a split second, realizing Harry's game, catches his bow in midair and plays in the right moment. Harry grins—Jan has passed this little test. Harry doesn't care about the audience or the guest conductor, Royalton Kisch, 'Kisch for Cash', as he is known, one of a series of conductors who buys the orchestra's services for self-aggrandizement. Most surely with such a contract, a Tchaikovsky symphony is bound to follow.

It doesn't take long for Jan to assimilate the last three symphonies of Tchaikovsky. All three are performed every week. The musicians maintain a cheerful disrespect towards the music and a tinge of contempt for the man conducting it. In the Finale of the Fourth Symphony, after the opening salvo, a portentous tune is introduced; its lyricism invites words to be attached: 'Mother's got a boil on her arsehole,' a phrase most likely coined by orchestral players as soon as the ink had dried. Later on in the movement, as that tune gets fragmented throughout the orchestra, Norman Jones, Jan's fellow cellist, points out that all the neighbours are talking about it: 'Mother's got a boil on her, Mother's got a boil on her…'

Another of Kisch's favourites is Dvořák's 'New World' Symphony. In rehearsals, he looks every inch a businessman in his double-breasted suit and horn-rimmed glasses, and leads the rehearsals with a toffee-nosed disposition. He has garnered quite a following amongst the hoi polloi because, value for money, he throws in an extra overture (prelude, lude, and postlude, as it were) before the final work.

Frequently, he runs out of rehearsal time. 'Gentlemen, we'll just top and tail the Dvořák Symphony. You know my interpretation.' Indeed they do. The 'New World' is old hat.

In the concert—Kisch now in white tie and tails—arrives the first glimmer of comedy at the beginning of the slow movement. During the opening brass chords, Kisch's white waistcoat begins to come unstrapped. Maintaining a seraphic look behind those horn-rimmed spectacles, he begins to clutch at his chest with the hand not holding the baton. Normsk, visible at the front desk next to Hugh Maguire, begins to giggle quietly. The waistcoat sags to his stomach—more feverish clutching—as the strings play the melody 'Going Home'. Stifled mirth spreads. The vest now dangles at his crotch, the straps hanging down. The strings play soulfully on as if to the wounded *Titanic,* tears of laughter running down their cheeks. At last, the movement quickens to the oboe solo and the agitations of conducting cause the vest to drop to the podium. Simon Streatfeild, principal viola, quickly bundles it up under his chair. The orchestra plays on.

The orchestra looks forward to the next comic turn, but it doesn't arrive until the last page of the Finale. At the quiet coda, the motif, a triplet followed by a duplet, is handed down the string section. Three divided by two rhythmically can be a tricky thing. Kisch, unnerved by his vestlessness, arrives at this passage much too slowly. The violins, uncertain, play radada dum-dum. The violas, watching the deceleration anxiously, reply ra daa daa dumm-dumm. During the next deceleration, the cello section, like baseball players watching a very high ball to be caught, position themselves determined not to disappoint and play raa daa daa gedum gedumm. There is a low chortle from the trombone section. Then, as in Danny Kaye's recording 'Tubby the Tuba', they all play and the concert is over: 'We've done it, haven't we?' said the bullfrog. 'Oh,' said Tubby, 'how happy I am.'

Portrait: Norman Jones

In the LSO, Jan eventually moves up to number four cello and sits next to Norman Jones. Jan admires Norman's cello playing, delights in his sense of humour and together they egg each other on. He's slight of build, with a round face and spectacles, and has a bald pate with a long blond fringe around the sides. Occasionally, he spits on his hands and pulls up his hair: 'This is my imitation of a pineapple.'

Myra Hess plays Beethoven's 'Emperor' Concerto several times in her declining years. A square-looking woman with an expressionless face, she's gained authority at the expense of her vivacity. During the Concerto's expansive E-flat major opening, Norman leans over and whispers, 'We're stuck here for the next forty-five minutes.' He calls it the most depressing chord in music. In the cadenza of the massive first movement, there are quiet filigree passages. 'She can play that on my balls any time,' Norman murmurs. Whenever the joyful theme of the Finale is announced, rarely accurately, by the pianist, Norman and Jan, knowing that release is at hand, always sing together as they play the responding bass line.

Norman plays on two cellos—a Guadagnini with a sweet and nutty tone, and a Cristofori, which he prefers to play in the orchestra. Cristofori, a mechanic as well as a luthier, developed the first pianos at the end of the eighteenth century. Norman's cello looks unmarked, as if fresh from Cristofori's workbench. (Eventually, Norman is rear-ended by a fellow motorist and tragically, his Cristofori, lying in state in the back, has its table split from top to bottom.)

As well as playing in the orchestra, Norman plays in a piano trio and is nightmarishly busy. While the LSO assembles for a rehearsal at the Albert Hall at 10 a.m., Norman turns to Jan and says, 'We had a trio concert in York last night,' or 'Have to dash after this rehearsal—got a session in Ealing Studios,' or 'Tonight we have to be up half the night—got to learn a new trio for the day after tomorrow.'

(Much later in his career, Jan will reflect that Norman likely was told to keep an eye on Jan. Norman, infinitely more experienced, could point out the pitfalls while Jan learned the repetoire.

The violinist of Norman's trio—Sydney Humphreys, who was also leader of the Aeolian Quartet, very busy as well at that time—will tell Jan that the members of his ensembles would all get their diaries out, looking for a rehearsal time. Nobody wanted to give anything up—the chamber musicians relied on their other work for a stable income. They haunted the recording and film studios and if this work dried up for a while, one could see famous faces playing at the back of the orchestra string sections. 'So often,' Sydney will say, 'we ended up having to rehearse trios after midnight.')

Norman is an outstanding cellist; his fingers curl around the instrument as if he were born playing it. He can ace any passage as if it's routine. Jan has unbounded admiration for him. Like many of his ilk, Norman is totally unassuming and has no conceits, not even stated ambitions. He has no obvious stage presence; he could be taken for one of the stagehands rolling out the grand piano.

One morning at a rehearsal, he turns to Jan: 'I've got a gig for you. Are you free next Sunday afternoon?' Jan feels complimented and nods. 'Good. Three o'clock, dark suit. You're going to be my best man. Fiona, the girl I'm marrying, is shy and very modest. She's the kind of girl who comes down the stairs sideways.' Amongst the wedding guests are the other members of Norman's piano trio—Sydney, as well as pianist Robin Wood.

∗ ∗ ∗

Half a century after their wedding, Norman and Fiona travel to British Columbia to visit their son who's living in Penticton. Norman, who is virtually blind but still giving recitals, has just toured Japan. Annual visits to BC follow, and Norman and Jan periodically meet or telephone.

'Hullo, Jan,' says Norman over the phone. 'It's my ninety-first birthday. Sorry we can't meet this time, but I'll be out for my ninety-second.'

'You're still playing of course?'

'I still practise every day. I don't know why—my fingers have trouble pressing down the first octave of C major. Cello has always been my hobby. Did you know that I studied engineering?'

'I thought that, like Einstein, you didn't know how to count.'

Norman ignores this. 'It's been lovely earning a living playing my hobby. A few months ago, some guy in the pub asked me what I did. "Play cello," I answered. "How can you possibly make money doing that?" he said. I replied, "We musicians are bottom feeders but I was one of the four cellos accompanying the Beatles in 'Eleanor Rigby'." "Wow." The guy looks incredulous. "Let me buy you a drink." Funny that he should have that reaction. It was just another gig.'

Portrait: Handel at Hovingham

In the summer of 1959, after a lapse of forty-five years, Lady Read revives the Hovingham Festival in North Yorkshire. Known to her family as 'Golly', Lady Read had been a violist in the music profession. Her long, narrow house—in fact, three cottages in a row—is clamorous with preparations when Jan, in his early twenties and still in the LSO, his fellow musicians and their manager and violist, Quin Ballardie, arrive from London. Sir Herbert, Golly's husband, famous poet and art critic, keeps himself aloof, silently sitting on the sofa and smoking his pipe, his large poodle Hector at his side.

Golly wishes to replicate Baroque performances and so has recruited the London musicians together with the Pobjoy family, an extensive family of amateur musicians well known in the surrounding region.

The Hovingham Festival features several concerts, one of which is 'Handel at Hovingham', a series of musical scenes held on two levels at various points in the Riding School of Hovingham Hall—ancestral home of the Worsley family. These scenes are held together by narration. The logistics are formidable as Golly and her assistants push and cajole musicians from station to station.

Quin sits with his viola wreathed in cigarette smoke, viewing the whole enterprise with amused malevolence. 'Do we have a Pobjoy?' he asks in a voice as loud as the narrator. Dressed up, everybody tends to look the same under spotlights. 'Not another Pobjoy,' Quin exclaims at the next site. The Pobjoys, regardless of the instruments they play, are all girls with their hair in ringlets. 'Where's Pobjoy?' Quin demands of a girl in ringlets. The collision of professionals and Pobjoys causes Jan some embarrassment.

As the night progresses, Quin's garrulousness becomes more pronounced. Mind you, the men look pretty silly. Dressed in seventeenth-century style, they are required to wear wigs. Looking in the mirror, Jan thinks he resembles a cocker spaniel. When a cellist wears a wig, Jan rapidly discovers, the fingers get caught up with the hair. As his fingers move up and down the cello, so does the wig. No wonder music of that period usually stayed in the first position!

After the last performance, Golly throws an extravagant party. She hires a Dutch street organ— an elaborate machine with a row of puppets clashing their cymbals on top—that wails long into the night. Hector the poodle seeks sanctuary behind the sofa where his master, Sir Herbert, puffs serenely on his pipe.

Golly's brother-in-law is a professor of Spanish at Edinburgh University. On a visit there years later, Golly is entertained by Jan and some of his colleagues. 'And how is Sir Hector?' politely inquires a spouse of one of the musicians.

'Oh, he died. He swallowed a golf ball.'

'Oh … my!'

INTERLUDE: SIR MALCOLM

'Why do you begin that with an up-bow?' asks Fred.

'Suits my bow arm,' replies Normsk.

'It's bass-ackwards, leaves me up skunk creek at letter A'.

'Well, you could tuck in the two sixteenths in the bar before. In any case, my bowing goes with the rise of the phrase. Sometimes it's difficult to explain. Sir Malcolm Sargent, Flash Harry as he was known—'

'The staid *London Times*,' interrupts Phil, 'in a review of our tour across Asia, even had as its headline, "Flash in Japan".'

'The conductor of the Scottish National Orchestra was known as Flash Haggis,' adds Jan.

Normsk theatrically clears his throat. 'Yes, well, Flash came back from Austria—"Gentlemen, I bring you greetings from the Vienna Phil"—with a new bowing for the dotted tune of Schubert's C Major Symphony. Down-up, down-up, down-up, down-up *down*.' Normsk bows in the air. 'Then—up-down, up-down, up-down, up-down, *up*.

The violin section laughed and Hughie called it a silly bowing. Sir Malcolm was clearly upset.

'Then there was that time,' Normsk continues, 'at the Proms, we were playing Schubert's *Unfinished*—the slow movement. At that unaccompanied violin passage, Flash asked for only the first four violins to play it—in the Albert Hall! Not only that, he wanted the whole thing in one bow.

'There was that fourth violinist we called the "Pearly King". His bow always got the pearlies when the going got tough. Well, we creep up to this passage and we begin it very softly. Inevitably, his bow begins to shake and it's catching. We all begin shaking. I was leading because Hughie was away that night. At the end, of course, Sir Malcolm tried milking the applause. When the clapping appeared to subside, I got up and led the orchestra offstage. Sir Malcolm in the wings was white with rage: "You killed the applause!"'

Fred makes his Pekinese dog face at Normsk. 'Never milk the applause!'

'You remember that he had an apartment right opposite the stage door of the Albert Hall,' says Normsk. 'Before the concert he had a limousine pick him up, drive him round the Albert Hall and drop him in front of the stage door. One time there was some orchestral problem concerning Sir Malcolm. A committee of us was sent over to meet with him. "Come in, come in," he said. I could see signed photographs of royalty displayed on the grand piano as he offered me a chair—a Louis Quinze. There was an explosion of antique wood as I sat down. A very sad Sir Malcolm offered me a hand to get off the floor.'

'You know that story,' Phil remarks, 'about Beecham, Sargent and a bus conductor traveling out of London in a train carriage. Beecham was holding forth to the other two until he had to get out at Doncaster. As the train went on its way, Sargent turned to his companion and said, "Do you know who that was? It was Sir Thomas Beecham." "Cor," said the man, "fancy him talking to a couple of ignorant buggers like us."'

SEVENTEEN

Polovtsian Dances

Three years after the Hungarian Revolution, Zoltán Kodály travels to London to conduct a concert of his own music with the LSO. Public sentiment still makes Kodály a symbol of the uprising—upon his appearance for the concert in the Royal Festival Hall, the entire audience stands up and claps for ten minutes. After one of the rehearsals, Jan plucks up the courage to knock on Kodály's green room door to ask him for his autograph. Jan hears a grunt—he takes it for acquiescence—and walks in. Moments later, he wishes he hadn't. What Jan hasn't realized, and what the official photographs of Kodály with neatly trimmed beard obscure, is that Kodály's eyes are badly aligned—the left veering left, and the right, upward and right. The effect makes him look furious. Jan hands Kodály the score of the Second Quartet, which Kodály graciously signs and unfuriously hands back. Jan scuttles away with his treasure.

Another distinguished guest with the LSO is Heitor Villa-Lobos, who comes to conduct his own music. His published works are almost innumerable; he's written more than anyone, rivalling Bach and Telemann in his output. No wonder he can't remember details of his earlier works when questioned by the orchestra. Villa-Lobos, in his seventies with late-stage cancer, shows up at rehearsal with a plump, raven-haired beauty on each arm, cigar in his mouth and a flask of Scotch in his hip pocket.

Moving up the Americas, another distinguished visitor, Aaron Copland, comes armed with one of his symphonies and his ballet *Rodeo*. With his large thin nose and protruding teeth, Copland resembles a cheerful rodent. 'No, no, gentlemen. It's do da detit detit do da.'

'Oh really?' British musicians, nourished on Sullivan and Ascot, are discomfited by *Rodeo*'s cowboy rhythms.

The Copland symphony is more serious business than the ballet. The cellos have an eleven-bar rest. Jan makes a mental note to enter two bars after the timpani. At the concert, Jan comes in one bar early. 'Spectacular domino, Jan,' says fellow cellist Jack Long, 'crashing in like you were falling through a greenhouse.'

✳ ✳ ✳

Jan's learning curve continues. Playing in an orchestra is sometimes a contradictory experience. Sonorous and rich though it is, the string sound can be disconcertingly quiet. Jan, playing Smetana's Overture to *The Bartered Bride* for the first time, encounters the fugue, which for the most part scurries along for thirty bars *pianissimo*. Jan, caught out in the morning rehearsal, untangles all the shifts, practising fast finger work through the afternoon. At the evening performance, Jan discovers that for all his left hand agility so recently won, he can't play soft enough to allow his fingers to fly. When the Overture is programmed six months later, Jan again practises the fugue through the afternoon. This time, he makes sure his bow articulates all the notes at a barely audible level and successfully nails it at the concert. Wisdom accumulating.

How does everyone else get around all those notes without apparently trying? Jan presumes that they are better than he is, more experienced, know things that he doesn't. His left arm is sore from playing so much unfamiliar music. The orchestra performs at the York Festival, playing—along with other pieces—Monteverdi's *Vespers*, after which Jan forgets his sore muscles. Monteverdi's music is gorgeous and, for Jan, undemanding. Working for a week in York Minster is also edifying—instrumentalists and singers are placed about the building to enhance the antiphonal effects so that the audience—like the one in St. Mark's, Venice—is engulfed in sound. When Alfred Deller, the countertenor, rises to sing, two well-dressed ladies sitting near the front look around to find the soprano, then realize that the sound is coming from this stocky, bearded gentleman. They clap their hands to their mouths.

The orchestra is scheduled for a run-out concert to Leeds. All the old lags in the know book off. The list of musicians is posted and Jan is pleased to see he is number three cellist. Then he notices that Doráti is conducting, also that Borodin's *Polovtsian Dances* are programmed to end the concert. Oh my God! he thinks, remembering there is one calm bar where three solo cellos have to play harmonics—he will have to play his A harmonic alone for four beats.

On the day, he gets up early, takes the Underground to St Pancras

Station and catches the train to Leeds. The A begins to prey on his mind. Before the rehearsal, Jan lunches off very dry fish and chips, preoccupied, then makes his way to the town hall for the rehearsal. The stage is set for the orchestra with stuffed burgundy chairs complete with burgundy skirts. From the stage, the auditorium also presents a sea of burgundy. Jan sits down and wonders when in the rehearsal Doráti will get to the *Polovtsian Dances*. Probably it will be last, like the order of the concert.

The rehearsal proceeds slowly. Doráti stomps and yells a bit and Jan's apprehension grows. Toward the end of the afternoon, Doráti calls for the Borodin. Now it's coming, thinks Jan. They play for several minutes. Jan turns the page. There is the A. Doráti faces the cellos. The three cellists—Jan among them holding his breath—play. The conductor gives them a quizzical look but moves on. Jan feels the muscles in his shoulders tense. If it feels so bad now, what will the concert feel like?

Outside after the rehearsal, Jan walks round and round the town hall, his anxiety thickening. It doesn't occur to him to practise. The audience is arriving. Back in the hall, the men—Marie Goossens has the day off—change into tails. They move onto the platform. The circle of that whole note A seems larger than the whole afternoon. Doráti walks out. The concert begins. As each piece finishes, the A looms nearer. Intermission arrives. Jan paces up and down backstage, his temples throbbing and his hands cold. The audience reassembles for the second half. The house is full. Fuller than full. Jan checks on his A in the back of his folder. It seems to be throbbing, too. Doráti re-enters. The music begins. Jan plays but he hardly hears the music. His heart pounds. He can hardly see the music. The moment for the Borodin arrives. Oh God, please God! Jan turns the page—there is the A again, a big shimmering circle, as big as the harvest moon. Doráti gestures to the cellos and the world suddenly becomes quiet. The three soloists play. Jan holds his breath just as he did in the afternoon and plays. At the end of four long beats, his bow shakes a little. It's over. Jan suddenly hears the music again.

The audience spills into the street. Jan threads his way through the crowd to the railway station. British Railways, ever mindful of public discomfort, has so arranged that the next train for London departs at 2 a.m. Jan buys a pint of beer and a pork pie and sits on the platform bench. He worries over his note. His performance wasn't good—well, it was good enough except for that shake at the end. His heartbeat is normal, his head clear, his hands warm, but he is miserable.

He arrives home at the same time that he had left the previous morning. He can sleep now. As he gets into bed, he realizes that he has spent the last twenty-four hours being sick about playing a whole note A harmonic, something a very young cellist can do after a few months of lessons. This is something he will have to face. His teachers have been good. He must not have listened to them. He will have to retrain.

Profile: Cellos

Jack Long, assistant principal cellist of the LSO, is obsessed by cello sound. Although he's forever changing his cellos' strings, sound posts and bridges, his realization of an ideal sound is forever frustrated. English string players are still hotly debating the relative merits of metal strings versus gut strings. England's green and pleasant land is munched upon by contented sheep, which obligingly bequeath strong, rich gut—lush lachrymae, less liver fluke. Jack Long, caught in the middle of the argument, changes his cello strings from metal to gut almost daily. 'Gut's better,' he says, looking for corroboration.

Jack brings a Fendt, an English cello in mint condition, to a concert. At the end, when the conductor gestures the orchestra to their feet to acknowledge the applause, Jack as assistant principal is standing close to the podium. The conductor bows to the audience and, giddy with public approbation, as he's turning to leave the podium, steps right through Jack's cello. Jack stands there, looking down at the wreck, mouth wide open and speechless.

Harold Beck, principal cello, who's been parachuted in from the Hallé Orchestra in Manchester, sells Jack one of his cellos. In deference to a colleague, he gives Jack a deal on the price. Described as an example of the Montagnana school, the instrument has a lustrous varnish. Jack, in the quest for the perfect instrument, buys it. He changes the strings, moves the sound post, adjusts the bridge, decides he really doesn't care for it and offers it up for sale.

Jan is still playing the yellow student cello given to him as a teenager. Norman Jones, his stand partner, is given to subversive remarks *sotto voce*: 'I'd buy Jack's cello if I were you.' Jan needs no further endorsement. Jack Long kindly passes on the sweet deal (to Harold Beck's disgust, Jan finds out much later) and for Jan it's love at first play and love for the rest of his career. The cello has a particularly resonant bass, ideal for playing string quartets, but it has no maker's label pasted inside.

Jan takes it down to Hills', the instrument shop that's been in Bond Street since before Samuel Pepys's time. The man who examines it is rather dismissive. 'Well,' he pronounces, 'it's not what you think it is.' Actually, the man hasn't asked what Jan thinks. Jan lets the comment go; he has an instrument of a professional standard, that he's acquired for an affordable price.

* * *

The man behind the counter is Malcolm Sadler, who later leaves Hills' to form his own luthiery, Ealing Strings. When not behind the counter in Ealing, Malcolm chases down clues to hidden string treasures. Dealers in old violins are forever poking around antique shops, estate sales and attics of Scottish castles. The inquisitiveness often pays off. Scottish fiddlers and their ken didn't play on any old box; they had good equipment.

Years later, the Quartet on tour will travel with Malcolm, who's combing Canada for violins and acquiring other treasures along the way. At the Banff Springs Hotel, Malcolm re-examines Jan's cello. 'Well,' he declares, 'that has all the features of Panormo. Vincenzo Panormo.' They descend for dinner. Malcolm, bespectacled, joweled and lumbering, cuts a Dickensian figure and is in an expansive mood. He orders several bottles of wine and the hotel dining room is empty by the time they're ready to leave. The bill is paid. The poor young waitress is pining to go home. 'What's your name?' Malcolm asks.

'Anne.'

Without a word, he reaches into his jacket pocket and pulls out an antique gold locket on a chain. He gives it to her. She thanks him and Malcolm says, 'No, open it. There's a catch underneath.'

She opens it. Inside is etched 'Anne'—magic.

INTERLUDE: INTIMATE LETTERS

The Quartet rehearses Leoš Janáček's *Intimate Letters* at Phil's house. They'll soon perform it at Carnegie Hall. The aroma of baking bread ensures an early coffee break. However, they're still coping with the rhythmic flourishes of the first eight bars. These give way to an unaccompanied melody played ponticello by the viola—the edgy sound suggesting the anxiety of love.

The music, a roller coaster between tumultuous passion and anguished yearning, transports Jan fifteen years earlier to his flat in London:

He's listening to *Intimate Letters* on his record player. He discovered the quartet for the first time a few weeks before, and the novelty of the music is gripping him. He's still in the LSO, but has been offered a position in Edinburgh. The mixture of melancholy and tenderness in the music suits Jan's mood exactly. He feels drained by indecision, uncertain of himself, unsure of his ability to meet professional expectations, torn between his love for Edinburgh and his commitments in London.

He meets his cousin Rodney at the Boileau Arms, the family watering hole, a pub five minutes' walk from the family house that Guv built.

(Rodney, as a child, had been threatened with tuberculosis. The doctor prescribed beer as an antidote. Guv would take Rodney down by pushchair to the Boileau Arms for a pick-me-up and bring home a bottle of Guinness for Bar. Rodney has been drinking beer ever since.

Sometimes in the summer, when Colin reappeared from California, pleasant evenings were spent drinking beer in the Boileau's garden. Here, Jan got tiddly on his first pint of bitter and many years before that, Colin got used to the taste, coming in as a young man and forcing himself to drink it every evening, until, at the end of a month, he enjoyed it.)

Jan sets down his pint. 'Miles Baster is reorganizing the resident string quartet for Edinburgh University and asked me to be the cellist.'

Rodney is aghast. 'Why do that? You've established yourself in London. You're a member of the LSO. You're in the Academy of St Martin.'

Jan deflects Rodney's remarks. 'Funny. We had an Academy rehearsal this morning at Nev's house. I was so early, Molly and Nev were still in bed.'

'In Edinburgh,' continues Rodney, 'nothing much happens except the Festival. I know that your mother and brother are there, but you belong here. You were raised here, you went to school here. Don't be a fool!'

'Rodney, this is a difficult decision for me. Miles had just phoned me when the orchestra had a run-out to Oxford. I spent the day in a dither. I don't altogether feel I belong here. London is hotching with wonderful musicians all hanging on to their turf. Despite lots of work, things move slowly. I don't feel that I'm really good enough to hang on to my position.' Jan looks down at his glass. 'Despite good teachers, I don't think I've thought out the principles of playing for myself yet. It just seems I've got to go away and work it out. Lots of people have taken jobs in the provinces and they return to London the richer. It's better than mouldering in a cello section here and eventually being moved back before being moved out.'

'Oh well,' replies Rodney, 'as Guv would say, "It's your life, son." I'll see you at the Festival when the London Phil plays there in August. Bound to be raining, dang me! By the way, Glenna and I just bought a house in Bledlow Ridge, a stone's throw from Radnage.'

Jan returns to his flat and turns on his record player. Back to Janáček. In the Finale, his ear is caught by soaring trills played ponticello by a solo violin. In contrast to the viola's solo at the opening, this sound, although edgy, suggests exuberance. Jan hopes he can learn this quartet when he settles in Edinburgh.

* * *

At Phil's house, the aroma of bread just baked is too much for Fred. At the end of his cadenza, two pages away from the end of the Finale, he groans, 'How can you possibly trill *fortissimo* and play ponticello at the same time?' He puts down his violin. 'Forget Carnegie Hall. Let's get at that bread.'

EIGHTEEN

The Haydn Quartets

* 1959 *

The Edinburgh String Quartet (ESQ), raw, inexperienced, made up of young men who hardly know each other, has a relatively short time in which to prepare for their inaugural concert at the university. It is a foregone conclusion that they will open the program with one of Haydn's quartets. Already nervous, they calm themselves by sight-reading a different Haydn quartet at the beginning of every rehearsal. The days are counted off as they play through eighty-three quartets. (Today, they would be required to play sixty-eight; musicologists have since deemed that fifteen of Haydn's quartets were misattributed). Then, like Frederick the Great playing Quantz's three hundred flute concerti, they will begin all over again.

Although it's the morning in late August, they're playing with the light on and it's chilly. The first violinist Miles Baster's flat is at the top of a stone building built in 1615; if Jan cranes his neck, he can see the castle perched above the rock face. Next door is a rope shop. (In 1736, someone from a rioting mob took a length of rope from this shop to hang Captain Porteous. After the lynching, a less-riotous person remembered that the rope had not been paid for. The shop displayed his coin until recently, when it was stolen.)

* * *

Haydn was sent at the age of eight to join the choir at St. Stephen's Cathedral in Vienna. There, because of his talent, he was taught the three Rs and was grounded in music, an education that sufficed him for his illustrious career. When his voice broke, the Empress Maria Theresa complained that the boy 'crowed like a cock' and influenced the church to dump him at age seventeen into the streets.

Over the next ten years, through industry and good luck, Haydn attracted the attention of and was hired by Prince Nicholas Esterházy. As

Kapellmeister, Haydn wrote music, often for visiting dignitaries, tried it out on the house orchestra, coached the singers and rehearsed opera productions. These weren't always his own. Other composers—Salieri, Mozart—were represented; *The Marriage of Figaro* was produced at Esterházy. Sometimes while he shaved in the morning, Haydn gave a harpsichord lesson.

The Esterházy estate was large. Guests were given maps to find their way from village to village. The names of some of the visitors resonate down history—the Empress Maria Theresa, Horatio Nelson with Emma Hamilton after the battle of the Nile. Haydn wrote a mass for them, which they neglected to hear; they went to the casino instead.

To Jan, Haydn seems a familiar figure; such a kind, genial personality seems to shine through contemporary reportage. (To George, the Prince of Wales, a sometime cellist, Haydn responded diplomatically: 'Your Highness plays like a *Brince!*'). Haydn was a musician who had a full life, if outwardly an uneventful one. He forged his music in comparative seclusion. For lack of other influences, he was forced to become original, slowly and with constant inventiveness. His music always refreshes.

✳ ✳ ✳

When Jan arrived in Edinburgh, he brought with him stacks of 78s that he picked up for pennies— now that LPs hold sway—at the Gramophone Exchange in London's Wardour Street. Jan's collection is mostly of string quartets. He notices that these recordings, at seven minutes a side, influenced an acceleration of tempos to fit performances on an economical number of records.

The Léner Quartet recorded its repertoire at the Wigmore Hall at the end of its career. Theirs were leisurely performances, born of long experience on concert platforms. In contrast, the Budapest Quartet adapted their performances to fit the seven-minute duration of a 78. Jan considers them the snappiest. He's particularly enamoured of their performance of Hugo Wolf's *Italian Serenade*, which they zipped up on one side of a record. (Years later, driving down Georgia Street in Vancouver, Jan will catch sight of the Budapest Quartet hailing a taxi. Except for the cello case, the men with their leathery faces and carrying what could be imagined as gun cases could be mistaken for the Mafiosi.)

The ESQ tries to emulate the Budapest's performances of the *Italian Serenade* and Haydn's 'Quinten' Quartet for their concert. Little do they realize that they are ratcheting up the speeds as they learn their program. These problems tend to feel one week as irresolvable as they seemed the previous. Spurred by Jan's obsession with bowing, everybody in the group plays continuously a little louder.

The dreaded concert day arrives along with the first frost. The ESQ rehearses in the Reid Hall in the morning. Already jittery, they feel confused by the hall's acoustics and their ensemble seems ragged. Now in their soup and fish, they pace up and down the Reid Library, which serves as a green room.

'How do you like my tails?' Miles flicks cigarette ash off his lapel. 'I asked my tailor to make them extra long. I think it gives me authority.'

Jan feels upstaged. His are second-hand and shabby with the old sweat of LSO concerts. Julian, the second violinist, clips on his white tie. Miles turns round. 'Don't you tie your own? That's so infra dig.'

Sidney Newman peers round the library door. 'Five minutes.'

They open with Haydn's op. 76, no. 2, his D Minor Quartet. Named the 'Quinten' for the falling fifth intervals in the theme, the work was written in Haydn's retirement years while he was still at the height of his powers. It is masterly, inventive, as well as imaginative. After the opening statement, Haydn switches to the relative major key, providing an exuberant counterpoint to the pair of falling fifths, which thrust up in the opposite direction. This leads to a passage of syncopations which can prove the undoing for the unwary, particularly in the coda where Haydn mixes a rhythmic cocktail to accompany the first violinist's rapid sixteenths.

'What happened at the coda?' demands Miles as they leave the stage. 'You all came in right on top of my lead after the pause.'

Brian Hawkins, the violist, is offended. 'You weren't clear.'

Miles continues, 'Anyway, probably nobody noticed. We recovered after a couple of bars.'

Jan privately doubts that. The whole music department is here along with the city VIPs and the newspaper critic, as well as his former teacher Joan Dickson, with her musical family. She is bound to phone him.

They scamper through the *Italian Serenade*. Hans Gal, the eminent Viennese composer who had the double misfortune of fleeing the Nazis and then years later trying to teach Jan counterpoint, comes round to the green room after the concert. 'Wull,' he says, then pauses. 'The *Italian Serenade* is about lovers. Good lovers are not fast; they are slow.'

* * *

Whatever the tempo, Scotland needs a group that's mobile enough to meet its demands. Chamber music life in Scotland picks up where the previous ensemble left it. The Scottish Arts Council has arranged concerts for the ESQ from Gordonstoun to Invergordon, and the musicians often have to drive back to Edinburgh after a concert to attend morning rehearsals of the Reid Orchestra. The roads are not built for the speed their car is going. On the other hand, their car is the only one on the roads. One starlit and very cold evening, Brian spots a nocturnal rainbow. Julian stops the car and the quartet steps out to contemplate the great, white arc. It's described the next day in a newspaper article as a rare phenomenon caused by ice crystals in the air—once in a blue moon.

Concert conditions are sometimes less than perfect. Local halls might be unlocked after months of disuse. In Fort William, the hall is so cold that the musicians decide to step across the road in their tails and overcoats and visit the cinema, to return exactly at the moment they are due on stage. A quartet's needs are simple—adequate downward lighting and four straight-backed wooden chairs. The town of Melrose complies with the request except that the chairs are the folding type, fixed in a row as if from a theatre. On a side trip to Dublin, they play for the Ballsbridge Society where Colin had said there once was a notice saying, 'No knitting during performances.'

Performing with the ESQ is not without its highlights. Larry Adler, who plays the harmonica with an upper lip like that of an anteater, persuaded Ira Gershwin to part with his brother George's *Lullaby for String Quartet.* Adler arranged it for harmonica and strings, and he and the ESQ premiere this at the Edinburgh Festival. As well as the Festival program, a number of unofficial, fringe events spring up. Through the influence of Jan's old school chum John Bassett, assistant to the Festival's director, the doorbell rings late one evening at Jan's mother's apartment and in burst the 'Beyond the Fringe' people. Dudley Moore commandeers the living room piano to the delight of a bevy of young female admirers who had burst in with him.

The ESQ is invited to play on the Isle of Man. This necessitates an overnight train journey from Edinburgh to Liverpool, followed by a boat journey midmorning to the island. On arrival in Liverpool, they decide to wait out the time by having a leisurely breakfast at the Adelphi Hotel. Having eaten, Jan notices a familiar, craggy-looking face behind a slice of toast and marmalade. It is Michael Tippett and his friend Karl. (Years later, Jan will look back on this meeting and conclude that Tippett was probably in Liverpool for the premiere of his Third Symphony.)

The musicians walk over and introduce themselves. Jan is excited; Tippett has remained a hero ever since that premiere of *The Midsummer Marriage*.

'Excuse me, you're Michael Tippett?' asks Jan.

Tippett looks up.

'I so admire and love your music. We were,' says Jan, remembering to look round and include his colleagues, 'wondering if we could learn one of your string quartets.'

'But of course.'

'Which one would you like us to learn?'

'Please learn the first one. Nobody is playing it.'

They do, and in time, record it. (Jan will come across, decades later, a double LP of premiere recordings produced for Tippett's eightieth birthday and see that it includes the ESQ's recording of the First Quartet on the Waverly label. 'No details of this performance were available,' declare the liner notes.)

Miles is an earnest Catholic. It doesn't take long for him—new to Edinburgh—to make friends with Arthur Oldham, who directs the choir at St. Mary's Cathedral. They initiate an Easter performance by the ESQ of Haydn's *Seven Last Words*. To Jan, a reluctant Presbyterian, Catholic customs are obfuscating. But when in Rome, do as the Romans do.

The ESQ is to play in front of the altar. Before the concert, Jan sets up four chairs and four stands, genuflecting each time he crosses and recrosses the altar. He heads to the vestry to collect the music, but Miles is already coming out with it. 'Those chairs are too high,' he says imperiously. 'We need something lower.' Frustrated, Jan points questioningly to a prie-dieu. 'Those over there,' says Miles, ignoring him. Miles was not put in the world to carry chairs, so Jan, self-conscious now that the cathedral is filling up with people, replaces the chairs, genuflecting on each trip. As the ESQ walks out to play, Jan genuflects for the last time and the new Tortelier bent spike of his cello crashes into the marble tiles.

After the performance, the priests invite the musicians back into the vestry. The eldest, thinnest (and holiest, Jan finds out later from Arthur) priest produces a bottle of whisky. 'You must have a dram,' he says. The musicians are all too glad to comply. 'Have another.' The priest cocks the bottle. The ESQ has played slow music for eighty minutes. They accept the second dram. They have at last slowed down.

∗ ∗ ∗

As successive Easters pass, Haydn's *Seven Last Words* will enter Jan's soul. Each movement with simple imagery speaks directly to Christ's utterance, directly and profoundly. Haydn was a devout man, praying before he composed and writing *Laus Deo* at the end of every score.

After Haydn's last tour of England in 1792, he returned to Vienna with more than 3,000 pages of manuscript. Back home, he wrote *The Creation*, *The Seasons* and a number of masses for the Esterházy daughters, who were discreetly pensioning him. It was the end of the journey that had begun with the young Kapellmeister writing for Prince Nicholas's instrument, the baryton. Haydn secretly learned this cumbersome instrument and played it better than Nicholas, to the prince's chagrin.

Again, the world has moved on—how did these long evenings go? Master and servant playing duets? Was Haydn subservient, or did they meet as musical equals? Did Prince Nicholas ring for coffee and cake or a carafe of wine to be shared?

Jan, in his later years, provides tea and cake for senior students at Langley Community Music School after they play Haydn string quartets on Sunday afternoons. Over the years, the quartets have become embedded in Jan's psyche and in his musical lexicon, and he wants to pass on this very particular love affair to young string players. 'But they all sound the same,' says a young cellist during one of these sessions. Jan smiles and pours the tea.

Portrait: Haydn's Skull

Jan as a boy comes across a newspaper photograph showing Haydn's skull in a glass case. Apparently, upon Haydn's demise, a phrenologist friend requested his head. He wanted to examine the bumps that had contributed to such an original man. The skull was exhibited in the *Gesellschaft der Musikfreunde* in Vienna until 1948, when it was returned to Haydn's body.

It is Easter in Sarasota. The Quartet's manager, Leigh Cross, has arranged that they will play Haydn's *Seven Last Words* at a church.

'I talked to this minister on the phone,' Leigh told Jan before the Quartet left for Florida. 'He had a Southern drawl and between his uh-huhs I hope he got the idea that he's to announce the phrase and then give a homily before each movement. I have a gut feeling he thought I was talking about hominy grits. In any case, I've sent him the program. But you better check up on him when you arrive.'

At the church, Phil and Jan, replacing the armchairs with straight-backed chairs at the last minute, quickly mention the program to the minister.

'Don't worry, the ushers are handing them out now,' he drawls reassuringly.

Homily follows homily and all is well until the Quartet finishes playing the Sixth Word, 'It is finished', which has the sound of finality. The Quartet waits for the minister to announce the Seventh Word and his closing homily on 'Into thy hands I commend my spirit'. He doesn't move. They look at him expectantly but he has adopted a sanctimonious stance looking out into the church. After an uncomfortable pause, Phil and Jan exchange glances and they start into the Seventh Word and the final rending of the veil.

Leaving the church, Jan picks up a program left on a pew and realizes that Leigh Cross had omitted the Seventh Word. He shows it to Phil in the parking lot.

Phil laughs. 'Haydn's *Six Last Words* according to Cross.'

NINETEEN

The Schubert Quintet

It is 1970 in West Vancouver. Jacqueline du Pré arrives late to the party at Normsk's with two Strads. Normsk hands her a glass. 'Drink up,' he says. 'You're one behind.' Several drinks later, the Quartet with Jackie proceed to the basement to play the Schubert Quintet, the party project.

Jackie, who that afternoon played the Schumann Concerto with the VSO, takes one of the Strads out of its case. 'Here,' she says, turning to Jan, 'you play this.' The instrument looks in mint condition, its russet varnish casting a halo of light. To his eternal regret, Jan refuses; in a confined space and with everybody less than sober, he is afraid it might get damaged. Strad in hand, Jackie commands into the din of battle. The first casualty is the dynamics; the hushed *pianissimo* of the two cellos introducing the second subject in the opening movement is trodden under, and thereafter the playing becomes increasingly strenuous. The boisterous Finale, however, matches their spirits and after fifty minutes of Schubert, they pack up their instruments and head upstairs for more drinks and the *pièce de résistance*, Normsk's curry.

Jan heads to the bathroom. This prompts Jackie to regale the party by singing Dvořák's 'Humoresque': 'Passengers will please refrain/from flushing toilets while the train/is standing in/or passing through the station ...' By the time Jan comes out, she's on the phone to the pianist Fou Ts'ong in London. For another fifty minutes he recites love poems to her. She'd asked Normsk for the phone number, which he had because the Quartet had recently accompanied the pianist in a performance of three Mozart piano concertos.

Next morning, the Quartet returns to the basement to rehearse Haydn amidst abandoned glasses. They are distracted by a gurgle from the downstairs toilet; a tsunami of West Vancouver sewage is surging towards them over the floor. They take off shoes and socks, roll up pant legs and, with shovels, bat the turds out of the French doors into the garden. Such is the catastrophe that a new culvert has to be cut.

A month later, Normsk receives a staggering phone bill.

And once a week for the next five years, precisely at 11 a.m., a man from the works yard visits the front of Normsk's house to inspect the new manhole.

* 1960 *

When the Griller Quartet pays its last visit to Europe, Colin is invited to Edinburgh to play second cello with the ESQ next to Jan in Schubert's Cello Quintet. Its spirited Scherzo embeds a trio, led by the violist and second cellist, with a very serious demeanour in the middle of it, and sometimes, the long silences punctuated by shared upbeats, the ornamentation plus the repeat, can conspire to turn seriousness into rigor mortis.

For the ESQ rehearsing the trio with Colin, the path to the morgue is set right away when Brian plays alone with Colin. Brian shows uncertainty in the initial upbeat about whether he should lead or defer to Colin. In the midst of this section, booby-trapped as it is with ornaments and upbeats, there is a danger of the tempo collapsing so that it can't be revived. Colin's idea of the tempo is to take off twice as fast as Brian, to the astonishment of Jan and the others.

Colin stops playing and turns to Brian. 'Schubert writes alla breve, cut time,' he says. 'He's written "Andante Sostenuto", not "Adagio".' For the rest of the trio, all the inherent problems vanish.

'Shall we order five early lunches?' says Brian, putting down his viola and sighing with relief.

'I'll have a ploughman's lunch with an IPA,' says Colin, smiling. He mostly takes the back seat of the second cellist in rehearsals, except at the beginning of the second rehearsal, when they're back at the beginning of the piece. They play through the exposition and arrive at the solitary dominant seventh chord at the double bar.

'I don't think we should play that,' Colin observes in the pause that follows.

'Really?' Miles picks up the coffee mug sitting under his music stand.

'Well, I take it we're not going to do the repeat.'

'No,' says Miles, sipping coffee, 'it's long enough.'

'That chord only makes sense if we're going back to the beginning,' says Colin. 'It's a non sequitur if we continue into the development. I think Schubert forgot to write a first and second ending. After all, he died before the work was performed.'

— 138 —

Colin turns to Jan. 'By the way, son, we don't have to be so loud at the unison after letter A. Schubert never heard how powerful two cellos can be.'

(Jan remembers how loud the two cellos were when he first played the Schubert Quintet in 1957 with his former colleague, Anne Crowden, as second violinist. The cellos, however, weren't a match for her riotous laugh—Anne's sense of humour offended many an Edinburgh matron: 'Och, she's no better than she should be.')

The Quintet's seraphic slow movement erupts in the middle section with scale passages laced with a swarm of accidentals for the second cello. 'Cellists shouldn't be too literal about the notes,' Colin observes. 'Think, rather, of the key the run is in. It begins on the leading note—E major-B major-F-sharp major-C-sharp major. You're heading to the bottom of the circle of fifths.'

'So we better practise our scales so we don't head for the second cellist's graveyard,' says Jan.

✳ ✳ ✳

Apart from death and taxes, there are two certainties in the life of a cellist—that they will be asked to play Saint-Saëns's 'The Swan', as well as Schubert's Cello Quintet. Because of its unique scoring, this work stands alone amongst the masterpieces of chamber music. Schubert chose an extra cello for his Quintet, unlike Mozart, who chose an extra viola for his great string quintets. The sonorities of two cellos can, in not-so-sensitive hands, threaten to engulf the other players, but the instrumentation provides a wide palette of colours which Schubert controls with great skill. Near the end of the work, there are hushed curtains of sound, magical, like the aurora borealis. Schubert was putting the finishing touches on the Quintet two weeks before his death at the age of thirty-one.

The Quintet is an enormous structure. Schubert's songs, on the other hand, are deft—short and seemingly effortless piano introductions set each scene as Schubert explores the minutiae of human experience. The songs are the epitome of the Romantic movement. Jan was introduced to this musical world at university. Elf was leader of the choir of St. George's Church and extra duties periodically required her to sing solos, with Jan accompanying, at Presbyterian socials. Depending on the levity of the function, she would either sing Schubert's 'Who is Sylvia?' or Aaron Copland's arrangement of 'I Bought Me a Cat', one of those accumulating songs. As the collection of animals grew—cat, cow, pig, horse—Elf would forget the order as she sang down the feeding chain.

Besides the Cello Quintet, Schubert wrote of course the famous 'Trout' Quintet—after his 1817 song 'Die Forelle'—at the request of Paumgartner, a wealthy patron, who wanted a piece like Hummel's for piano, violin, viola, cello and bass. Its charms has pianists—and double basses, who are chamber-music-deprived—clamouring to perform it.

* * *

In the mid-1970s, the Quartet gives a performance of Schubert's 'Trout' at Courtenay Music Camp on Vancouver Island with Robert Rogers, pianist. The CBC comes up from Vancouver to record the performance. The musicians pass up a salmon dinner by Mitch, who presides over the kitchens at Vanier School, in order to have a balance test at the theatre. The students are bused up to the auditorium and the musicians walk out to a full house.

Halfway through the first movement, a child rushes up the aisle and out of the theatre. At the end of the movement, several more hurriedly leave. At the end of each movement, clusters of students head for the exit. 'Is our performance so bad?' Jan asks himself as they begin the fourth movement—variations on the song 'Die Forelle'. Concert etiquette is abandoned as after each variation, rows empty. By the Finale, the theatre is two-thirds empty. Returning to Vanier, the musicians find the cafeteria full of blankets, stomach pumps and prostrate students attended by staff. The salmon, not the 'Trout' was bad!

Schubert's two quintets bookend his significant instrumental chamber works; while the 'Trout' Quintet is his first mature offering, the Cello Quintet closes his career.

* * *

At the close of Colin's career, Jan sits in Colin's kitchen where his father holds court to visitors—musicians, old students, friends—offering them a glass of cheap California wine. Jan doesn't know how Colin can drink the stuff. It's really only fit to sprinkle on fish and chips. Colin sometimes plays chamber music in the sitting room with friends who are amateur musicians. Jan marvels at how on a student instrument—the Amati by this time is in New York with Colin's ex-wife, Bonnie—Colin with broad fingers on a hand that resembles a baseball glove, can still draw out a sound as resonant and resinous as the one he made on the Amati. Once, alone in the kitchen with Colin, glass in hand, Jan recalls playing the Schubert Quintet together in Edinburgh. 'Joan used to say,' says Jan, 'that the cello should establish the intonation from the bottom up, the root of the harmony, that the cello should always be heard clearly.'

'Clarity is one thing, son. But I don't think the cello should be loud. As the bass line—quite the reverse. You have to give room for all voices to be heard. Quartets are not competitions, they are conversations. Musicians must accommodate.'

Portrait: Elsa

The Schubert Quintet is often featured at summer music camps due to a surfeit of cello students. At Naramata, the Quintet is played by Elsa Fisher, an octogenarian cellist, at the bottom, led by a preteen boy playing violin at the top. Both are very talented. Between rehearsals, Elsa happily engages in water pistol attacks with the younger students, and in the fall and winter leads the cello section of the Okanagan Symphony. Even later, she plucks up the courage to attend the Shawnigan Summer School of the Arts to play for János Starker, who evidently is surprised and impressed. Not only is music an international language, but it has no barriers when recognizing talent.

Portrait: Jacqueline du Pré

'Where did Jackie go after that party in the basement?' asks Normsk.

'I think she was to go on to Hawaii from Vancouver, but she cancelled that part of the tour because of pain in her bow arm,' says Jan.

'The first intimation of trouble.'

'Still, from Hawaii, she was returning to London to prepare for *Pierrot Lunaire*,' says Jan. 'We had just performed it and at the party she was asking me about Schoenberg's writing for cello.'

'But after the party, how many times did she return to Vancouver?'

'Just the once,' says Jan.

'Oh, yes,' says Normsk, 'but she was just travelling with her husband, Daniel Barenboim. She had flu and was in bed in the Hotel Vancouver. Despite the flu, she was her cheerful self. I don't think she had yet been diagnosed with multiple sclerosis.'

'I think the whole Quartet was there,' says Jan.

'That's right, we played Scrabble at her bedside and emptied a bottle of vodka. I guess Daniel was giving a recital that night. He and Jackie were the golden couple. Then the devoted young stars of classical music. They hadn't been married that long. You remember her telling us that before their wedding, while the Rabbi was indoctrinating her, another Rabbi was instructing Daniel on the art of lovemaking.'

'Poor Jackie,' says Jan. 'To be struck down so young!'

———————

INTERLUDE: DANCER

'Why do winds always have to be so sharp?' asks Normsk. The Quartet has spent the morning rehearsing the Brahms Clarinet Quintet on the North Shore. 'Let's go down to the Tally-Ho for a beer and sandwich.'

A waitress sets down two beers unasked. 'This summer in Penticton,' Norman begins, 'Jenny and I went to the big hotel in the middle of town for lunch. We were shown a table right by a rostrum. Pretty soon, this young girl comes out and begins her stripper routine. We had ringside seats and I felt embarrassed for Jenny. At the end of the performance, the dancer puts on her housecoat and suddenly looks over at our table. "Hullo, Norman!" she cries.

'"Oh my God!" I put my hand up to my face. The girl comes over to our table.

'"Don't you remember me? I used to attend Courtenay Music Camp."

'"Glad to see you are still in music," I managed to reply.'

TWENTY

Mendelssohn Octet

A few years after settling in Vancouver, Jan, in his forties, is driving from a symphony rehearsal and as usual turns on the car radio, always tuned to the CBC. The music is breathless, the bustling of notes very familiar—it is the closing of Mendelssohn's Octet. There is applause as the string players finish their E-flat chord. The announcer cuts in, 'That was a performance originally given to a live audience at the Edinburgh Festival.' Jan is amazed; he's just heard himself with the ESQ and the Lyra Quartet and of course it was a live audience, there aren't too many dead ones. The CBC evidently can stretch a long hand into the BBC archives.

* 1963 *

In Edinburgh, the Margand String Quartet (MSQ) and the ESQ consult their diaries, looking for a date to broadcast the Mendelssohn Octet. When musicians consult their diaries, the problems multiply exponentially with every musician and country that is added.

They agree that only a date in late April will work. But there seems to be no time to rehearse. 'Well,' suggests Jan in his best French, remembering that the ESQ is to tour the Netherlands for a week in December, 'we can come to Paris from the Netherlands and rehearse with you after December 13.'

Michèle, the first violinist, looks at her colleagues. '*D'accord,*' she says.

The all-female MSQ looks stunning. They play well, too. Four elegant, chic, vivacious young Frenchwomen are having an enviable career. In September, they arrived for a tour in Scotland from concerts in Egypt. With looks like that, how can they fail, thinks Jan.

After the MSQ leaves Scotland for France, Jan thinks about offsetting the costs of going to Paris in December. He writes to the British Consulate in Paris—would they be interested in a concert of English music to be performed there in the middle of December? Jan receives an answer from the cultural attaché, Charles de Winton: yes, the consulate would be interested in an evening concert on Sunday, the 15th of December.

In September, the ESQ returns to its routines for the concert season. As winter wears on, Julian seems to get very tired, his face becomes flushed and he seems to struggle with the routine. Their tour of the Netherlands is upon them and Jan travels down to London by train overnight in order to visit a few favourite places. He leaves his things at the family house in Hammersmith and goes out. The ESQ is to take the overnight ferry and play a school concert at 3 p.m. the next afternoon in Apeldoorn. Jan returns at 5 p.m. to find a message waiting for him: 'Please phone the Cummings' house as soon as you get in.' Julian had visited his family after a lapse of the winter season. His parents took one look at him and sent him to their family doctor, who immediately had him hospitalized for tests as a suspected diabetic. Julian isn't going anywhere for a while.

Jan has a crisis on his hands. He spends the evening on the phone. The office of their Dutch agent, Mr Vickers, is, of course, closed. Hours pass. At last, on a redial, a lady answers. 'Well, it's not surprising you can't get through. It's December 6, St Nicholas Day. We celebrate it like you celebrate Christmas Day. Don't worry. I'm a singer. I know what to do. I can contact Mr Vickers and I'm sure he'll have no problem postponing your tour until your violinist is better.' A flood of relief overcomes Jan.

On phoning his colleagues the next morning, it is agreed that they'd best hang around London and then leave for Paris for the octet—now turned septet—rehearsal previously agreed upon. Feeling that the urgent stuff has been dealt with, and disinclined to add to his aunt's phone bill, Jan sends a telegram to Charles de Winton informing him that they will be unable to play at the consulate. Ten days later, the three members of the quartet book into a grotty hotel in one of Paris's narrowest streets. Next morning, Jan is awakened by a knock on the door. 'Telephone, Monsieur, *salle d'attente, rez-de-chaussée.*' Jan goes down to the lobby in his pajamas and picks up the phone.

'Ah, Mr Hampton. Charles de Winton here. I thought I might find you in Paris. What do you mean by it?'

'I sent a telegram,' Jan splutters. 'I thought I had explained!'

'Well, the concert has to go ahead. Come to my office. I'm sending round a car.'

Jan hurries back upstairs and wakes up Miles and Brian. 'We have a problem.'

They wait in the lobby. Pretty soon, a large black limousine with a Union Jack pennant fluttering on its hood dwarfs the street in front of the hotel. The chauffeur opens its doors and they climb in. The British Consulate has an imposing front door; it opens onto a spacious hall beyond which is a wide staircase leading to the first floor and the cultural attaché's office. Charles de Winton sits behind his desk, demanding an explanation. Jan carefully tells him the details of Julian's condition and of their obligation to rehearse with the MSQ.

'The concert has to go ahead,' repeats Charles de Winton. 'There has been a postal strike in France. Your telegram only arrived yesterday, Friday. I've issued special invitations.' He motions towards a pile of gold-embossed cards on his desk. 'This concert is tomorrow night. I can't retract all those invitations.'

'We can't possibly play without our second violinist.'

'I don't understand why a quartet in your position doesn't carry substitutes.'

'I have an idea,' says Jan. 'We're rehearsing with the Margand String Quartet this morning. I'll see if they can play the concert.'

'Very well. But they have to play the same program.' Jan privately thinks it unlikely that a French quartet will have Purcell, Tippett and Elgar up its sleeve, but he's glad that the conversation is terminated and the musicians make their way to their rehearsal. At the Margand house, the problem has to be tackled before bow is put to string.

'Eh, bien,' Michèle says, 'we are free to play tomorrow night. We can't play your English program. We are working in a new second violinist and we have a limited repertoire at present. We can play Devienne, Dalyrac and Debussy.' She looks at her colleagues. 'D'accord,' she says reluctantly.

It will have to do. Jan carefully writes out the program, the names of the instrumentalists, the quartets they'll play and the movements.

'Right,' says Miles. 'We need to rehearse the Mendelssohn now, Julian or not.'

The two quartets feel each other out as they play through the Octet's opening. After stops and starts, they reach the wonderful point at the first ending to the exposition where Michèle rises to the very top of her register before returning to the very bottom, the note which opened the work.

After coffee and eclairs, they sit down to tackle the Scherzo.

'Trop fort,' Michèle says before they even begin and everybody laughs.

The opening sixteenths, jostled with the trills of the first violin, conjure a potion entirely new to the musical world. Mendelssohn met with Goethe on five occasions and was much taken with Goethe's *Faust*. While writing the Scherzo, he had the Walpurgis Night scene on his mind—the nocturnal scuffling of the spirits is played fast and secretively, the dynamics staying virtually *piano*.

Michèle stops playing. 'Our spiccato sounds like the Battle of the Ardennes,' she says, glaring at Françoise.

Jan resumes playing, trying his best to keep his saltando from puncturing the soufflé. He looks over at Michèle, who seems to play effortlessly, dusting the normally murderous trillwork with pixie dust.

Lunchtime looms.

'By the way,' Michèle asks, showing Jan to the door, 'for our concert tomorrow night, could we get four complimentary tickets?' Jan groans inwardly. This will call for more diplomatic skill than the cultural attaché has himself. But Jan has a hunch; if he arrives at the consulate just after midday, chances are that the staff will be out for lunch. In France, lunch is *de rigueur*. The hunch proves correct. Jan opens the big front door. There is nobody around in the hall. Mr de Winton's office door is wide open. Jan lays the program prominently on his desk. The stack of invitations is still there. Jan takes four. There seems to be nobody in the building. Jan leaves unchallenged and returns to the rehearsal. At the end of the day, the Margand and the Edinburgh have worked through the Mendelssohn Octet. There's no point in hanging around. The Edinburgh contingent catch the boat train that evening.

* * *

The Octet, written when Felix Mendelssohn was only sixteen years old, is held strongly in the affections of string players for several reasons. It's fun to play and though it is a virtuoso showpiece for the first violinist, everybody gets thrown a tidbit. Socially, it fills a felt want when string players congregate, and is particularly useful for chamber music programs and music camps; its freshness, confidence and assertiveness of youth lives on.

At least two of the Octet's movements can be described as a chamber violin concerto. Mendelssohn certainly knew about the violin so it is unsurprising that his Violin Concerto, written some twenty years after the Octet, has passed into violin lore. This concerto probably heads the ever-lengthening list of pieces Jan would be happy never to hear again. It is the curse of a professional musician that some works are played disproportionately more than others. Ultimately, however brilliant the rendition, it can't disguise the fact that to the jaded professional, the Mendelssohn Concerto appears too frequently each winter like the common cold.

In contrast, in over seventy years of repeated listening, Jan finds it remarkable that with the Octet, not only could Mendelssohn surpass Mozart with this instance of teenaged precocity, but that the piece matures along with the listener. Mendelssohn provided an alternative soundscape to Beethoven; the Octet shimmers with magic.

After that, Mendelssohn became a pretty dull fellow. While Beethoven is always inquiring, Mendelssohn's melodic material—for example in the late Quintet op. 87—seems predictable and laboured, in need of editing. A quick read of his career highlights seems to reveal why—he just took on too much. How he managed to compose between obligations is a miracle. That he went into serious physical decline in his thirty-eighth year is tragic.

✶ ✶ ✶

In Edinburgh during the following concert season, Brian Hawkins, the violist, announces that he will go and seek his musical fortune in London after the upcoming touring season. He and Mavis have one child and another on the way. The ESQ salary clearly will not support a family any time soon. A tour to France, after the recording, will be the last thing the present ESQ will do together.

After the tour, back in the U.K., Brian moves his family to London and ingratiates himself into the music scene. A year or so later he travels with the ECO to Paris. At a reception after the concert, Brian finds himself facing Charles de Winton. Politely, he inquires after the Margand concert at the British Consulate. 'Adequate but not capital,' comes the reply.

Portrait: Otakar Ševčík

When Jan in the ESQ plays Mendelssohn's Octet with the Lyra Quartet for the Edinburgh Festival, he becomes acquainted with Granville Casey, the leader of the Lyra. 'Off to the pub we go,' says Granville after a rehearsal of the Scherzo, and they set off to the White Horse. Setting his drink down on the counter, Granville lights another cigarette and, exhaling smoke, says, 'The Scherzo is a contradiction in terms. You're asked to play *pianissimo* while bowing spiccato and saltando.'

'I'm sure Ševčík had an exercise for that,' says Julian.

'Oh, yes, number 1001,' says Brian, laughing into his beer.

'Well, actually I studied with Ševčík in his later years,' says Granville. 'I was surprised to find that he concentrated on the left hand during his classes, never mentioning the bow. At midmorning, we would all descend to a street café. There, in the Prague sun, we sat around our tables. A fly fell into Ševčík's coffee; the old man picked up a teaspoon with a palsied hand and chased the fly around the cup. We all looked on, not daring to help. Finally, Ševčík abandoned the chase, stirred in the fly and gulped down his coffee.'

INTERLUDE: PARIS

Jan, on a visit from Edinburgh, meets his cousin Rodney at the Duke of Wellington in London.

'The beer's very good right now,' says Rodney. 'Bitter, that is. I'm sorry I didn't see you at the Edinburgh Festival. Turned out that all the rehearsals were in London. We ran up for a dress rehearsal and played the concert. Left first thing the next morning.'

'That's the way it goes,' replies Jan. 'The LSO were up and away in the same fashion. I went to the Usher Hall to see my old colleagues. As you know, it was the Russian Festival. The LSO was rehearsing the Symphonic Suite from Shostakovich's *Lady Macbeth of the Mtsensk District.* The only people in the house sat on individual chairs placed at the front—Rostropovich, Shostakovich and a guy I didn't recognize but it was probably Richter. Shostakovich was really agitated. I've never seen a person more tense and nervous. He kept puffing on these Russian cigarettes, more cardboard than tobacco; he'd littered the butts around his chair. Apparently, one of the LSO guys told me, the parts were full of mistakes. Russia is not signatory to the Stockholm Agreement on Copyright. These parts were pirated and the orchestra was playing wrong notes in good faith.'

'I forgot to ask,' says Rodney, changing the subject. 'Before you went to Edinburgh, you spent a bit of time in Paris.'

'Yes. I had a few lessons with Paul Tortelier. Of course, I had no money. I lived in this crappy hotel—De la Nouvelle France—and ate paté and cheese with baguettes for the most part. The hotel was at the top of this street, which became, like a rat's tail, thinner and thinner down towards the Seine and to Les Halles, which is Paris's Covent Garden. My free entertainment was walking down that street. As the street narrowed, the little shops crowded in, their wares spilling out on the streets. At the bottom, there was more chaos around Les Halles. There were three open barns, for fish, for meat and for fruits and vegetables. I loved walking through and looking at everything.'

'How was Tortelier?' asks Rodney.

'I think he was disappointed in me. I got stuck on the Boccherini Concerto. He was very French—long-faced under wiry grey hair, long-nosed and a small mouth, which he sucked in when about to play. Long everything. In the thumb position, his fingers were extraordinary. They went down on the string absolutely straight; the last joint didn't bend at all. Talking of bending, despite playing a Testore, he experimented with sound modifications, drilling holes up the feet of the bridge and of course, coming up with the bent spike. I brought one back from Paris.

'Back in Edinburgh, the only luthier was on holiday so I took the spike to be fitted at the bagpipe shop. The guy assured me he could do the job: "Och, many festival musicians come in here. One person came in wanting his Torti bow fixed. I replaced the screw. First time I had seen a Torti bow." In order to put the spike in, the guy had to remove the strings, bridge and tailpiece and make the bushing wider. After it was done, everything was put back and I began to retune the cello. As the strings were coming up to pitch, there was a sharp explosion. Oh my God, I thought, the sound post has gone through the back. I examined the instrument. No damage. It was the tailgut slipping into its notch as I raised the string tension.'

A Ticket to Ride

'Come out west, son,' Colin tells Jan upon hearing that the ESQ is dissolving. 'It's a lovely place and there are ample opportunities.'

Jan plans to dip a toe into the Pacific and return if things don't work out. More quixotically, he's recently become engaged to Emmy—raven-haired with brown eyes like lamps. She loves the sun, she loves the desert. If Jan decides to stay, she'll follow him out later.

The Blue Star Line freighter bound for San Francisco lies low in the water, seeming somehow not big enough to ply the Atlantic. Andy helps Jan clamber aboard with two cellos and a suitcase. Jan sent the boxes of music ahead. The record albums have stayed with Elf. 'I won't hang about,' says Andy, but before he can turn to leave, an elderly woman suddenly appears at Jan's side. 'Are you fellow passengers?' she asks with a thick Glasgow accent. She is slightly heavy-set—evidencing a Scottish lifetime on a farinaceous diet—and is wearing a knitted hat.

'My brother is,' says Andy with a knowing smile. 'I'm just leaving.' He turns to Jan. 'Bye, laddie,' he says, and Jan watches him descend to the wharf, his grey raincoat blending into the concrete dockside.

The woman turns to Jan. 'Och, I like a wee drink before dinner. I hope you'll join me. I don't like to drink alone.'

She takes his arm and they step over the threshold into the corridor. From the forward deck, someone is whistling 'A Ticket to Ride'.

* * *

The officers have arranged an introductory cocktail party for the seven passengers on board. 'I wish I could get off this boat!' complains the American girl, Liz, who is returning to California from her finishing tour of Europe. She's upset since discovering that the boat will be making only one stop en route. Through the gin haze of his predinner cocktail with Morag, the woman from Glasgow, Jan observes the officer nicknamed

Brian the Freezer—because he's in charge of refrigeration—surveying the field and approaching Liz to replenish her drink. 'Too late now,' says Brian, taking Liz's empty glass. 'We're out of sight of land. Where are you from?'

'That girl is too tall for that officer,' remarks Morag to Jan. 'Och, there's the man with the drinks. Laddie, could you just reach over and get me another wee dram?'

As the voyage progresses, it seems that for Morag, drinks before dinner is becoming a substitution for elevenses. Jan tries to spend the morning practising Bach in his cabin but invariably when the sun is approaching the yardarm, there is a knock on his door. 'The bar's open,' calls Morag. Booze is cheap; the crew member at the bar is kept busy bringing up buckets of ice from Brian's freezer.

One evening, Brian intercepts Jan and invites him into the crew's quarters, a much more restricted and communal place. Here, more bottles are opened and off-duty officers, lounging on Brian's bunk, talk about their adventures circling the globe. Jan, questioning his special status here, thinks perhaps they need a new audience. It is a world far removed from string quartets. The young captain, who keeps a parakeet in his cabin, is about to retire to study theology and become a pastor. 'You can't stay in this life more than beyond thirty,' he says. 'If you do, you're stuck in it for the rest of your days.' All of the officers are certainly very young and single. Brian keeps these nightly conversations on topic. Relieved from thinking about refrigeration, he can think about the other topic occupying his mind—seduction. 'Women are prone to drop their panties on boat trips,' he says, offering Jan the bottle. 'I reckon I can make at least one conquest on every trip.'

'How's it going with the California girl?' asks one of the officers.

'A bit uphill,' admits Brian.

* * *

The crew is invisible but audible below decks. It is Beatlemania—Jan can hear scraps of 'Ticket to Ride', 'She Loves You' or 'I Want to Hold Your Hand', sung or whistled offstage.

Nightly conversations always feature a report on Liz. It becomes clear as the boat steams into warmer waters that Brian has misjudged his quarry. She's getting off in Los Angeles and he's only managed to fondle a breast.

'I may need your help tomorrow,' he tells Jan with a nudge.

The next morning, the boat is due to arrive at Long Beach, their first port of call. Jan moves up on deck to watch as the ship slips slowly up the channel, past expensive yacht clubs and green lawns to the docks beyond.

Brian sidles up to Jan and anxiously points out that the officers have discovered they've mistakenly put the clocks an hour ahead of the local time. 'I'm hoping to meet up with my LA girlfriend on the dock,' he says, looking at his watch. 'Can you keep Liz occupied on the other side of the boat?'

Jan finds Liz at the prow of the boat and inquires after her family. With the help of Morag come to say farewell, he manages to maintain small talk until out of the corner of his eye, he notices Brian disappear with a girl between the wharf buildings.

The ship is tied up on American soil, as it were, but Jan is not technically landed. He goes to bed early. At midnight, there is a knock on the cabin door. It's Brian the Freezer. 'Jan, Jan. You've got to get up. There's a party at my girlfriend's and there aren't enough men.'

Against his better judgment, Jan dresses and follows Brian down to the dock. An open convertible is parked alongside full of blondes. To Jan, all American girls are blond. These blondes chatter away and as Jan gets in, the girl behind the wheel takes off. Once on the elevated freeway, she puts her foot to the floor. After a month at sea, driving on the wrong side of the road with the lighted streets whizzing past diagonally below, Jan feels sick and remembers that he left his passport back in the cabin. If they crash, he'll have some explaining to do. Eventually, the car slows, turns down to a suburban area and stops in front of a bungalow.

On entering, Jan's worst fears are realized. In the spacious sitting room, chairs line the walls as if for a dance, with only a few chairs occupied. Brian disappears with a girl into a bedroom at the far end. Jan wanders into the kitchen, where a young couple sits at the kitchen table. The man reaches into the fridge and hands him a can of beer. 'It's Coors,' he explains. 'I haven't heard of it,' says Jan, sitting down with them, anxious to keep the conversation going. 'Coors,' the man continues, 'is the best beer. It's the absolute best. I don't drink anything else, do I, hun?' He turns to the girl, unaware that she has begun to play footsie under the table with Jan, who despairs. He is a prisoner here until Brian comes out and arranges a ride back to the boat. 'What other kinds of beer do you have in the U.S.?' asks Jan.

Brian emerges from the bedroom about 5 a.m. Behind him, a girl is in tears. They leave the house. Jan follows them outside, where the fog has moved in. The small yard is swathed in grey and beads of moisture cling to the leaves of the banana tree, reminding Jan of the Edinburgh Botanic Garden on a wet afternoon. 'Oh why, oh why did I come here?' thinks Jan miserably on the drive back to the boat.

It's one day's sail from Long Beach to San Francisco. On his last evening, Jan and a retired couple—the only passengers remaining—watch as the sea becomes suddenly alive with dolphins, surrounding the boat and seemingly diving all the way to the moonlit horizon.

It is lighter than usual when Jan wakes up, and the boat is motionless; he must have overslept. He looks out of his porthole. There, on the wharf, looking for him, is Colin.

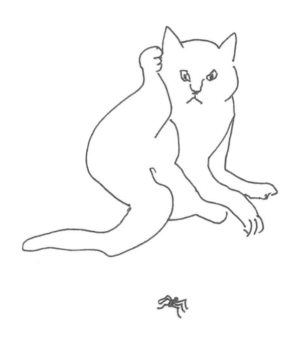

Book Two

RVW

TWENTY-ONE

Pacifika Rondo

The distance from the land of Walton and Vaughan Williams to the continent of Copland and Carter can be measured, not in nautical miles, but in decibel levels. Vehicles zip endlessly on the multi-lane, elevated freeways which stride across the Bay Area at roof level. Police sirens whine all night. Fire trucks and ambulances clamour for attention. Even the garbage trucks back up to a parody of Beethoven's famous Minuet. The peep of the London North Eastern Railway pales in comparison to Amtrak's rich horns. The London double-deckers run silent compared to the clanging of the San Francisco trams.

The first order of business for Jan after getting off the boat in June is to join the Musicians' Union. This requires an audition. 'Don't worry, son,' Colin says. 'When Bonnie joined, they asked her whether she wanted to stand or sit to play the cello.' Colin's second wife, Bonnie, also a cellist, is currently away playing on the East Coast for the summer.

There are times when Union procedures are not appropriate to the music profession. On his first gig, Jan discovers that there is a ten-minute break in every hour of rehearsal—no more, no less—clocked by the Union steward. You can't play through a Brahms symphony, nor do you have time to buy a cup of coffee. The gig in question is an outdoor concert atop Mount Tamalpais. They play *Pacifika Rondo*, a pentatonic piece by Lou Harrison featuring some Asian instruments. Harrison is one of an enquiring group of American composers pursuing avenues away from the European tradition. John Cage and Terry Riley, for example, have opened new ways of thinking about sound—mixing Western and Eastern and found instruments, using quarter tones, equal temperament, Indian ragas and electronic equipment. Another piece on the program is *Fables*, a narrated piece by Ernst Bacon, which is acerbically witty.

Gone are the stuffy Sunday night concerts at the Royal Albert Hall. Stepping off the boat to the West Coast, Jan is confronted by fearless, searching, unprejudiced and vibrant musical activity. However, on the mountaintop under the scorching sun, Jan's appetite for Bacon is compromised by a large crack opening up on the belly of his cello. In the heat of the day, the crack moves visibly up the instrument towards him.

Later, at Colin's, Jan surveys his two cellos. The crack on one has to be fixed and the purfling on the other—a souvenir of Panama—has to be reinserted. He has to take both instruments to the luthier Jan Kortenaar. Jan studies the street map. The Kortenaar shop is kitty-corner to the opera house. New to right-handed driving, Jan prefers to trust his own two feet rather than to attempt driving Bonnie's car with three.

(When Jan arrived at Colin's in early June, Bonnie had left her car in the garage. Jan eyed it dubiously—a giant chromium-plated creature lurking in the shadows like a predator waiting for a takeout dinner to walk by. The car, a stick shift, has a mysterious feature—the handbrake is released by a foot pedal. In a city like San Francisco, where several of the hills are almost perpendicular, starting away on a green light is of some significance. Three feet are needed to drive this car, and Jan, who continually stalls it, plans his routes around the city very carefully in order to avoid the steeper hills. Don't drive to Chinatown!)

He decides to park by the Amtrak station and walk to Kortenaar's shop. It's only a few blocks. It is a foggy morning. Jan finds it disconcerting that it can be so cold in the middle of summer. He wears his hairy English jacket. After parking, he walks—a cello case in each hand—along the street that leads to the opera house. The street is straight, relentlessly ascending and the blocks longer than they appeared on the map. Halfway along his journey, the fog evaporates and the sun comes out. Jan begins to sweat; by the time he arrives at Kortenaar's shop, he's soaking.

Kortenaar examines the instruments. 'I think we should loosen the plates,' he says. 'When instruments come from Europe, they have been living in a uniformly damp place. Here, it is much drier. The wood will shrink a little and we need to relieve the tension. That's why you've got this crack.' He runs his finger along it. 'You have something else you can play for a couple of weeks?'

'I'll use Colin's spare,' says Jan.

'By the way,' says Kortenaar, 'it's a real privilege to work on the Amati cello—your father brings it in from time to time. It's had some woodworm damage. I don't think he knows that.'

On Colin's advice, on leaving the luthier, Jan pays a visit to Germain

Prévost, who lives close by. Germain had been the violist of the Pro Arte, one of Europe's finest string quartets. He meets Jan at the door. 'You're soaking. Take off your jacket. I'll find you a T-shirt. 'ere's a towel.' Jan is very grateful. 'Why did you walk?'

Jan explains.

'Ah, yes,' says Germain. 'When at last I learned to drive, I 'ad this beeg car. I could just see over the steering wheel. I drove it for a while and pretty soon, I see a light in my mirror. I tried to avoid the light but it kept following me. It was a cop—'e pulled me over. "Oh officer," I said, "this ees my first day driving." The cop handed me a piece of paper. "And 'ere," he says, "ees your first ticket."'

Germain makes coffee and they sit at the kitchen table. He is inclined to be talkative. 'Rest awhile. You 'ave a long walk back to your car. You should play in the Oakland Symphony. I do, even though I thought I'd retired years ago. I bring the section in wrong sometimes, but it's more fun than playing *quatuors*.' Germain looks into his coffee cup. 'Mrs Albert … you know? Well, she owns a bank. She wanted me to write my memoirs. I thought about it for a while, but it brought back unhappy memories—one night, travelling in a Pullman coach, I overheard Onnou and Maas discussing about replacing me.' He sips his coffee. 'I told Mrs Albert I didn't want to do it. There were good things—we had special audience with the Queen of Belgium. She asked Onnou if we would play a Haydn quartet. We only 'ad one Haydn in our repertoire at that time. "Certainly, ma'am," Onnou bluffed. "Which one would you like?" Luckily, she chose the one we knew.'

The phone rings. Germain answers in French. The phone rings again. This time he speaks in English; it's a Russian colleague. Jan contemplates the range of cultures that contributes to the American people. Germain returns to the table and offers Jan more coffee. 'Of course, every *quatuor* argues through rehearsals and it is strange what different solutions to familiar problems each ensemble devises. One occasion, we were in London. Maas got phoned. The cellist of the Budapest 'ad suddenly taken ill. Could 'e take 'ees place? The concert was at the Conway Hall at seven o'clock. There was not time for a rehearsal. The Budapest was opening with Beethoven's opus 95. You know 'ow eet begins with this fist-thumping gesture. Maas walks out with the Budapest, sits down, 'as 'ees bow ready to play fast and loud at the heel, and they begin with an up bow!'

Not long after this visit, Jan has the opportunity to meet Mrs

Agnes Albert in her home. Upon arrival, Jan notices a Bruegel painting—*Hunters in the Snow*—above the mantelpiece. Jan tries to remember where he's seen it before; is it real?

Mrs Albert, anxious to help Jan, arranges for a secret meeting with
Josef Krips, now director of the San Francisco Symphony (SFS).
Although there is no position available, any audition is supposed to have
the blessing of the local Musicians' Union. Jan enters what appears to be
the concert hall's janitorial closet and there is Krips sitting against the
back wall. Jan plays straight into his gaping belly button. Not an edifying
experience. (Krips had previously asked Bonnie if she would play in the
SFS. 'Well, I really only play chamber music,' she politely refused. 'But,'
returned Krips, 've all play chamber music, only ve all play it together.')

The weeks of summer pass and Jan is often alone in the house. It has
become apparent to him that possibly Colin and Bonnie's marriage is
straining at the ropes. Jan has his own problems to solve. He has
parachuted into San Francisco with no promise of employment. He has a
fiancée who will join him later in the season and they will have to settle
into a society where the sole criteria for lifestyle choice is money. A car is
necessary. There are few transit options. Jan must pay tolls to cross the
bridges. Houses on the right side of the tracks are unaffordable. There
seem to be no libraries or medical services, and no assurances of stable
employment. Jan's socialist leanings are a by-product of the welfare state.
He is at odds with the hedonistic society he's found in California. In Edinburgh, he had walked everywhere. He's already discovered that urban
America is unwalkable. He knows the streets of his former home from the
curbstones upwards. Sometimes, lying in bed at night, assaulted by police
sirens, he walks his route across Edinburgh.

* * *

The last week of summer, Jan and Colin set off in Bonnie's car to Yosemite
National Park for the California Youth Symphony Camp. Colin is to
coach the cellos and for good measure, Jan is invited along to coach the
basses. For the first time, Jan leaves the Bay Area to experience rural
America. The ever-beckoning spaces of the North American continent
were one of the inspirations for his leaving Scotland. Under bright sunshine, Jan drives to the end of the bay at Vallejo, through hills of dried
grass to Stockton, along the levees between fields of sunflower and
tomato to the hills, which begin to be dotted with green oaks. They climb

past Sacramento, the capital city, and on to Colfax where they stay the night in a small cabin built by Bonnie's father. Now that he's an invalid, nature is claiming it back. On the window, Jan glimpses the biggest beetle of his life. It has long, crenellated whiskers, like a lobster.

The next day, they drive down Highway 49, the gold rush road, with abandoned towns and villages reincarnated as tourist traps. Despite the souvenir shop signs, there are few cars on the road and the dry landscape holds an intimate beauty Jan hasn't expected. They stop to buy bourbon in Angels Camp.

'Lovely town,' mutters Jan, driving slowly.

'Associated with Mark Twain,' says Colin. 'Did you ever read "The Celebrated Jumping Frog of Calaveras County"?'

Jan shakes his head.

'They have a competition to see which frog can jump the farthest,' says Colin. 'The favourite can't move, because they filled it with lead shot.'

The shadows lengthen in the late afternoon sun. Colin takes a good swig before passing the bottle to Jan. 'Son, you've probably guessed by now. Bonnie's been away all summer. She's been increasingly away as her musical activities have widened and she is becoming well-known. Our paths are diverging. She will be home soon to start teaching at the university. Even so, we have talked about separating but you don't have to worry. By the way, she's to have the Amati. You and I get the house.'

They pass the bottle between them. The landscape turns greener and mountainous as they began the long descent into Yosemite Valley.

✳ ✳ ✳

Outside of happy hour, Aaron Sten presents himself as an authoritarian figure to the California Youth Symphony. He conducts them with a rod of iron. There are sectional rehearsals in the mornings. Jan takes the basses outside. Despite being on the valley floor, with the sun dappling through the redwoods, it is cold. They're studying the *Symphonie fantastique* by Berlioz. The basses warm up to the 'March to the Scaffold'. The whole orchestra rehearses through the afternoon, playing impressively. The evenings are given over to recreation. Colin and Jan retire to their cabin on the edge of the campsite, where they spend their evenings drinking cheap red wine and peeing in a bucket which Colin, an early riser, empties and swills out before anybody else is stirring. They sleep on the verandah under an enormous starlit sky.

In the middle of the week, the orchestra is rehearsing as usual when, in the middle of 'The Witches' Sabbath', Aaron sets down his baton. Somebody or a group of somebodies had been rowdying the night before. Aaron embarks on a lecture, symphonic in scope, symphonic in structure. They are all heading for the fires of hell unless those responsible come forward.

Jan, standing at the back with his bass section, watches the smallest player, who's standing in front of the Coke machine, reach into his pocket for a coin. Holding his bass and bow in one hand, he drops the coin in at an opportune moment during the diatribe. Never taking his gaze off the conductor, he stuffs his hand up the aperture at the bottom of the machine and tries to ease the can's noisy descent. This takes an agonizingly long time. With can and bass bow in one hand, he tries with his free hand to flip the opening catch. The diatribe is rising to its final climax. He flips the catch and takes a discreet swig. The can is passed surreptitiously through the basses up to the leader. Aaron's lecture comes to a close. There is an embarrassed silence. Then Jan notices that the boy has a very large insect embroidered on his jacket. 'Nice bug,' Jan observes. The boy spazzes out, dropping his bow. 'Get it off me! Get it off me! Ugh!'

* * *

It is late September, and Jan reflects that in Edinburgh the chilly mists are rising, whereas here in California, the summer fogs are receding and autumn isn't going to arrive. Jan is playing in the Oakland Symphony's opening concert of the season. First on the program is Copland's *Appalachian Spring*, a sop for the invited dignitaries. Jan is familiar with this music, as Copland was really the first American composer to claim the affection of the British public. Weary in the aftermath of the Second World War, English listeners found his music fresh and open, having a spaciousness unachievable by composers living within the confined borders of Europe. Jan, playing at the back of the cello section, thinks about how this program seems to cross and recross the Atlantic; he remembers playing this same music in the LSO under Copland, who gestured as he conducted with his long fingers. The leisurely chords of the opening strings capture the essence of Copland and the lure of the American landscape, with its widely spaced intervals and slowly unfolding harmonies.

After the interval, they play *Three Places in New England* by Charles

Ives. This is Jan's first time playing Ives. During the second section, 'Putnam's Camp, Redding, Connecticut', Ives, recalling a childhood memory, conjures up two marching bands who pass each other without giving way—a moment of wonderful noise. The cacophony continues after the concert on the freeway as Jan heads home in his old Buick, which burns a can of oil on every trip.

In October, Jan's fiancée, Emmy, arrives from Edinburgh with his extra cello. Unlike Jan, she loves everything hot and sunny and accepts the American way of life, her large brown eyes unblinking. She accompanies Jan on his peripatetic teaching schedule around the Bay Area. Jan drives the Buick, a heavy old beater bound for the knacker's yard. It suffers from engina and overheats as it travels the hot plains towards Davis. At the beginning of every journey, Emmy buys a large bottle of Coke which warms up in competition with the engine. She also discovers fast food and takes a novelty on each journey, the smell of heating engine mingling with that of breaded shrimp.

Jan's teaching schedule pays for the cans of oil, but not much more. In between, he plays in the Oakland Symphony (OSO). Inspired by its conductor, Garry Samuel, the OSO has since 1959 garnered national attention by programming predominantly twentieth-century works, and becoming a competitor to the larger, more staid SFS. The OSO has the artistic edge over the latter, which under Josef Krips, pursues straight-ahead—largely German—repertoire. Coming from London where *Scheherazade* was programmed at least once a week, Jan finds the OSO's repertoire to be exhilaratingly contemporary and is amazed to find that such uncompromising modernity commands full houses. Schoenberg rubs shoulders with William Schuman, Andrew Imbrie cheek by jowl with Seymour Shifrin.

Jan's diet of chamber music follows in the same spirit. Donald Pippin runs a series of Sunday night concerts at the Old Spaghetti Factory in San Francisco, and Jan is a regular performer. Here, in a backroom behind the restaurant, aficionados, armed with a pint of pale beer, take the opportunity to listen to a very wide range of music. Donald wears his erudition and his pianistic ability very lightly. He can wear little else, with spaghetti being slurped behind the curtain. His concerts range from Rameau to Rorem, and again, Jan, used to the rather ecclesiastical audiences of England, is stimulated by the fresh American approach to the genre.

One evening, Jan is invited to perform the Ravel Duo and also hears Donald and the violinist play Leon Kirchner's Sonata Concertante for Violin and Piano. After the initial atonal shock has passed, Jan is persuaded by its romantic swagger; it has a thrust that appears to be in short supply in the European atonalists. The music, though, is somehow reminiscent of Berg. Jan hears a lot of consonant harmonies.

Bonnie—herself a fearless cellist—returns from the East Coast and repossesses her car just as Jan has finally mastered its little ways. (Decades later, Jan will have a phone conversation with Bonnie, recently retired from the faculty at Juilliard after a distinguished career spent in the centre of the contemporary American music scene. 'Maybe it's because the '60s and '70s were my coming-out decades, but I think the music coming out of the West Coast was very vital and significant. There was a lot of experimenting by younger composers. Their two mentors—Milhaud at Mills and Bloch at Calm were very open to new paths, particularly Milhaud.'

Bonnie's phone delivery is as tumultuous as her career; she speaks quickly with intense volubility. 'I don't know whether the visual dynamics were important to many of those composers. Most of them seemed quite heedless of the instrumentalist's limitations. Out of frustration, I said to one of them, "I'm going to write a piece especially for composers." Whoever it was didn't like the inference.'

'Who?'

'Can't recall. Seymour Shifrin for instance was very picky. I played a piece of his which was full of double stops, very difficult, but he insisted on his bowing which made them all but impossible. I practised it till my hands hurt, at which point I handed back his music and told him to find a cellist who could play it.')

* * *

As the sun climbs high in the California sky, Jan's first concert season closes, the college students wilt and eventually the school district succumbs and the kids are out on their long, long summer vacation. Much too long, thinks Jan. He and Emmy decide to vacation in Colfax. They can soak up the hot sun and cool off in the glacier-fed river. A week later, their neighbour from the next cabin strolls across the field of dry prickles and hands them a slip of paper. 'You're to phone this number. It's long distance. Canada, I think. Dial zero first.' Jan dials the number. A familiar voice answers.

'Oh, Jan. Glad we tracked you down. It's Simon. Norman and I have come out to Vancouver. We're playing in the symphony here for Meredith Davies. Norman wants to form a string quartet and needs a cellist. Would you be interested?'

INTERLUDE: COPLAND'S HEAD

'We'd better tackle Ives,' sighs Normsk. 'That concert is sneaking up.'

'Shall it be "Discussions" or "Arguments"?' Fred has a glint in his eye.

'"The Call of the Mountains",' Normsk says firmly. 'We had a heck of a dinner party last night.'

'That's stupid,' Phil exclaims. 'We can play that movement. We need to practise "Arguments" slowly to get the rhythm, let alone the notes.'

'Seems the notes don't matter, some of them are crazy,' returns Fred. 'I wonder whether his insurance policies were a similar jumble.'

'I don't know,' adds Jan. 'The music kind of evokes New York round the turn of the century.'

'Were you there?' asks Fred.

'I imagine early urban clangour.'

'Oh, for *Appalachian Spring* or Barber's *Adagio*,' groans Normsk.

'What about *Quiet City*?' replies Jan.

'Were you in the LSO when Copland collapsed?' Normsk asks, turning to Jan.

'No ...'

'We were recording in the Kingsway Hall, Copland conducting. Anyhow, he collapsed. There was a room up a flight of steps from the orchestral area, which was used as a green room, so Nev and Simon took the arms and the legs, I held Copland's head. Trouble was, I had to go up the steps backwards. At one point I slipped and dropped his head. It went clunk on the step. He was unconscious anyway so later, he appeared to be none the worse for it.'

'Except he went atonal after that,' says Fred. ' "Arguments" ...'

TWENTY-TWO

Romeo and Juliet

Jan, in his seventies, browses at Chapters bookstore, thinking that these days, the store seems to sell more hardware than hardcovers. However, he exits with a retrospective of mountaineering photographs by Galen Rowell. Jan was drawn to the book because he'd known its author. Galen's biography includes a snapshot of his parents in earlier years. Jan experiences a shock of recognition when he sees Galen's father, who had been a professor at Berkeley. When Jan, with Colin, met him at the faculty club in 1963, Jan was surprised to hear the man ordering buttermilk. Jan also knew Galen's mother, Margaret, a well-known cello teacher in the Bay Area. In 1966—before becoming a renowned mountaineer—Galen was running a little garage in Berkeley. Jan purchased a Chevy from him for 300 dollars to make his journey north to Vancouver, Canada.

* 1966 *

Early in September, Jan, Emmy and two kittens set out in the Chevy. True to the age, it is pickle-coloured with chromium fins. They drive through dusty fields. The kittens pant from the heat on the floor of the car. The flaxen hills begin to get steeper and fir trees first dot the landscape and at last obscure it. The burning hives of sawmills appear, producing a pervasive smell wafting through the car windows not unlike stale sewage. As they make for the Canadian border, America seems featureless and unable to come to an end.

Colin, who seemed disconcerted at Jan's departure, had said, 'If you look at the map, son, there isn't much up there,' and now Jan, looking out the window, is afraid his father might have been right. Vancouver, as Brian the Freezer had predicted, turns out to be foggy. Jan and Emmy hunker down at the Sylvia Apartments downtown, overlooking English Bay. The kittens, cool and happy to be unconfined, climb the curtains. Jan settles in and waits for the symphony season to begin at the end of the month. Normsk is still holidaying in London. Simon, Jan's other London contact, is also away, so Jan and Emmy have slipped unheralded into Vancouver life. Jan is relieved at this—he doesn't want to give the Musicians' Union any hint of collusion between himself and his former colleagues, who are principal players with the Vancouver Symphony Orchestra (VSO).

* * *

September in Vancouver is warm and brilliant, the summer lingering longer than in England. In the offices of the Vancouver Musicians' Association, the president glares balefully at Jan and barks like a guardsman. 'Are you a member of the Federation of Musicians?'

'Yes.'

'Which local?'

'San Francisco.' Jan glances around the room. All the members sit quietly staring at the table like so many browbeaten schoolchildren.

'Why did you come here?'

'Because I didn't care for San Francisco and I know people here.'

'British people?'

'Um—'

'Did the Vancouver Symphony bring you in?'

'No.' Jan shifts uncomfortably in his chair.

'It's a bit coincidental that you've arrived just at the beginning of the season.'

'Well, I'm hoping to find work.'

A quiet voice beside him—a blond woman—says, 'Do you remember me? I'm Judy—we were once stand partners in London.'

Jan is taken aback by this. He can't remember the occasion. It was nothing he regularly had been booked for—it must have been a one-off gig. He racks his brains amidst an uncomfortable silence and suddenly remembers. 'Oh, yes—we played *Peter and the Wolf* together!'

She smiles at him, the first friendly indicator of this interview.

Jan senses that the tide has turned.

'Do you intend to audition?' the president asks brusquely.

'I hope to. If they ever hold auditions.'

'To avoid collusions,' the president says pointedly, 'such notifications are done through our office. Welcome to Local 145. Thank you. You may go. Next business.'

Jan walks, relieved, into the September sun, his first obstacle behind him. Getting into his car, Jan remembers more of the *Peter and the Wolf* concert with Judy in London. He laughs, recalling that at the abrupt ending of the piece just after the narrator tells the audience about the duck still quacking in the wolf's stomach, Prokofiev surprised both Jan and Judy, and they played one beat more after the conductor had finished. 'Oh crap!' Judy had said loudly in the pause before the applause began.

A month after Jan's arrival in Vancouver, he and Emmy move from their downtown apartment to a rented house in North Vancouver. The two kittens are happy for more space. After three weeks of sunshine, the rains come. How it rains! As a Brit, Jan felt he was always short of three months of sun each year, but at least in England it rained gently if frequently. The rain falls relentlessly on Vancouver—pounding rods of water for forty days and forty nights. No, make that eighty.

* * *

The musical range of Prokofiev's ballet *Romeo and Juliet* is extensive, from the innocence of C Major scales played by the high instruments describing the young Juliet, to the violins' frantic sizzling of rapiers as Romeo and Tybalt fight, to the percussive fighting of the Montagues and the Capulets interrupted by a cacophonous chord from the top to the bottom of the orchestra which signals the prince's decree. Prokofiev's orchestrations can be as quirky as his harmonies.

(Years after his arrival in Vancouver, in the Queen Elizabeth Theatre [QET], from the back of the cello section, Jan will watch with amusement as R. Murray Schafer, one of Canada's prime composers, gives an introduction to a school concert presented by the VSO. The program will include Prokofiev's Suite from *Romeo and Juliet*. To demonstrate the pomposity and intractability of the families Montague and Capulet, Murray, the least pompous of men, will march around the auditorium, his nose in the air, while the orchestra plays.)

A Russian colleague once told Jan that Prokofiev didn't orchestrate his own music, probably because his initial ideas were always notated in piano score. This appears demonstrably untrue; Prokofiev was always looking for new colours. He may have found the labour irksome, so perhaps hired someone to do some of the grunt work. The colleague also mentioned to Jan that when they began rehearsing *Romeo and Juliet* in 1940, the musicians shook their heads at one another and thought Prokofiev had gone senile; the music seemed to them old-fashioned.

Prokofiev's language had smoothed out in his later works such as *Romeo and Juliet* and the Cello Sonata, aiming at a transparency and simplicity for the proletariat. *Romeo and Juliet*, however, is a very rich score and, like *Peter and the Wolf*, is a regular favourite with the public.

* * *

'How have you settled in?' Normsk, upon his return to Vancouver at the end of September, asks Jan. 'How was the Union interview?'

'A little tense but fine,' says Jan.

'Did you meet Judy? She's on the board.'

'Yes,' says Jan with a laugh. 'We finished *Peter and the Wolf* together.'

Normsk and Jan have come to Simon's house in North Vancouver for dinner to discuss the possibilities of forming a string quartet. Jan thinks that Normsk has changed somewhat since his London days. It's something about his mouth; he looks unhappy.

'Well, I've come out here to form a string quartet, not to be a concertmaster,' says Normsk, uncorking a bottle of wine. 'It'll take a little time. We need a strong second violin. The assistant concertmaster position is open. I hope I've persuaded Ray Ovens to come out. Maybe next season.'

Simon turns to Jan. 'I eventually plan to give up the viola and become a conductor, but that's around the corner,' he says. 'Norman and I have discussed this.'

'Meanwhile, I'm going to form a Baroque string group, like the Academy of St Martin,' says Normsk. 'Judy said she'd leave Vancouver if I didn't. I've promised a few players.'

Simon refills Jan's glass. 'Quite a nice wine. It's not your Eau d'Kelowna. Did you know I'm conducting the Vancouver Youth Orchestra? The children are wonderful—it's the parents that are a pain.'

'The phone goes all the time,' moans Liz, Simon's wife.

'We hope to raise the standard of education and opportunity here—organize an orchestral summer camp at Courtenay next summer and we have a committee working on establishing a community music school in Vancouver. Mrs Koerner heads it.'

'A name to conjure with,' says Normsk.

'The committee is being advised by a specialist from the U.S., a Dr Zipper,' comments Simon. 'No flies on Dr Zipper!'

It doesn't take Normsk long to find players for the Baroque Strings.

Judy schedules the rehearsals. Normsk rehearses the group obsessively ('light, feathery bows'), looking for romantic shading and special lyrical moments. (The early music concept has yet to reach Vancouver.) They are learning all the concerti grossi of Handel and Corelli, twelve from each composer, and are looking to play concerts.

Simon, in addition to his other activities, is involved in negotiations to move the VSO from the QET to the Orpheum, a Spanish Renaissance Revival cinema lying empty. This will be an arduous process taking several years. (The QET, built in 1958, is a symbol of civic pride. Graft and budget constraints altered the original design from a rectangle with a high roof, to lower and wider dimensions by adding another aisle of seats. These altered dimensions resulted in disastrous acoustics. As a wind player observed, the people that build auditoriums also build airports—acoustic engineers like to fire guns to test the acoustics as if Vancouver listeners would be hearing nothing but the *1812 Overture*. When string soloists visit the QET, they begin a rehearsal confidently but as they hear no returning resonances, they begin to fight themselves, fight their instruments and struggle with the orchestra.)

In 1974, several years after Jan's arrival in Vancouver, he enters the renovated Orpheum Theatre to play Prokofiev's *Romeo and Juliet* with the VSO and its newly appointed conductor, Kazuyoshi Akiyama. (Incidentally, during the renovations, a powder puff belonging to Pavlova came to light.) Having played *Romeo and Juliet* several times below ground in the pit of the QET, Jan savours the colours Akiyama draws from the orchestra in the new acoustic above ground. *Romeo and Juliet*, a full-length ballet in the Tchaikovskian tradition, illustrates Prokofiev's broad musical range. Tchaikovsky, in his *Romeo and Juliet* Overture-Fantasy, wrote one of the the greatest Romantic themes that epitomizes the bitter sweetness of young love. Prokofiev challenges that in his twentieth-century way with the opening phrase of the ballet, its edgy harmony expressing the anxiety of tender love.

* * *

Prokofiev wrote about his travels in his diaries, including an account of his circuitous route to the United States in 1918. Uprooted by the revolution, he travelled by train from Petrograd through Siberia to Vladivostock, arriving in New York via Tokyo, Honolulu, San Francisco, Seattle and then, to Jan's surprise, to Vancouver in September 1918. What's remarkable to Jan is that Prokofiev, despite chaotic travelling conditions, is neither inconvenienced, nor is his muse disturbed.

In the spring of 1936, Prokofiev moved his family back to the Soviet Union. Acute longing for the homeland seems to be a peculiar Russian trait. In a letter to a friend, Prokofiev wrote about his need to experience again the turning of the northern seasons. *Romeo and Juliet* premiered in the Soviet Union in 1938, two years after Prokofiev's return home following eighteen years abroad.

Stalin welcomed Prokofiev back. One of the composer's conditions was that he would be free to tour abroad, but after another visit to the United States in 1938, his passport was revoked. Prokofiev died in 1953 on the same day as Stalin. Since the composer lived near the Red Square, it was impossible to move his body because of Stalin's obsequies.

* * *

Thanksgiving 1967—Jan sells one of his cellos in order to purchase a house in North Vancouver. He phones Colin.

'Contrary to what you said,' says Jan, 'there's a heck of a lot going on up here.'

'Tell me.'

'Lots of concerts, broadcasts, recordings ... we haven't got the quartet started yet, but Ray Ovens is coming out with his family from London in September. And we've started a cello club modelled on yours in California.'

'You sound settled, son.'

'It feels like home.'

Portrait: VSO

A month after his arrival in Vancouver, Jan starts playing at the back of the VSO cello section. Almost as soon, he senses a restlessness within the organization. Previously the plaything of the financially and socially elite, it seems to be outgrowing a certain parochialism that pervades its structure. Jan feels uncomfortable because the principal cellist, Ernst Friedlander, was ill and died shortly after Jan's arrival. Jan feels people think it's somehow his fault. Paranoia takes hold, increasing as Jan and his colleagues in the orchestra anticipate a forthcoming audition for the principal cello position. Jan had been blithely unaware of orchestral politics in London. There, it was easy to find other work. In Canada, you'd probably have to move five hundred miles.

Meredith Davies presides over this sea of private agendas with laconic humour: 'It's the sax and the single flute problem' and to the bass drummer, 'Really, that sounds like a duck falling into a wet blanket.' A good communicator with the audience, his British presumptiveness can be less than sensitive. 'The twelve tone system reduces notes to immemorability. They all seem the same. Like so many Chinese.' Not a good thing to say in Vancouver. His remarks probably arise from a cheerful disrespect for the audience who still clap between movements. 'The silent pause is bound to be ruined by the purple-spotted purse snapper,' he says, and when he deletes the waltz from *Eugene Onegin*, 'Halfway down your programs you will see Eugene One-Gin. We're not playing it.'

* * *

On stage at the QET with an audience of Meredith and the principal string players, Jan feels his audition for the principal cello position is going well.

'What other orchestral solos have you prepared?' asks Meredith from the front row.

'How about,' Jan says, smiling impishly, 'the cello solo from the "Emperor" Concerto.'

Meredith frowns. 'I don't recall that one. Could you play it?'

Jan plays two bars of low tremolo on the C string. From behind Meredith, Jan hears Norman laugh.

Portrait: CBC

The CBC Vancouver Orchestra, directed by John Avison, is thirty years old when Jan arrives in Vancouver. It attracts and supports excellent musicians, who, having settled in Vancouver, initiate other musical ventures. Like Jan, many of the instrumentalists also play in the VSO and freelance. Every week, the orchestra records an hour's program of Canadian and other—mainly twentieth-century—music with a generous filler from the classical era, frequently a Haydn symphony.

Jan parks his car in the Georgia Hotel parking lot and heads to Studio G, the unattractive space where the orchestra will record through the day, finishing at 5 p.m. 'First the "sig" tune,' announces Avison. They play the first several bars of Barber's *Adagio for Strings*, which is freshly recorded every week. 'Now the Canadian piece which we'll record movement by movement.' Well, of course, thinks Jan, how else would you record it? The Canadian piece causes trouble. It is in manuscript and has many bugs in it. Avison fields a torrent of questions from the players with a mixture of expertise and inspired guesswork.

After lunch, they move on to Boccherini's *Il Notturno di Madrid* and at ten past four, the final work, Haydn's Symphony 'Le soir'. 'Oh my God,' thinks Jan. 'How can we possibly record this in fifty minutes?' At the end of the first movement, a voice comes from the control box: 'There are various fluffs, I think we should record it again.' Jan moans inwardly and thinks again, 'How can we possibly do this?'

(The voice in the control room belongs to the composer Robert Turner, who has the further distinction of being able to speak without moving his lips. Robert Turner as producer should be credited with maintaining and furthering the CBC Vancouver Orchestra's reputation for supporting Canadian music and young Canadian musicians.)

'And now for the slow movement.' It is 4:35. Halfway through the slow movement, a horn crows. 'Back to the beginning,' the producer says. 'There are no splicing places.' Jan marvels that there are no signs of panic. 'Do you do overtime?' he whispers to his colleague. 'Practically never.' Jan curls his toes in his shoes as the orchestra approaches the offending horn passage. They reach the double bar safely—4:45. Next, the Minuet. 'I'll give two on the finger,' announces Avison. 'Two beats before the downbeat,' explains Jan's partner. 'Once more,' says the conductor, frowning at one of the bassoonists, 'because the *fagotto* forgot.'

Angelina, Avison's wife, who leads the second violins, says something surreptitiously to her desk partner. Avison looks down at her. 'Don't talk behind your violin. You'll blister the varnish.' When Avison gives a downbeat, he has an odd habit of rolling his eyes upwards so that his irises disappear. 'Looking for his brains,' Jan's partner explains. At 4:55, they arrive at the Finale. 'No repeat,' announces Avison. They sight-read onto tape. 'Thank you,' says the producer. It is exactly five o'clock.

Spring—daffodils in Vancouver, corn stubble just visible above snow in other parts of the country—is touring season for the CBC

Orchestra with a group that is smaller in numbers than that which regularly meets in the studio. Jan finds himself in North Battleford, Saskatchewan, in the locker room practising before a concert in the high school gymnasium. When on tour with this group, Jan has the opportunity to play the *Classical* Symphony by Prokofiev. Because of its restricted orchestration and easy accessibility, this group of the CBC Orchestra frequently tours with it. The *Classical* Symphony captures the elegance of the eighteenth century; Prokofiev intended it to be the one which Haydn would have written had he been reincarnated in the early twentieth century. This symphony is mercilessly exposed like a Haydn string quartet, especially in the violin department. The second subject of the opening movement sounds deceptively simple with octave transpositions boomeranged into space by grace notes. One slip of the finger and the whole world has heard it.

Sitting on the slatted bench in the locker room with concert tails hanging from the shower stall, Jan makes sure to study one passage in the Finale before the performance; there is a frantic Alberti bass-like challenge to the fingers and bow that needs attention immediately before going out on stage. It calls for extreme electrical response of the muscles to navigate it which Jan does, looking down at his open music on the floor with a view of stray gym socks in sight.

Portrait: Arthur

Arthur Polson invariably arrives early at the theatre. He parks his Chrysler in a staff parking stall to make the quick getaway while the singers are still taking their curtain call. In the orchestral green room, he warms his fingers with a frantic study that takes them all over the violin. Then he sits, his violin tucked under his arm, and talks. Arthur cuts a Humpty Dumpty figure that betrays a career of indulgent but discerning tastes in cuisine and the cocktail cabinet, punctuated by an occasional cheroot. His violin also reflects his taste, a Guadagnini with ribs like tiger stripes. In his hands, the violin sounds strong and steady, a musical rope that all the orchestra can grab on to. Arthur has been a leader most of his life. He has fine judgment about rehearsing detail according to the amount of time available. When Meredith Davies began importing

English musicians, Arthur felt it was time to leave Vancouver, only returning after leading the Winnipeg Symphony for twenty years.

Arthur chats amiably in the green room. 'I was born in Vancouver, bottom of Burnaby Mountain. I went to Capitol Hill Elementary School. (Jan imagines a small, rotund schoolboy.) My father would take me fishing in the Burrard Inlet. One time, he pointed out an albatross soaring above us. I began the violin at the age of four, was playing professionally in my teens. My first gig, I was told the rehearsal was ten to one, so showed up at 12:50. I joined the CBC Orchestra then but every week there was other stuff. There was usually a variety show—band singers, special soloists and always new arrangements. Then there was chamber music of all kinds. The organist, Hugh McLean, had a radio show, *Music in G*, under his supervision. We virtually sight-read chamber music onto tape each week.

'In the early days, the broadcast went out live. One time, the orchestra was waiting quite a time for the red light. Everything was still and quiet. Those were the days you collected silver foil from cigarette packets to buy guide dogs for the blind. Somebody had rolled a big ball of foil and lobbed it into the air. It fell on the timpani with a loud thump. Everybody was galvanized to attention, especially the timpanist, who had been dozing. "Who did that? Who did that?"

'Before TV shows, there was usually a meal break so that crews could sweep the set and retouch the flats. One time, they had painted the floor and various sets with quick drying brown varnish. The string quartet had left their instruments on their chairs. When they returned from their break, they found them covered in brown varnish.'

Arthur looks at his watch as the stage manager calls the half hour before showtime. 'House open now.' Arthur gets up. 'Time to overlook the part,' he says, laughing at his own joke.

INTERLUDE: SCHOOLS, VIOLAS AND SHRIMP

The Quartet is booked for several days of school concerts up and down the Sunshine Coast. They rent an apartment at a new development in Halfmoon Bay, which stands roughly in the middle of their musical operations. Each season, a quartet member takes on the task of explaining things to the children. Jan is frankly ill at ease in this role; the novelty of a string quartet holds the interest of the children initially, but then one has to work increasingly hard to maintain their interest. Children are conditioned to think that music is background noise. It follows them in elevators, airports, grocery shops and hotel lobbies—you talk against it, talking it out of your consciousness.

Fred programs Beethoven's last quartet. Beethoven gave it a prefix, *Muss es sein?* ('Must it be?'). Fred sings the motif—'*Muss—es—sein*' and looks up at the children. 'Now many of you will think this is about a moose.'

Phil is in charge of the school concerts on the Sunshine Coast. He tackles the problem differently. At the top of the concert he holds up his viola and asks, 'Do any of you know what this instrument is?' and then explanations follow.

Their Sunshine Coast tour coincides with the shrimp season. All the way up the road, private houses belonging to fishermen advertise shrimp for sale. The Quartet stops at one, and the house owner opens his freezer in the garage and shovels shrimp into a bag. Though frozen, the shrimp—numb but not dead yet—have a disconcerting habit of shifting within the bag.

The rented apartment has cooking facilities and Phil comes into his own. School concerts have to be over by 3 p.m. Thereafter, the day is dedicated to cuisine. Phil cooks shrimp in garlic butter, shrimp in brandy, shrimp in Pernod and cream. 'When my father was a chef in London,' he says, 'he would buy the freshest produce, the best meat and the best seafood in season. He would have it delivered to the hotel and oversee the preparation and the sauces. He'd come home for a small nap in the afternoon, then return to town to supervise the receptions and banquets scheduled for that evening. Then the whole thing would begin again. Along the way, I learnt a few tricks from him.'

In households where cooking is taken seriously, preparation is often accompanied by glasses of wine at the elbow. Consequently, at the presentation of another heavenly dinner by Phil, members of the Quartet and other participants are well-lubricated and the Quartet struggles to make a 9 a.m. appearance at the high school in Sechelt. Phil gets up to do the introduction.

'Does anybody know what this viola is?' he asks.

'A piano?' drawls a soft voice from the bleachers.

Portrait: Phil

The Quartet proofreads a program.

'Etter,' teases Jan, 'Sounds like a Basque separatist. There was never a program printed without some screw-up. My favourite was when we were playing Mozart's "Hunt" Quartet and the program called it Quartet in G Major, the "Aunt".'

'Could have been worse.'

'Actually, Etter is old French-Swiss. We have a crest,' says Phil. 'When we lived in London, we would go back to Vevey once a year. I can still remember the fresh smell of butter and strawberries when we got off the train. I spoke only French until I was sent to school. When I got a job in the City of Birmingham Orchestra, Margarita and I lived in the Irish district. Everyone called us Mr and Mrs O'Tear.'

PE

TWENTY-THREE

In Nomine

When Ray Ovens arrives from England to play assistant concertmaster in the VSO, the Quartet—Normsk, Ray, Simon and Jan—can finally begin rehearsing. The first few sessions are given over to getting used to one another by playing through Haydn, Mozart and Beethoven. By the beginning of the second week together a working routine has been established which includes generous coffee breaks.

'What should we call ourselves?' asks Ray.

'What's wrong with the Nelson Quartet?' asks Jan.

'Sounds as if we all have one eye, and one arm with Lady Hamilton hanging on it,' says Normsk.

'Vancouver Quartet.'

'Been used.'

'British Columbia Quartet.'

'Too presumptuous.'

'Quartet of Canada.'

'Much too presumptuous.'

Finally, Simon suggests the Purcell String Quartet (PSQ).

'PSQ...' Norman muses, 'for pipsqueak.'

'Why not?' persists Simon. 'We're English. Purcell was English. He wrote some of the first and finest string music in four parts and there's a range, the Purcell Mountains, in BC.'

The search is called off.

* * *

In the name of Purcell, the PSQ examines a variety of repertoire with a view to introducing themselves to the public with a series of concerts at the Vancouver Art Gallery. It decides, as a tribute to its namesake, to reach back to 1680 and play six of Henry Purcell's *Fantasias*. One fantasia will be featured in each of six concerts along with other repertoire.

These extraordinary pieces, made up of alternating slow-fast sections, are brief and profound. Since Purcell wrote for an ensemble of viols—where the two inner parts weave tenors—rather than for a string quartet with alto and tenor, the music has to be rearranged and some of the parts redistributed. This is done by VSO bassist Bill Fawcett, who gives Normsk a series of small sections of manuscript amendments, which the quartet members are to paste over the original parts.

At rehearsal, Normsk feels in his pocket and pulls out the by now crumpled manuscript cuttings. He hands one of these, rather longer than the rest, to Simon. 'The fantasia for our opening concert. You now get to lead in the final fast section.'

Simon places it on the music stand. 'Do you remember when we played this for that little ensemble gig we did for the LSO?'

'Oh, don't!' moans Normsk. 'Four minutes of acute embarrassment.'

'To the unwary,' continues Simon, 'this music looks easy because Purcell writes in white notes twice the value of modern notation. But it isn't, because the shortest value, usually quarter notes, can go like the wind.'

'And if you do get 'em in the right order, then counting the rests, whether they're hanging or sitting, can be your undoing,' adds Normsk.

'Anyway,' continues Simon, 'the cellist came in wrong and stayed wrong the whole piece. As you know, the *Fantasias* are usually in contrasting sections, slow-fast-slow.'

'Or the other way round,' says Normsk, 'like Thurber's cast iron lawn dog.'

'The cellist was so confused that he couldn't even get back in when the tempos changed.'

'Moriarty switched the bars.' Normsk does a Goon Show imitation. 'It was a relief to get outside and find the Green Line buses still running.'

The night arrives for the PSQ's first concert. In the opening fantasia, violist Simon is to lead from the penultimate slow section into the final fast passage. The performers arrive at the uncertain half-close and look to Simon to lead into the final section. Simon sits stock-still, his eyes on the music, registering nothing. Without his lead, Jan and the others are powerless to save the situation. The audience, confused by the dangling half-close, begins clapping. The quartet lamely arise from their seats and bow. Back in the green room, Simon explains that the lead-in—a crumpled piece of manuscript—somehow got folded behind the printed music and there was nothing in sight that he could play.

* * *

Purcell is the flavour of the season. The newly formed Baroque Strings are preparing a program of English music for their first LP. This includes Purcell's two *In Nomines* and his *Fantasia Upon One Note*—the note C being played on the double bass by the aforementioned Bill Fawcett. One of Purcell's *In Nomines* is in seven parts, and is a particularly wrenching piece of music with grinding harmonies that seem more attuned to the twentieth century than the seventeenth. The recording sessions with the CBC take place in St. Andrew's Wesley, a large church in the heart of downtown. Because of traffic noise, the first sound check is slated for 11 p.m., presuming on comparative silence by midnight.

Purcell, like many of his contemporaries, used *In Nomine*, the Salisbury plainsong, as a basis for his arresting music. In the wee hours, the Baroque Strings build Purcell's austere edifice not unlike the spacious stonework rising above them. By 4 a.m., it's all in the can just as the grinding of the garbage collection trucks starts up for the day. So far it's the only traffic on the road as Jan heads to the Second Narrows Bridge in the pouring rain.

A collaborative production of Purcell's opera *Dido and Aeneas* is mounted at the Playhouse Theatre. Jan's first experience with this opera was at Bedales. The sailor's song with its lyrics, 'Take a boozy short leave of your nymphs on the shore,' was particularly appealing to the sixth form boys who sang it round the quadrangle. Dido's *Lament*, the aria 'When I am laid in earth', is one of the great moments in English music and is, like *In Nomine*, built from the ground up.

Below ground at the Playhouse Theatre is a pit designed for a pygmy orchestra. In this case, the pygmies are the PSQ and add-ons like Bill Fawcett. Jan always arrives early to stake out his territory; his chair must be positioned so he doesn't hit the concrete wall with an up-bow and damage the harpsichord with his down-bow, while still maintaining visual contact with Normsk.

This visual contact with Normsk must be maintained as the PSQ rehearses Bartók's Fourth String Quartet, the tough companion they've paired with Purcell for the second of their Art Gallery Series concerts. Rehearsing for six concerts, at three works per concert, the PSQ is required to learn some eighteen works. Plotting rehearsals through busy schedules of other musical distractions, such as commitments with the VSO and the CBC, begins to require an ingenuity comparable to their previous negotiations as freelancers in the London musical scene.

But finally the public performance and broadcast of Bartók's Fourth brings the PSQ public attention. 'Surprisingly good,' declares a local critic. Critics are parsimonious with their praise; they know that at a slight whiff of appreciation, they will be quoted worldwide. They hand out compliments like a pinch of caviar between an orgy of fried fish suppers. To some extent, the PSQ's thunder has already been stolen—the Orford Quartet from Toronto had its debut months earlier. But, thinks Jan, surely Canada is large enough to accommodate a different string quartet operating on each side of the country.

Portrait: Zonk and Other Effects

Over at the VSO, Meredith Davies has designed a series of contemporary music concerts called 'Zonk' which features, among others, a piece by John Tavener called *The Whale*. This includes a repetitive passage which is meant to be unrelievedly boring and features the composer jerkily and with exaggerated movements attacking the piano. Messiaen's *Chronochromie* is also excerpted; Normsk remembers playing the section for six solo violins for an enormous fee in London: 'It sounded like a room full of violins practising their bits.'

Canadian music is given its due. This includes a piece by Lloyd Burritt which, at the end, asks for a sudden cut-off, the players frozen in playing position silhouetted by strobe lights while a tape plays loud electric noises for three minutes. At the performance, the tape fails and the orchestra, highlighted in silence, can't maintain its position for mirth.

Not to be outdone, the CBC Orchestra records a contemporary piece which requires the violinists to put down their bows and pick up metal frog clickers. These click when pressed between the fingers and click again when released. At the end of this section, the violins have time, during the following slow and quiet section, to put the clickers down silently and pick up their bows. During the recording, the violins click away. But Ron, in the first violins, accidentally presses in his clicker as the quiet section begins; it's as if he's pulled the pin on a hand grenade. If he releases the clicker, he'll ruin the recording, but neither can he pick up his bow to participate in the next section. He waits out the recording, violin in left hand and clicker in right.

The same program features Artur Balsam—who had previously been Heifetz's accompanist—playing Beethoven's Second Piano Concerto. As is his custom, Jan arrives early and finds the soloist warming up, so waits quietly in what passes for an anteroom. Soon, Avison enters and embarks on a hero's welcome. He strides with arms outstretched across Studio G to the piano. 'Ah, Art*uro*!' he cries. 'How are you?' As Avison reaches the keyboard, Artur holds his hands against his chest, 'My hands are cold. I hate Baldvins and the acoustics are terrible,' he says in a quiet, rasping voice. Avison, lost for words, resembles a fish gasping for breath.

They go on to discuss the musical points in the concerto. 'Er, how do you finish the cadenza?' Avison asks.

'I trill as usual for four beats but I end with a slow *Nachschlag*,' says Artur.

'Good. That solves the problem of a karumph.'

'A what?'

To the unsuspecting, karumphs are lurking elsewhere in the Concerto. Beethoven requires the pianist to play a musical loop-the-loop, where there's a chromatic free fall and a chromatic ascent which can disorientate a conductor trying to bring the orchestra back in at its apex. At the rehearsal, Avison fails to recognize the note that signals the orchestra's re-entry. Face is saved because, in his anxiety, he splinters his baton against his stand light and there is a noise like the *Queen Mary* hitting Pier 49.

'Ohhh,' says Avison in sepulchral tones, 'daaaamn.'

''Fraid we'll have to go back to the piano entry,' says the producer.

They start again. Tensions rise as the pianist approaches the offending chromatic passage. Avison, taking no chances, steps off the podium to watch Artur's fingers ascend the keyboard. The orchestra comes in on time, if too loud.

The six-inch elevation that a podium affords a conductor can give him delusions of grandeur. Meredith Davies, in a fit of bloody-mindedness at a Pops rehearsal, makes the tenor repeat Sullivan's song 'Tit Willow', ad nauseam. 'How many tits has a willow anyway?' ponders Audrey, an elderly cellist, to anybody close enough to hear.

Conductors can at times be cavalier; they are well aware that they have to command respect from eighty or so musicians who all think they know better than the conductor. They sometimes forget that they owe their bloated salaries to the bleeding fingers of their orchestra. Toscanini, Szell, Solti, et al. are silent now. But then they were never heard in the first place.

There are, of course, moments of grace. Avison tells of the time he was dining in Ottawa at the Chateau Frontenac. He spied the Governor General eating alone at another table. Avison went over and introduced himself: '... I'm a conductor.' The Governor General seemed puzzled. 'CP or CN?'

In another moment, Jan is obliged to call Mario Bernardi—a later inheritor of the CBC podium—who is a long time coming to the phone. 'Sorry, my wife called me in from the garden. I'm building a wall. Sometimes I think these are the more durable achievements in one's life.'

INTERLUDE: VSO RECEPTIONS

Normsk rosins his bow. 'Do you remember how in Victor White's years as manager, the VSO always had a reception after their Sunday afternoon subscription concert?'

'Do I ever,' answers Jan.

'It was a different mansion each time, each bigger than the last, but the bartender was always the same. An elderly man, hired for the afternoon, I suppose. He had a memory like an elephant. When you'd drained your drink he had a tray discreetly at your elbow. "Gin and tonic wasn't it, sir?"'

'My first reception was memorable,' says Jan. 'The hostess of the house greeted me in the front hall and apologized because her husband was not present to officiate. "He's at the Grey Cup match," she explained. I must have let down my guard because she said, "Well you can take that look off your face. Some of us like football matches as well as concerts."'

Normsk wipes the rosin off the wood of his bow.

'I remember the occasion. The concert started late because of the traffic. That was the reception they played the Bruckner Viola Quintet for us on LP, knowing that we were trying to form a quartet. Only they played it at the wrong speed. Mind you, if it's Bruckner, the faster the better.'

'Victor White was a fine socialite,' observes Normsk. 'As VSO manager he was well-connected. Do you remember every Christmas he'd come out as Santa Claus? "M-e-r-r-y Christmas, V-S-O!" He'd use his operatic voice, then hand out candy canes to the audience. He was very good at the Symphony Ball. Grand occasion and it raised money for the orchestra. He'd come out in a tailsuit and lead off the dancing, waltzing impeccably to Johann Strauss. Except for that one time when unaccountably he and his well-dressed partner fell flat on the floor holding the same impeccable pose—horizontal instead of vertical.'

'Talking of such,' says Phil, 'we always had to wait about for the refreshments to end and the dancing to begin. They summoned us and one time, a tousled head popped out of a bass bag—Bill Fawcett had been asleep, fending off the flu.'

'Playing Strauss waltzes was a freebie for the orchestra players selected,' says Jan. 'We were always thanked by the Ladies Committee. One year they gave their thanks with a fancy bar of soap to each musician.'

'Do you think there was some kind of a hidden message?' asks Fred.

'Do you remember the last Shaughnessy reception we went to?' Normsk asks. 'It was a warm afternoon and it seemed like all the socialites were gathering to celebrate something. The old bartender was there but he never offered us a drink because we were playing. We stole away when the speeches began.'

'We stole away without our music stands,' Jan says. 'I went back to collect them the next day. I parked in front of the house and walked round the side to the garden where we'd played. There were our four Manhasset stands in a row by the back door. I didn't think I should just take them without explanation so I rang the doorbell. There was no answer. I looked in the window. All the furniture was hidden by dust covers. The place was deserted. All of the bar trolleys and barbecues were gone. I glanced at the kitchen through the window. It looked as if it had never been used. I rang the bell a second time and I heard a shuffling. An ancient caretaker opened the door. He wore slippers and looked at me wild-eyed, his lower lip hanging slack. I explained why I was there and he nodded towards the music stands and firmly shut the door.'

TWENTY-FOUR

Schafer One and Two

Normsk, now with a shock of white hair, picks up a book—*My Life on Earth and Elsewhere*, by R. Murray Schafer—from the coffee table in the living room of his converted fisherman's hut in Sooke. He and Jan, who will never retire, are having a glass of wine after a day's coaching at the Sooke Harbour Chamber Music Workshop, where they've coached every spring for the last eleven years.

'He's just published his autobiography,' Normsk tells Jan. 'He was out here before Christmas. The Victoria Symphony was playing a new piece of his. He was signing books in a pub—the Bard and Banker—so I lined up with everyone else. When I got to the table he didn't look up.

'"Name?"

'"Norman Nelson," I answered. He began writing. "We used to know one another," I said.

'He looked up. "Norman! For Godssake, you've changed! I wish I were back in those days. We had such fun. The quartet had such a sense of humour."

'Hugh Davidson, long retired from the Canada Council, was also at the signing,' continues Normsk. 'He came up to me and said in a stentorian tone, "Hugh Davidson." I thought he didn't recognize me either so I said in an equally stentorian tone, "Norman Nelson" and he replied meekly,"Yes, I know."

'Anyhow, we get a line in Murray's book—"What a beautiful experience, listening to my First Quartet played by Norman Nelson and his team."'

* 1 9 7 0 *

R. Murray Schafer looks at the PSQ intensely with his lazy eye as they read through his First Quartet up in the Department of Communications at Simon Fraser University (SFU). (Jan will later discover from Normsk that Murray's eye is in fact a glass eye.) Murray's eclectic mind and keen ear

MS

for the sonic environment provide rich material for his music, even though he gives away very little when the composition is in gestation. His Quartet is in one movement. They reach the final pages and Normsk puts down his violin.

'Murray, what do you mean by this mark?'

'I use the Bartók snap mark to indicate a review of previous episodes,' says Murray, seated by a window that gives a panoramic view of Vancouver below. 'I use these reviews rather like photographic snapshots until the camera runs out of film.'

'Like this,' says Normsk, pulling his string from the fingerboard like an elastic band and letting go.

'Yes, but I want it to be toneless.'

This provokes a snapping competition amongst the players like so many turtles.

'How's this?' asks Jan. He places his finger on the C string primary harmonic and snaps loudly.

'That's it,' says Murray. 'Now, how to show the film running out.'

'If we all slide our thumbnails along our bottom strings,' suggests Phil, 'it produces a quiet, slithering sound.'

'That's exactly right,' says Murray, 'and then the quartet plays the final pizzicato.'

The PSQ has commissioned R. Murray Schafer's First Quartet and are looking to premiere it at Vancouver's Art Gallery Series and eventually in the U.K. They've reconfigured after a couple of false starts in which Ray has returned to England, Simon has become assistant conductor of the VSO, and Phil and Fred have joined the quartet.

The opening of Schafer's First Quartet sounds like wasps in a jam jar, the players locked together and trying to free themselves. There is nothing in the quartet literature comparable to this. The PSQ uses it to open their school concerts, commanding immediate attention from a gymnasium full of children. To a preteen, the Beatles are as remote as Beethoven. They respond best to contemporary sounds, unlike their teachers who regularly ask the PSQ not to play anything later than Haydn or Mozart and only half a movement at that.

The snapshots ending of Murray's First Quartet reviews the episodic nature of the piece, while its structural cohesion is about players being locked together or breaking apart. After the congestion of the opening, individual players examine the new landscape with thoughtful phrases—they link up loosely in a passage of moiré rhythm where one instrument, a click faster than the instrument in front, slowly catches up and passes. The movement enters a long, slow unison by all four players—along the way, each breaks into an improvised cadenza. As the unison gradually accelerates and gets louder, each succeeding cadenza becomes more frantic and culminates with the acoustic shock of the first cello snap.

* * *

'Can you drop by my office tomorrow?' Murray asks Jan. 'I have to ask you something.' Jan obliges. In the office, Murray sits at a low table. On it is a large white sheet covered with oversized, calligraphic images. Conspicuous in the middle lies a small piece of manuscript paper with a couple of bars of music written on it.

'Is it possible to pluck these harmonics?'

'Is it fast?'

'Not very.'

'The primary harmonics are resonant, the secondary harmonics are more tricky,' says Jan. 'Depending where they are, they might not sound very loud. The best way to deal with them is to pluck like a jazz bass player—right hand plucks down as the left hand releases upward on impact.' Jan flicks his fingers on an invisible cello. 'Stravinsky asks for such harmonics in *Pulcinella*, but plucked in double stops.'

'Thank you,' says Murray. No explanation is forthcoming.

* * *

In 1972, the PSQ joins Murray in the Centre for Communications at SFU. The director, Nini Baird, had known of the Griller Quartet residency in Berkeley when she was a student there, and quietly made arrangements for something similar for the PSQ. The passing around of the diplomatic pouch calls for skillful persuasion of a number of agencies amid secret negotiations, lest it all fall apart. Thus, at fairly short notice, the VSO has to replace three principals. (The orchestra manager was not very happy when Normsk, Fred, Phil and Jan went up the hill to SFU, but the next twelve years there will be the most constructive ones in the PSQ's career.)

For the cost of one chair of learning, the PSQ residency is set up to play a series of formal evening concerts, balanced by casual lunchtime concerts held anywhere on campus. In the absence of a music department, there is a free weekly chamber music workshop for anyone to attend. Additionally, the university arranges two tours into the province each season and handles other concerts as they come in.

The PSQ finds the work inspirational; they are working in some of the most beautiful, unspoiled country anywhere. BC is a vast province of mountains, valleys, rivers and lakes, islands and coastlines. The PSQ traverses it by ferry, disturbing a myriad of birds as it negotiates passages between Gulf Islands, by car up steep passes and circuitous roads, round lakes, by seaplane over rolling waves in the Georgia Strait and even by helicopter to tight landing spots in precipitous valleys.

* * *

The PSQ gives Schafer's First Quartet, along with Barbara Pentland's Third Quartet, their European premieres at the Wigmore Hall in London. To play at the Wigmore Hall, as with the Carnegie Hall in New York, is a performer's rite of passage. The Wigmore is a very modest hall with an art deco full frontal nude behind and above the platform that listeners can examine if they get bored with the coming-out recitals. Behind the nude is the cozy green room, replete with photographs of the famous who have been through the process. The doorman is about to open the door to the platform, the PSQ has music in hand; they are to open with Haydn, when Normsk suddenly says, 'Oh my God, I left the Schafer Quartet in my room.' The doorman is kind. 'Give me the hotel's phone number, sir. I'll make sure a taxi brings it round at once. Berkeley Square, you say? Shouldn't take too long.'

The PSQ walks out on stage. Jan is too nervous to worry about what will happen if Schafer's manuscript doesn't arrive on time; everything seems so unreal. Twenty minutes later, as the applause dies down, they return to the green room. 'Taxi's just arrived, sir. Here's your music.'

Relieved, they walk out on stage. The PSQ always relishes shocking the audience with the chaotic cacophony that opens Schafer's Quartet. As the music calms down, Jan feels the attention of the galvanized audience is held as they listen to the quartet exploring new aural territory. The PSQ begins the accelerating unison that will drive the piece to its conclusion. Jan has written out his so-called improvised cadenza. He is uncomfortable with improvisation, as many classically trained musicians are. He has given thought to how he should leave off this series of cadenzas—slowly moving away from the unison as if he is lost. The music speeds up to its frantic conclusion, released by a loud snap.

Many years later, Normsk will laugh over the forgotten music incident. 'For good luck, I'd worn my wife's underwear to that concert. When I sat down, it squeezed me and I was in discomfort throughout the evening.'

* * *

It is the autumn of 1976. 'Murray rang up last night,' Normsk informs his colleagues. 'He's finished his Second Quartet for us. It's called *Wales*.'

'Mammal or country?' asks Jan.

'Or wails, as in pails?' suggests Fred.

'Dunno, I didn't catch all of what he was saying,' replies Normsk.

Murray's Quartet no. 2, *Waves*, is a by-product of his World Soundscape Project, an international collaboration and examination of humankind's uneasy relation to sound and noise pollution. Murray has just initiated it; he and his students analyze wave patterns of the Atlantic and Pacific Oceans and discover that, while asymmetric, the waves crest between six and eleven seconds. The music metronomically mimics this pattern, undulating accordingly until at the close, the players sneak out one by one still playing, leaving the cellist to clap a spyglass to his eye to see where his colleagues have gone.

Waves goes on to win the first Jules Leger Prize for new chamber music in 1978. That year, the PSQ plays it in Rideau Hall, supposedly in the presence of Pierre Trudeau who, it turns out, has more important things to do. Perhaps fortune is smiling. Before the concert, the PSQ arranges the extra music stands behind the door to the staff quarters, left ajar for the disappearing trick. During the performance, a staff member dutifully closes the door so the departing strings can't exit. Jan, however, still has to search for them with his spyglass, only to see them playing on the spot like rats in a trap.

Portrait: Dvořák American

Antonín Dvořák drew upon African-American melodies during his three-year stay in America to write his Quartet in F Major, op. 96, currently nicknamed the 'American'. Jan has a copy of the BBC *Radio Times* weekly program c.1943 listing the Griller Quartet broadcasting Dvořák's 'Nigger Quartet', the epithet generally used at that time. The 'American' Quartet is arguably the most frequently performed quartet in the literature.

Such is its popularity that it is the natural choice for the PSQ's performance at the Olympic Games in Montreal in 1976. The lunatic extravagance of the Olympic Games is usually justified by the employment created by the amenities that the host city must necessarily acquire. The Games pay lip service to the visual and performing arts by showcasing the host region's culture and Montreal is no exception. The PSQ is duly sent to the Olympic site, and—to justify the travelling expenses—to Old Montreal to play an outdoor concert.

On arrival at Dorval airport, Fred, who assumes the role of the worldly-wise tourist on such occasions, reaches for one of the hotel's white telephones. 'We have a booking at your hotel. Do you have limousine service from the airport? ... Purcell Quartet ... *Quatuor* Purcell ... You don't? Try under Simon Fraser University ... We must have a room ... You only have one ... Twin beds? ... Can you put two cots in there? *Bien.*'

The next morning the PSQ, in white jackets and black bow ties, waits in the shelter of the hotel entrance. It's a wild day—a strong wind sends the rain clouds scudding across the sky. 'Surely they'll be sending a limousine,' says Fred, eyeing a bus in the parking lot. A group of Aboriginal dancers begins congregating around them, complete with headdresses, feathers, beads, drums and beaters. Everybody stands about. Fred spies a young man in a trench coat, immediately identifiable as an upwardly mobile bureaucrat. Fred sidles over to him. On return, Fred says, 'Yep, we're all going on that bus.'

On arrival at the Olympic site, everyone is put through a security grilling worthy of an agent trying to cross the border to Albania. The dancers are through. Normsk is through. Then Fred. Phil follows. When Jan offers up his ID card, the man at the wicket frowns. 'Your name doesn't match the name on the manifest—Leo Andrushkin.'

'Purcell Quartet,' says Jan, 'Look up Purcell Quartet, SFU.' The man at the wicket is joined by another man in a trench coat. He turns away and talks into his lapel. 'Okay. It was a mistake. Go in.' Jan joins his colleagues and they are led across the site by yet another young man talking to the lapel of his trench coat. They walk through a maze of concession marquees, all flapping in the breeze. The young man stops at a large marquee, its roof flapping violently in the wind and making explosions like rifle shots. It's a hot dog stand. The lone occupant behind the counter, wearing a very high chef's hat, sets out hot dogs on the electric heater to be cremated.

'Are we to play here?' Jan asks, incredulous. The man in the trench coat nods and consults his watch. 'You play in ten minutes,' he says, and leaves. The PSQ dubiously unfold their music stands. Due to the inclemency of the weather, nobody visits the site. The quartet plays Dvořák's 'American' Quartet, casting their pearls before cremating swine.

'I hope we've enriched your day,' remarks Fred, sneaking a hot dog, to the vendor as they are led out once again by the trench-coat men.

The wind has not died down the following morning as the PSQ is shown a stage that has been erected in the middle of a square in Old Montreal. On it are four heavy duty music stands. 'I'll bet there'll be a larger audience than yesterday,' says Fred, raising his voice above the wind. Jan lays his cello case on the cobbles—if he leaves it standing the wind might carry it off. They climb onto the rostrum. Immediately, a stand blows over. Young men in trench coats run forward to sandbag the music stands' feet and to distribute clothes pegs amongst the musicians.

With their hair blowing in their faces, the quartet pegs down the music and starts in on Dvořák's 'American' again for the occasional passerby. Ah, Olympia!

Portrait: Il Tramonto

Robin Blaser is teaching a course on Shelley at SFU. It is proposed by Gerald Newman, also in Literature, that his wife, Joyce, should sing Respighi's setting of 'Il Tramonto' (The Sunset) to Robin's class. It is scheduled for three Mondays hence. There is difficulty finding a time to rehearse with the singer; the following Friday morning seems to be the only available slot. Accordingly, the PSQ arrives at Gerald's house in West Vancouver at 10 a.m. After they've been rehearsing some twenty minutes, Normsk observes to Fred that they seem to be playing an awful lot of the same notes. He glances over at Fred's part. 'Oh my God, you're playing a first violin part. I must have left the second violin part at home. I'll go and get it. Be about half an hour.'

'I'll make coffee,' says Joyce.

Jan is the only member of the quartet who has played 'Il Tramonto'. He can hardly claim to know it. It was his first CBC experience in Studio G with Hugh McLean, who sat on a high stool conducting an ensemble that sight-read the work, recording it phrase by phrase to be stitched together later. That memory is enough to make Jan realize that with only one—no, half—a rehearsal, Respighi is ripe for a rough ride. While they drink coffee and wait for Normsk, he and Phil cue the vocal rhythm line into their parts.

The following week, Jan receives a phone call from Gerald: Would the quartet mind if he records their performance? Jan replies that he doesn't think so. It's just a class. He puts down the phone and forgets about it.

On the Monday evening in question, Normsk arrives late for their weekly workshop. He's been adjudicating at a local festival and has been wined and dined by the local sponsor; Normsk is feeling no pain. At the end of the workshop, the door bursts open. Robin and thirty people come in, followed by Gerald with an assistant carrying boxes of equipment. They erect several microphones, run electric leads into junction boxes and plug jacks into sockets. Normsk looks on in disbelief. 'What is all this? What is going on?' Joyce takes her place. 'We're ready,' Gerald calls. Jan looks at Phil. This is going to be a nightmare.

The cellist has an advantage over the rest of his quartet colleagues—he doesn't hold the instrument under his chin. He can hear without obtrusive vibrations of the instrument and he is free to move his head. Jan endeavours to indicate the nooks and crannies of Respighi's music and twenty minutes later they arrive at the final bar, more or less in one piece. Jan is euphoric. They've done it. Fred has a glint in his eye. 'I think we should play it again,' he says wickedly. 'Oh, yes,' chorus the listeners. So they do. The sunset lingers.

INTERLUDE: ANDY

Because blood is thicker than water and water is thinner than beer, Jan crosses the Atlantic for a visit to Edinburgh and meets his brother, Andy, at the Greyfriars Bobby. Andy has a shrewd eye for second-hand cars and real estate. Music is a sideline but he developed a taste for jazz early and spent some of his evenings subbing and gigging with his saxophone around Scotland and into Scandinavia.

Andy sips his beer. 'I modelled myself on Sandy Brown. Our band had a drummer who had a short fuse. We did a few gigs at the Commodore. It was a large dance floor with a small stage area. The drum set was stage right and the Gents was on that side. Every time guys used the washroom they had to pass the drums. They could never resist snapping the cymbal with their fingers or doing a backwards kick as they passed the drum. The drunker they got, the bolder they became and the more apoplectic our drummer got. At last he said, "The next guy that touches the traps, I'm going to fill him in." Sure enough, this guy comes up to the set and attempts a paradiddle. Our drummer gets up and hits him on the chin and he flies across the dance floor. All of a sudden, everyone stops dancing, stares at the stage and the crowd begins moving towards us. We just ran for the door to flee for our lives.'

TWENTY-FIVE

Pentland Three and Four

Jan searches for vocal music in the Barbara Pentland Room at Langley Community Music School. It is a large studio and houses Barbara's Steinway grand piano, which has been well-used; its tone has lost some of its resonance. Inside, some of the hammers have stickers on them for identification when Barbara required the pianists to strike notes inside the lid. The school received the instrument courtesy of Bob Rogers, who was executor of her estate and who recorded all of her piano music. ('All on first take,' Bob said to Jan once, 'though there was one effect of half-lifting the sustaining pedal to diminish the sound that I could never get—it was an oddity that was particular to her piano.')

Jan, not often in the vocal studio, looks around. The piano arrived accompanied by several items that Jan recognizes from the music room in Barbara's house—a large etching of a woman's head from multiple views, an abstract chalk drawing in volatile colours, a unique music stand of trellised metal, on it an old metronome with one foot missing (Scottish: Jan remembers that its tick always went in Strathspey rhythm, however one tinkered with it) and the prize of the collection, a painting by BC artist Bertram Binning. Above the piano is an imposing photograph of Barbara herself, surveying the room through her horn-rimmed glasses with a typical look—as if she's about to give a measured remark.

* 1972 *

Jan can feel Barbara Pentland's microscopic gaze on him as she looks from her score to the PSQ playing through her Third Quartet. Barbara's music room, with Steinway, writing desk covered in onion skins and cabinet stacked high with large metal reels of tapes, leaves little room for her and the quartet. Jan expects Barbara to stop them at any moment, but inevitably Normsk stops two pages in.

'Barbara, does that double sharp apply to the G in this bar?'

'Of course,' says Barbara dismissively.

'I just asked because Fred is holding a G-sharp.'

'Well, I've put a line over your note meaning to pull on the dissonance a little bit.' She turns back to page 1. 'Fred, you should begin your crescendo a little earlier in bar 6.'

'Oh!' exclaims Fred, as if he's just divined the meaning of the Dead Sea Scrolls. He furiously extends the crescendo into his part.

As the rehearsal is reaching its close, Barbara's husband, Hally, enters with cigarette in hand. 'I have a tape of a recent performance of Barbara's *Symphony in Ten Parts.*' Everyone makes for the living room. Hally comments on passages as if they were Beatles tunes. 'Listen to that, a superb effect,' he says, turning the eternal cigarette in his fingers.

'Oh, yes!' agrees Fred enthusiastically, removing the tongue out of his cheek.

Half an hour later, Barbara says goodbye to the quartet from her wooden front steps as Jan negotiates his cello around the old Morris car that is parked in the gravel driveway and that has probably only known one owner. Hally appears from behind and asks Barbara, 'What should we have for dinner?'

'I thought pizza,' says Barbara.

The culinary arts are not, Jan thinks, a priority in Barbara's household. As he drives away with the *Symphony for Ten Parts* in his ears, he remembers playing it in the VSO when they included this piece in a program presented at the QET. At its conclusion, Barbara came on stage to acknowledge the applause. After exiting to the backstage with the conductor, Meredith Davies, she tried to return to the auditorium, only to be stopped by the usher who wouldn't allow her to re-enter. No ticket.

* * *

With Barbara's blessing and well-rehearsed, the PSQ travels to London to give Barbara's Third Quartet its European premiere. Following the Schafer premiere, the PSQ has a week to prepare for a second visit to the Wigmore Hall. In the intervening days, Jan visits his in-laws. Emmy's parents, Alec and Frances, are staying in a diplomat's house in St. John's Wood. They have afternoon tea in the garden.

Howard Hartog, head of Schott's Music Publishers in London, has also dropped in for a visit. 'So you're sponsored by the Canada Council,' he says to Jan in a deeply condescending voice. 'Is Hugh Davidson still head of music there?'

Jan nods. He feels socially discomforted making small talk with his in-laws and is intimidated by Hartog. (Jan as a student had met Hartog at Schott's store and found him, with his bushy black moustache, a daunting figure. Jan had asked if there were any recent cello works of Skalkottas. 'Recent!' Mr Hartog had snorted. 'He's been dead ten years.')

Hartog is more affable this time as he sits in the sun smoking a cigar. He is professionally interested in Canadian musical life. 'There's a fellow—I won't mention his name—who's now very high up in the Canada Council, who used to work for me at Schott's. He didn't last too long—he left an original manuscript of ours in a taxi. Is your quartet playing any …,' asks Hartog between cigar puffs, '… *Canadian* music?'

Jan grips his cup and saucer. 'Yes, new quartets by Murray Schafer and Barbara Pentland.'

'Yes, I remember Barbara Pentland. She had a piece played at the ISCM Festival in Stockholm. The press never mentioned the piece but said that Barbara Pentland was very pretty.'

Frances, with her grey hair piled up, cuts an Edwardian, statuesque figure. She stutters. 'H-h-h-h-oward and I g-g-o back a long way—t-t-t-o when we were students.'

'Good Lord,' says Jan, genuinely surprised.

'W-w-w-e once went out for a drive, a party of university students,' explains Frances. 'When it was t-t-t-time to go home, we found there had been a leak in the radiator and it was dry so all the men p-peed in it.' Jan is aghast. Frances is a cultured, sensitive woman and accomplished artist. He smiles, again not knowing what to say.

Frances turns to Howard, who is now looking more warthog than Hartog. She laughs. 'A-a-nd now I'm a grandmother. Jan and Emmy have two small boys, Rob and Judd.' She reaches into her purse and produces a photograph. 'There.' Howard, drawing on his cigar, affects interest. Seeing the boys reminds Jan of Judd's birth at the Lions Gate Hospital in North Vancouver. 'Emmy was the only person in maternity when Judd was born,' says Jan to his in-laws, 'so they put on Brahms's First Symphony over the PA. He arrived in the middle of the Finale.'

Jan's in-laws kindly attend the PSQ's second concert at the Wigmore Hall. Jan predicts that they might have trouble digesting the musical language of Barbara's Third Quartet. It is a good example of her mature style—works cast in one movement with rigorous, economical lines, but allowing aleatoric episodes where players are allowed to improvise within strict limits. These episodes cause Jan even more discomfort than he has with the improvisations in Schafer, since they are imposed into such a highly controlled context. It seems Barbara writes music with a scalpel rather than a pen; its icy quality might prompt the Wigmore's art deco nude to search for her fur coat.

Both Canadian premieres—the Schafer and the Pentland—are received with a yawn of indifference by the British press.

* * *

Jan hears on more than one occasion from Barbara, who was born in Winnipeg, that her generation of composers is the first to articulate a truly Canadian voice. By that she means that previously, what passed for Canadian music was largely in the hands of imported English musicians or Canadians who had received their apprenticeship from colonials shackled by their European traditions. In a career that never compromises her artistic values, Barbara is aware that her music seems austere and she has no illusions about her generation's predicament—shedding colonialism and slowly pursuing the difficult role of musical pioneer.

Barbara's music is clear, economical, uncompromising and is often described as glacial. Glaciers can be awe-inspiring; they expand, contract, glisten in the northern sunlight; they grind inexorably at mountains, creating valleys and lakes of fathomless slate blue. This sensibility in Barbara's music may symbolize Canada in the public imagination just as *Tapiola* symbolizes Finland or *Appalachian Spring* the United States. Ultimately, Canada may not be musically identified by anything geographical but by something unutterably northern like the aurora borealis. It is likely that in the future, Barbara's music will not be as immediately identifiable of place as that of Sibelius or Copland, but she consciously embarked on a pioneering journey and we, her listeners, travel with her.

* * *

Despite Barbara's role as Canadian explorer, her domestic life is steeped in European culture. Her mother-in-law is Elza Galafrés—a distinguished elderly lady, prominently dressed in white, with a white bag and white kid gloves. Adorned in small, brightly coloured Hungarian accessories, Elza always sits front and centre at the VSO Sunday subscription concerts.

After Elza's death in 1977, Normsk reminisces at the pub with Jan after a concert:

'Elza Galafrés, but known to us all as Madame Dohnányi—now there was a great old lady. She was the toast of Vienna when she was an actress at the turn of the century. She developed a notation for choreography. Bartók wrote *The Miraculous Mandarin* for her, which she refused to dance because of its lurid plot. She came from a prominent Hungarian family that had lost basically everything by the end of the Second World War. In her acting days she married the violinist Bronislaw Huberman. Later, she was married a second time, to the composer Erno Dohnányi.'

Normsk asks for another beer. 'For twenty-five years they were a prominent couple in the musical life of Budapest. Then Dohnányi, after a quarter century with Elza, fell for a nurse. One of her sons Hally Huberman eventually moved to Canada, married Barbara Pentland and was instrumental in getting Elza to emigrate. Elza came to Vancouver and married a radiologist, Clif Stewart. An autumnal relationship but I remember one of the last things she said to me, at the age of ninety: "You know, even now, I still get troubled by sexual longings."'

'Remember when she invited us to a Hungarian lunch at her home?' asks Jan. 'There was a painting of a valley hung over the mantelpiece.'

'Yes,' recalls Normsk. 'She acquired it before the war. But coincidentally, that was the valley where her younger son, Matthew Dohnányi, died of typhoid in a Nazi camp. Elza, with a coffin, searched the graves, found his body and gave him a Christian burial.'

'Ah, the threads,' says Jan. 'When I visited my mother in Edinburgh last summer, I looked up my old student friend, Christie Duncan. I was telling Christie about life in Vancouver and mentioned Madame Dohnányi hobnobbing with Kodály and all, and he said, "Yes, Elza Galafrés—we are related." I was blown away. Incidentally, I also called on the composer Hans Gal from my university days.'

'Ah, yes, the guy who edited the Dover Scores of Brahms's chamber music,' says Normsk.

'Yes, he was writing music, standing up at his apothecary's desk. Again, I was telling him and his wife about Vancouver. Mrs Gal was incredulous. "But it's a little logging town." Hans corrected her, "No my dear, it's a huge city with skyscrapers now."'

Jan laughs. 'Hans Gal and Elza Galafrés are basically old Vienna. It seems at odds that Elza should have a daughter-in-law writing atonal music.'

* * *

It is the summer of 1980. Far from the Vancouver skyline, Arnold and Carroll Beichman hold a pre-Okanagan Festival gathering on the manicured lawn of their English-style house at the end of Naramata village. The house stands back in mature ponderosa pines and a lawn runs between the trees down to Okanagan Lake, where the host has been known to stride naked for a swim. Here, down the years, have been many pleasant social occasions. The Beichmans are generous hosts and Arnold, a well-known American political journalist and author, seems to Jan like a mature version of Fred—larger than life, boisterous and very funny.

On this occasion, idle talk turns to purposeful discussion around next year's commemoration of the twentieth anniversary of the Okanagan Festival. At the PSQ's suggestion, it is finally decided to approach Barbara Pentland about writing a new string quartet. The Festival committee agrees to commission the composition and apply to the Canada Council for a grant.

Over the year, Barbara sets to work and finishes her Fourth String Quartet well ahead of the Festival's deadline, and the PSQ has it in their fingers before travelling to Penticton for the premiere. On arrival, they are shocked to discover that the Festival committee has omitted to apply for a Canada Council grant as previously discussed. Once a new piece has been performed, the Canada Council will not commission it retroactively. Barbara must be paid, the PSQ insists. The concert is three days away. Barbara is scheduled to arrive the following evening and there is to be a reception in her honour. No pay, no play, the PSQ insists, and convinces the committee to phone Hugh Davidson, head of the Canada Council, who manages to massage the money into the local bank.

Early the next morning, Jan heads to the grocery story to buy milk. As he turns to leave, Arnold enters. Arnold is the Festival's committee chairman for that summer. Straight away, he rounds on Jan. 'What sods you boys are. What a way to behave. I will not be hosting Barbara Pentland's reception.' Jan is taken aback. They are only protecting Barbara, who as a distinguished composer expects to be paid.

The concert goes ahead as planned. Afterwards, the PSQ improvises a reception for Barbara in the hotel orchard, at picnic tables set amongst the cherry trees under a starlit sky. The songs of Okanagan birds that Barbara wove into her Quartet are quiet. In the moonlight flutter giant moths.

INTERLUDE: VIOLINS

'Let's finish the movement,' Normsk says. 'The rehearsal will be interrupted shortly.'

'For Pete's sake, why?' asks Fred.

'Guy wants to show me a violin. Been in the family for over a hundred years.'

'They all say that.'

The doorbell rings. A man shuffles into the hall with a double violin case. Normsk gestures him into the rehearsal room. The man opens the case and gets out the first violin, which has the word 'concert' branded down the back of its scroll.

'NICE violin!' Fred roars, his eyes gleaming behind his glasses. 'What do you think, Normsk?'

'Well, actually'—the man uncovers the second violin—'*this* is the family heirloom.' Normsk takes it. The instrument has a burgundy varnish blackened around the bridge from rosin damage.

'Do you want the bow?' asks Fred, reaching into the case. The stick has a bun of horsehair, which has come loose from the tip, wrapped around its frog.

Normsk ignores Fred's jibe by picking up his own bow and beginning to play. Fred glances at the stamp on the bow. Sometimes a bow has more value than the violin it accompanies. Jan sees that the stamp on this one shows Romania, the country of origin. Fred puts it back.

Normsk plays all his favourite bits, then hands the violin back. 'It's very keen, isn't it?'

'Keen' is Normsk's euphemism for thin and shrill.

'If it was that keen,' chortles Fred later, 'why did you play it for so long?'

Some years later, after Normsk moves to Alberta, Jan, driving into Vancouver, turns on his car radio. The CBC is airing an interview with a violin maker in Edmonton; somebody is playing the violin in the background. The playing ceases and a distant, familiar voice says, 'It's very keen, isn't it?'

TWENTY-SIX

On Hearing the First Cuckoo in Spring

Jan is telling his student Jiwon about the print on the studio wall. 'It's a picture of Cookham, a little village on the Thames, painted by Sir Stanley Spencer. That boat is called a punt. When I was very young, my parents took me on it, for a trip about a week long.'

'Did you sleep in there?' she asks incredulously.

'Yes. My parents erected metal hoops and put a canvas overtop so it was like a tent.'

'Did you eat on it, too?'

'My mother cooked suppers on a primus stove, and we ate a lot of sandwiches. The swans would surround the boat and try to snatch the food from our hands. I was terrified of them.'

'Weren't you scared of falling in?'

'No, it's not like the Fraser River—the water is calm. It's fairly shallow and runs by well-manicured gardens and stately houses, fields with cows, beech trees with cuckoos and by towpaths for pulling boats.'

'What's a cuckoo?'

'It's a bird that always arrives with the spring in England. It sounds like this.' Jan plays a descending minor third on his cello. 'When I was a young boy, I had a record I loved to play on my wind-up gramophone.' Jan gets up to find the CD. 'It's by an English composer, Frederick Delius. It's called *On Hearing the First Cuckoo in Spring.*' The limpid harmonies transport Jan to the Chiltern Hills, the weeping willows hanging down and grazing the water, and the rhythm of Colin behind him paddling leisurely downstream.

* 1973 *

Jan and his colleagues in the CBC Orchestra are charging in Bombardiers—tank-like vehicles yawing their way across the ice—toward the community of Baker Lake. The ice is thinning in late May. Cracks appear, and the Bombardiers have to cross these at ninety degrees for safety's sake. Through the small window, Jan can see the white faces and wide eyes of musicians in neighbouring tanks, staring at the interlacing cracks.

This tour is worth a bullet in the chronology of Canadian culture; it's the first time an orchestra from Canada has ever visited the Arctic. This is due to the genius of George Zukerman, founder and owner of Overture Concerts. Besides being a bassoonist of international repute, George is an impresario with an uncanny ability to overcome setbacks. George employs two people—Helen, who drives endlessly across the country, encouraging and checking on the local concert societies, and Karl, who directs operations from an office in Vancouver. The fingers of Overture Concerts probe north, east and south and cover a fair slice of the continent. On the wall behind Karl's desk is a large map of Canada with little red flags pinned to it. Jan imagines these are stranded concert parties.

However well-planned the tours, fate frequently intervenes. Often, the gods are displeased. Months before Jan ever set foot in the Bombardier, Overture arranged for a Fairchild propeller plane to fly the CBC Orchestra from Vancouver to the western Arctic. When it landed on a gravel airstrip in the Far North for the first concert of the tour in Baker Lake, Jan couldn't spot a human being. George strode up and down the windswept gravel for a while. At last somebody emerged from a distant hangar and George disappeared, presumably to make contact. The orchestra waited inside the plane. The wind whined.

Suddenly and inexplicably, the crew erupted into activity. They took medical supplies, left the plane and ran across the gravel out of sight. The orchestra sat there in silence except for the wind moaning, blowing gravel along the runway. At last, the crew walked back, disconsolate, to explain that farther away, a plane carrying a cargo of copper rods had been circling to land. The rods had shifted in a gust of wind, rolling the plane, which plunged with its pilot—on his last assignment before retirement—through the ice and into the lake. No sirens, no flashing lights, just the whistling of the wind. The orchestra had some time to digest this news before George reappeared with the local contact; Bombadiers would take the orchestra across the ice to the concert at Baker Lake.

* * *

With the cracks in the ice to navigate, the orchestra arrives royally late at Baker Lake. But that matters not to the audience. Here, itineraries count for nothing. Inuit live in six-month, not sixty-second, cycles. The concert in the plywood community hall is a gathering; people walk about, music or no music. The themes of the opening Mozart symphony float on the steam between boots, babies and bearskins.

Following Mozart, the orchestra plays Delius's *On Hearing the First Cuckoo in Spring*. Cost dictated this piece's inclusion on the tour because of its minimal orchestration, despite the evident mismatch in scenic description. Although it is spring here, Delius's cuckoo has migrated far from its course; Jan finds the undulating rhythms of pastoral England at odds with the rocky outcrops of the Arctic. The thematic material, though, is a Norwegian folk song, 'In Ola Valley'. The young Australian composer Percy Grainger, who shared Delius's affection for Scandinavian music, brought it to Delius's attention. Delius then transformed it into a short, exquisite tone poem for small orchestra.

There are no hotels. Jan and Judy stay with a young couple, Carol and Roger, who are conservationists. (Emmy has recently moved with Rob and Judd to Alberta. The boys are preteens; Rob will celebrate his tenth birthday in a few days. 'Marriage and touring don't go together,' Jan said over the phone to Colin. 'Ain't that the truth, son,' replied Colin.) The conservationists' house is frozen-in eleven months of the year. In high summer, the barge arrives with supplies. The couples' estimations for shopping needs had better be accurate! Toilet facilities are practical, if crude—a garbage can with a pedal lid is lined with a heavy duty plastic bag. When the bag is full, it's left to freeze on the tundra. No garbage pick-up here—the farther north you go, the less civic pride.

Roger counts caribou. 'How can you possibly do that?' Jan asks.

'It's quite easy,' replies Roger. 'The herd migrates once a channel of water opens up in the spring. The channel is narrow enough that, in a boat, you can tag them swimming past you one at a time.'

After Baker Lake, they fly to Tuktoyaktuk where Cam Trowsdale, the concertmaster, wrapped up to his toque, climbs up on top of the community centre to play themes from *Fiddler on the Roof* on somebody else's violin to advertise the concert. Jan presumes he borrows a cheaper violin from his colleague because he doesn't want to wreck his own. The whole community drops what they are doing to come and listen to the concert.

Cuckoo is usually tucked into the middle of the concert, just before intermission. Delius admired Grieg, who incidentally had also set 'In Ola Valley' for piano. Delius stole a couple of Grieg's harmonic progressions but went much further, embedding the tune in luscious harmonies. The rich chromatics evoke poignant relief at the promise of a warm spring and of course, the cuckoo. Intermission in Tuktoyaktuk—steam turns to ice particles at the door. There are no windows in the hall, so Jan gets up to open the door, observe the monochromatic landscape and breathe the cold, dry air.

* * *

The western Arctic tour is so successful that Overture Concerts arranges an eastern Arctic tour for the following year. The orchestra's adventures are considered important enough so that André Fortier, representing the Canada Council, and his wife come along for observation. They all arrive in Churchill and are accommodated in a seedy hotel on the outskirts of town—if there is a town. All Jan can see out of the window is a white, featureless landscape punctuated by a procession of telegraph poles reaching to the horizon.

When travelling with the orchestra, Jan has learned to be prudent and dine early, ahead of the crowd. The restaurant occupies the tandem space to the bar, and a curtain divides the room. Mr and Mrs Fortier are also dining early. Mrs Fortier wears her suit *du jour* with fur stole and looks very chic in a Parisian way. The couple eats in silence. The drinking crowd is getting noisy. After a while there is some cursing, the sound of a scuffle and a glass breaking. A body falls backwards through the curtain, toward Madame Fortier. She takes no notice. Neither does the waitress. It is possibly a nightly occurrence.

In Norway House, as a publicity stunt, a small section of the orchestra plays for a local wedding. One of the wind players hurriedly arranges 'Here Comes the Bride' and writes out the parts. Either he made a mistake in copying or he's never heard Wagner's harmony; the arrangement is excruciatingly inept. On a cue, the musicians begin playing but the bride doesn't appear. Jan assumes she's on Inuit time. The orchestra plays it twenty-five times before the bride arrives. By this time, Jan's face is in a permanent wince.

Anyone doubting that Canada is a large country should fly west from Ottawa in a Fairchild prop plane. After fifteen hours of flying, it lands in Vancouver's South Terminal, the air inside the cabin fetid with old sandwich lunch boxes and overused toilets. Jan and Judy handle baggage duty for the last time and Jan says he will return with the van to take the timpani from the airport to the theatre in the morning.

The stage doorway at the QET is overseen by a bad-tempered little man who sits in a glassed-in cubicle just inside the stage door. He chain-smokes and his tie is perforated with scorch marks. He has an aversion to fresh air. If anybody leaves the stage door open, he yells at them to shut it, no please or thank you. Frequently after symphony concerts, women with pearls and furs, arm-in-arm with escorts, crowd the stage door, looking to speak to the conductor or soloist. The doorman accords no respect for the situation. 'Shut the door,' he growls.

Next morning, Jan collects the timps from the airport, parks the van in the loading zone, and, propping the stage door open with the 'No Parking' sign, takes the largest of the timps through to the stage area. No sign of the stage doorman, but when Jan returns for the second time, the sign has been moved to allow the door to shut. Jan repeats the process, carrying the smaller timp to the stage. On return, the doorman is inside his cubicle. 'Shut the door,' he snarls.

Two weeks of touring frustration suddenly surge up in Jan like milk boiling over. He goes ballistic. 'You rude, fucking idiot, you bloody fool, you're not fit to do this job!' Jan yells, slamming the glass cubicle with his palms and kicking the wooden door. The doorman cringes in his chair. 'I'm sorry, sir.' (Jan hasn't lost his temper since.)

Jan closes the back doors to the van, noticing Delius's *Cuckoo* on top of the stack of music. After returning the van to the office, he drives his own car home to West Vancouver, reflecting that while there are chevrons of geese here, the backyard songbird is not so audible as in England. He remembers that when he was a boy, the first appearance of the cuckoo with its distinctive call had the British public writing to *The Times*, eager to trump last year's date for its first appearance.

Cuckoos are common enough in Europe and no doubt Delius heard them in the village of Grez-sur-Loing, France, where he lived for many years. The cuckoo dines on caterpillars, larvae and insects, and so has to follow the food chain to survive. It is perpetually on tour. It can't settle down for long and raise a family—it has to leave its young to fledge with adopted parents. It follows the caterpillars all over Europe, borrowing nests, and finally arrives in England to serenade whoever happens to be living there—Celts, Romans, Vikings, Normans and those who come after.

The cuckoo has flown through musical history, its song immor-talized by Baroque, Romantic and Modern composers, from Daquin through Vivaldi, Bach, Handel, Beethoven, Leopold Mozart and Saint-Saëns to Respighi. And if it didn't find a place in Messiaen's ornithological catalogue, it must surely have left an egg or two in his aviary.

Various cuckoos migrate round the world. Jan hears them along the banks of the Thames and the woods beyond:

The punt is approaching Goring Lock. Elf points to the trees. 'Listen, do you hear the doves, but can you hear the cuckoo in between?'

Profile: George's Misadventures

Besides the culminating Arctic tours, George carefully choreographs tours to Canada's hinterlands around the Vancouver concert season, steering around every impediment with ingenuity, spontaneity and creativity.

A float plane carrying some of the orchestra to Vancouver Island is forced to land on the water due to poor visibility. They float about until they come across a fishing boat to find out where they are. Back on dry land, they have to take taxis up-island while in Nanaimo the audience and the rest of the orchestra wait for them. Those returning home for a morning deadline in Vancouver encounter another air incident. The plane, leaving Nanaimo after dark, is prevented from taking off because rabbits have chewed through the wires for the runway lights.

George's audiences are used to waiting. The itinerary for the orchestra's Alberta tour neglects to include the change of time zone. On arrival at Lethbridge—no time for dinner—Bob Meyer unpacks his bass in the wings of the stage and finds his instrument cracked due to the dry, cold climate. He pours a jug of water into it and walks out on stage to play the concert.

Bob's bass travels in an enormous hard case that Jan and Judy, who traditionally handle the baggage, christen Yorick. At Hay River, NWT, a small flatbed truck is waiting to pick them up. They place the orchestra's suitcases three-deep with Yorick lying across them on top. There is no space in the truck's cabin so they both climb on top of the suitcases and join Yorick, their backs against the cabin. The truck takes off at great speed down a road that appears to be asphalted onto the naked grass. Yorick begins to slide off. Jan grabs at the case, but there's nothing for him to grab on to. The suitcases are jiggling about and Jan has a vision of everything sliding off the truck and he and Judy being brained by Yorick. Jan yells to the driver to slow down. The driver doesn't hear. Jan knocks feverishly on the cabin glass, but much to his relief, the truck is slowing down, not because the driver heard him but because they are entering town.

At Uranium City, Saskatchewan, the recent closure of the mines doesn't preclude an annual ritual—an old car is driven onto the frozen lake while people make bets to predict which day in May the ice will give way under the car's weight. Sadly, the orchestra arrives a day after this rite of spring. A large pickup waits for the baggage. Again, there is no room for Jan and Judy except by standing with Yorick upright in the back of the truck, amidst the pile of luggage. This feels a safer journey than the one in Hay River. The driver stops at a pair of houses in a copse of woods: 'Just be a moment.' Jan and Judy wait, trapped amidst luggage, a black cloud of mosquitoes gathering above their heads. Twenty-five minutes later, the driver re-emerges. He's just had lunch.

The most idyllic of George's tours is of the Inside Passage on the *Northland Prince*, the mail boat that plies between Vancouver and Prince Rupert. The gods smile down on this trip. A week of perfect weather sees the boat make endless ripples down the placid water of fjords where sheer mountain faces allow streams to free-fall into the salt water below. The orchestra remains on the boat, only disembarking in their concert clothes to play in the converted cinemas of the coastal settlements. In situations like this, the normal professional etiquette is loosened. Back on board, musicians stay up too late, get drunk and chase their sexual peccadilloes. Thus, a wind player, rejected by his intended and locked out of his own cabin, wanders the ship in his underpants.

The CBC Orchestra is to fly to Massett in the Queen Charlotte Islands. George hires two seaplanes—the Grumman Goose. This creates a problem of nomenclature on the itinerary—are the planes two gooses or two geese? The orchestra waits on the wharf until the pilot tells them to climb in. Among those waiting in the rain are a violinist, who has a 'Proud Canadian' sticker on her violin case but is too proud to carry it herself, and the timpanist, who holds an attaché case full of drumsticks but leaves his timpani on the wharf for the less proud—Jan and Judy—to load. They haul a timpani into the nose of each aircraft. The planes rev their engines as Jan straps himself in. The planes begin to move. To Jan's horror, they move down rather than off and up as he expects. Of course, they are float planes and are going down the launch slope to the water!

It is raining in Massett, as usual. The orchestra sets up in the school gymnasium. The timpanist discovers that he left his attaché case back on the wharf—no sticks! What can be done? Somebody finds a pair of fisherman's knitting needles used for mending nets. At the concert, instead of going bonk, the timpanist goes bink.

By the end of the concert, the weather has worsened and Jan and Judy hurriedly strike the set and with the crew's help, place the timps back into the planes' noses. The musicians strap themselves in. 'Hurry,' says the pilot. 'If the sea gets any heavier, we won't be able to take off.'

At the tail of the plane, there is only one seat to allow passage out of the exit, with headroom requiring the passengers to duck in order to enter or exit. The waves roll in twenty feet apart. The planes, facing the oncoming waves, rev up their motors. Judy produces a bottle of vodka. Everyone near the back takes a swig. The plane picks up speed. It seems that it is waterlogged—water seeps in through the exit hatch. Gaining speed, the plane begins to lift, skipping through the crest of the rollers with accelerating thumps. Awash at the back, the musicians pass around the vodka for the second time.

George takes a swig and settles in his seat. 'I think next year we'll tour schools in the Fraser Canyon. We can take helicopters.'

INTERLUDE: DELYASS GARAGE

The PSQ is about to rehearse Percy Grainger's *Molly on the Shore.*

'Did the *Cuckoo* fly all the way to Tuktoyaktuk?' asks Normsk.

'Yes,' says Jan, 'but it lost a few feathers en route.'

'I think,' says Normsk, 'the distinctive element in Delius's *Cuckoo* is the way he uses the strings—he divides them so you have many voices pulling on those chromatics. Not quite so much in the companion piece, *Summer Night on the River*, but I like that, too. It's certainly more rewarding to play than eternal Bruckner. I also like that other piece Grainger gave Delius—"Brigg Fair"—even though I think it's too long.'

'When Jiggy was here last for that Percy Grainger recording,' says Jan, 'he was reminiscing as we queued up for lunch in the CBC canteen. Jiggy's grand-uncle, Balfour Gardiner, was very much part of the Delius crowd—he bankrolled the first performance of Holst's *The Planets*—so Jiggy knows a lot about Grainger. He was remembering the eccentricities of Grainger—his first impression was of the Australian with a towel wrapped turban-like around his head. Jiggy speculated that "Brigg Fair" was probably first sung by a yokel at thigh-slapping speed and down the years got slowed down, polished and emasculated so you get singers like Peter Pears getting all wistful over it. Jiggy did a passable imitation, pursing his mouth and producing a clergyman's hoot. Not as good as yours, though, Normsk.' Jan laughs.

'Jiggy told that story about Delius,' Jan continues, 'whose house at Grez-sur-Loing was long but only one room thick with a front and back door opposite to one another. Grainger would throw a cricket ball high in the air, run through the house, and catch it in the backyard.'

'Just like Ian Botham,' says Normsk.

'Grainger made his reputation as a pianist with his performances of Grieg's Piano Concerto,' says Jan. 'Jiggy used to tell the story of how at a lengthy orchestral ritornello, Grainger would sprint to the rear of the hall and return just in time for his entrance. He always made it back except on one occasion—there was an ice cream vendor at the back and he failed to meet the downbeat.'

Fred laughs. 'Must have been small halls because the Grieg isn't that long. Speaking of short pieces, shouldn't we be getting on with Molly?'

'Grainger's obsessive athleticism caused him to hurtle round the village pushing Delius in his wheelchair,' says Jan, opening his music.

'One time,' says Normsk, 'we were in Bradford and interested in seeing the house where Delius was born. We stopped at the gas station to ask. The guy at the pump said, "I don't rightly know but this is the DeLyass Garage."'

TWENTY-SEVEN

Mamangakis One

* 1977 *

The second violin chair at PSQ rehearsal is noticeably vacant. Fred, who was always large and loud, has left for Saskatchewan, and Chuckles, his replacement, self-effacing and thin, has not yet arrived.

'Probably missed the turning,' says Phil, making coffee.

Jan, eyeing Normsk, feels a tinge of apprehension. Because all violinists are born to be first violinists, those sitting in the second violin chair are looking for a career move. There is an in and out tradition for this chair in a quartet. However constant this syndrome, the departure of a member of an established quartet sounds a warning bell—if not the death knell—for an ensemble.

Chuckles arrives. 'Sorry, I missed the turning.'

His nickname, Chuckles, has followed him across the Atlantic because of his constantly sad expression. The downward curve of his mouth is misleading. Chuckles can explode into laughter when something tickles his very British sense of humour. The newly configured PSQ has recently set about relearning its repertoire. For a quartet, the repertoire is never completely learned. Whenever it resuscitates an old chestnut, all the old arguments about interpretation and technical solutions erupt all over again. There is less argument about modern works; the notes simply have to be learned.

The PSQ is to give the North American premiere of the Greek composer Nikos Mamangakis's First Quartet, *Tetraktys*, in Toronto. Four copies of the oversized score have arrived. There are no separate parts. Jan immediately perceives that each player has a varied and unsynchronized number of notes in each bar. A score is essential to avoid getting lost.

Jan opens his score and sighs. The manuscript is handwritten.

Chuckles sniffs. 'How are we to turn pages?'

'Good question,' says Jan, examining the score.

He observes that the notes have to be played up and down one string while bowing a drone on an adjacent open string. The Quartet has a slow middle section and the last part repeats the opening except, instead of a dense frantic sound, the notes are placed in clouds, thinning out with increased silences in between until the music peters out to a final silence.

Phil had recently met Mamangakis at a reception before the composer left Canada for his home in Greece, and had just received the score for *Tetraktys*. He'd asked about the chaotic jumble of notes at the beginning. '*Viertel*,' the composer had explained in German. *Viertel*, meaning count four beats to the bar.

Chuckles sniffs again. 'How can we possibly count four beats per bar when Normsk has seventy notes and I've got thirteen?'

'Sounds like an Australian test match,' says Normsk.

The first section, with its drones, clearly doesn't allow for page turns. By the end of a rehearsal full of stop and go, Phil and Jan decide that they will each cut out their own part and paste it underneath Normsk's part. They'll get it all on two pages and stick to Normsk right or wrong. Chuckles quietly makes his own arrangements.

Three weeks later, with cut-and-pasted parts in hand, the PSQ flies to Toronto. At the St. Lawrence Centre, the players take the stage for a dress rehearsal which is mostly about training powerful spotlights on the group, rather than rehearsing Mamangakis. Even though it's a new music concert, the Centre seems plausibly full. The PSQ walks out into the bright lights and attacks the Mamangakis. The fury of the notes has to be matched by the loudness of execution. Jan's fingers fly up and down the string while he grinds the bow on the adjacent lower string. Once his nerves settle down, he looks above his own music to Normsk's part. He can't find him. Where the hell is Normsk? Jan can sense that Phil, beside him, is equally uncertain. The first section will be ending soon.

Suddenly, Jan realizes that Normsk is playing slow notes, and jumps ahead to the slow section. Phil takes the cue and jumps too. But where exactly is Normsk? The music is quiet and slow now—it should be easy enough to find him. The search proves elusive. The section will be coming to an end. Normsk can't have that many whole notes left. Phil and Jan begin circling him like wolves round a moose. They are back on track. They lock on to Normsk.

But Chuckles, confused by what has been going on below him, is already into the third section. Jan and Phil hear his rapid arabesques so they press on in hot pursuit. Each person is to play their arabesques at random—short bursts of machine-gun fire followed by increasing silences. Chuckles is getting quiet. The rest follow him, quietening also. Only a couple of lines to go. But Chuckles has finished. He puts his violin down. The others play the final bars, bringing the Quartet to a hushed conclusion. As they finish, Chuckles, who feels he should be doing something, lifts his violin to his chin and plays one final, quiet arabesque all on his own. As is usual at new music concerts, the performance is received by uncertain clapping. Then, sure the ordeal is over, the audience breaks into determined applause.

'That was so sad!' Phil says once they reach the safety of the green room. A crowd of well-wishers push open the door and force their way in. 'Bravi! Bravi!' says the composer Robert Aitken. 'So much more effective than the dress rehearsal.'

The rest of the concert features Canadian music and, afterwards, all the participants gather at the composer Harry Freedman's house for a party. The house is full of people—a veritable who's who of the Canadian contemporary music scene—upstairs, downstairs and on the stairs. Conversations get louder. Jan's colleagues are nowhere to be seen. Jan is growing concerned; the evening was already very long and they have an early flight back to Vancouver next morning. Jan looks for a phone book to call a cab. As he does so, he sees Norma Beecroft, the composer, putting on her coat. 'Can you drop me off at the Four Seasons?' asks Jan.

'Of course,' she replies.

Early the next morning, Jan rises and phones his colleagues. No one answers. Jan takes a cab to the airport and, because of the time difference, arrives back in Vancouver for lunch. He discovers later that, having overslept, the rest of the PSQ had to wait for an afternoon flight.

* * *

Two weeks later, Jan is driving to a rehearsal at Chuckles's house with the car radio tuned to CBC. 'And now we go to the St. Lawrence Centre in Toronto for a concert of contemporary music. Here is our host, Norma Beecroft, to introduce the music.' A familiar voice comes on: 'The first item on the program is a quartet by Nikos Mamangakis. This incredibly difficult work is given a fine performance by the Purcell String Quartet.'

Jan switches off the radio. For the PSQ, the name becomes a cautionary term in their musical lexicon. 'Remember Mamangakis!'

Portrait: Crumb in Canada

Sue serves on the board of the New Music Society for some years. David Owen, oboist, has been deputized to meet the composer George Crumb at the Vancouver Airport. Crumb has been invited up to a New Music event. In the afternoon, Jan answers a phone call. A slow drawl, reminiscent of Jimmy Stewart, asks, 'Is Sue Round there? My name is George Crumb and somebody's supposed to meet me.' The delivery seems totally at odds with the composer of *Black Angels*. George Crumb arrives with no luggage—just one shopping bag which contains his toiletries and, one would hope, a change of underwear.

INTERLUDE: JOHN GAZI

'You remember John Gazi?' Normsk asks Jan. They're driving up Burnaby Mountain on a Monday evening to coach a student quartet playing early Beethoven.

'Of course,' says Jan. 'He was in the VSO for a few years.'

'He died over the weekend. Killed in a motor accident.'

'Oh, God. He was still young. What happened?'

'I'm not sure. He had been fixing up his car. It was a nice afternoon. The family was going to have a barbecue. He lit the coals and said that he'd just test drive his car round the block. He never returned. I think the brakes failed.'

There is a silence. Then Jan says, 'I remember he was going to come from the East Coast for an audition with the VSO. He had to postpone it for a few weeks. He had cracked a rib—fallen on a Ping-Pong ball and it had lodged between two ribs.'

'Extraordinary that.'

'But John provided a lovely joke to be added to the prize collection of musical humour,' says Jan. 'You asked him at his audition what he'd been doing previously.'

'I remember,' says Normsk, looking for a parking space. 'I couldn't believe that he wanted to vacate his seat in a string quartet to join the second fiddle section of the VSO. Then John got into a diatribe about how stupid the quartet leader was and to illustrate it, he said they were playing the Beethoven opus 132, rehearsing the seraphic slow movement, the "Hymn of Thanksgiving in the Lydian Mode". The leader starts off, very slowly, very smoothly. When he gets to the eighth bar, he suddenly plays a staccato quarter note, like a hiccup. Well, they rehearse the opening a few times and hear this hiccup and they don't comment. Finally, the violist enquires, "Why do you hiccup the third beat at my entry?"

'"Because," says the leader, "the note's got a dot over it."

'They all get up and squint at his music. Above the opening are Beethoven's words, you know—*Heiliger Dankgesang*, the Hymn of Thanksgiving, et cetera … in the Lydian Mode—well, in German, *der lydischen Tonart.*' Normsk pauses. 'DOT!'

Jan wipes his eyes. 'Oh, heavenly.'

TWENTY-EIGHT

Coulthard Octet

Jan is at Langley Community Music School, failing to find the score and parts of Jean Coulthard's Octet. Normsk has asked him to coach a movement at the annual chamber music camp in Sooke. Jan contacts the Canadian Music Centre (CMC). Not on file. They refer him to Berendol Publishers who eventually admit they've lost the only set they have. Jan calls up the Vancouver composer and music critic David Duke, who spent the last decade of Jean's life as her amanuensis, proofreading and correcting her scores.

'The UBC archives probably have it,' says David. 'They've modernized and have a new state-of-the-art system. Relevant archival material is stored in caskets like a funeral home. You press a button and the caskets trundle around on a loop, rather like a drycleaners. I'd go for you but I'm out of town on vacation for the next few weeks.'

Jan turns to his colleague Frances, who works at the SFU library. Miraculously, she finds a copy through interlibrary loan. On examination, Jan finds the usual mixture of errata and addenda. Later, Jan and David decide to have the work recopied. 'It is her masterpiece after all,' says David.

* 1979 *

It's a wet February morning, and the PSQ meets at Phil's house in North Vancouver to rehearse Coulthard's Octet, *Twelve Essays on a Cantabile Theme*, which they will record next month at the CBC in Vancouver with the University of Alberta String Quartet to celebrate Jean's seventieth birthday.

'Jean sent me the score,' says Normsk. 'It came in this very big envelope.'

Phil looks at the score over Normsk's shoulder. 'Good God, she's written Tom Ralston's initials against the first theme.'

'Well, it is dedicated to us and the U of A String Quartet.' Normsk points to the dedication at the top of the page. 'Ours is the second entry.' He turns the page. 'There's my initials and yours, Phil.' He stabs the viola entry. 'We get the second kick at the cat.'

Jan is flipping through his cello part. 'It may be a *cantabile* theme, but there seem to be an awful lot of notes later on. Let's play it through.'

'Remember, we've only got half of the information,' says Normsk. 'We should secure our entries in the fast movements, and particularly the fugue. Fugues are bad news, and we only have two days of rehearsals with the Alberta boys.'

Jean's Octet, comprised of twelve movements, is tinged with autumnal melancholy that is dispelled periodically by the livelier movements—'Winds of the Night', 'The Academicians' and of course the daunting 'Fugue'. ('It's so full of black notes,' comments Phil as they rehearse.) Standing out among the musical dozen is a movement titled 'The Wood Doves Grieve' in which Jean imagines the birds mourning the passing of Clementine Poston at Rooksnest House, her home in Stevenage, the locale of E. M. Forster's novel *Howards End*. Clementine's daughter, Elizabeth Poston, an esteemed English composer, was a long-standing friend of Jean's. The movement contains two passages of multiple descending glissandos played aleatorically, suggestive of birds flying, falling, calling or dying. This effect demonstrates that Jean, for all her melodic gifts, is not immune from contemporary technical devices and, when appropriate, can use them with imagination.

The rehearsal ends with the appropriately titled last movement, 'Farewell'. Over its *al niente* tones, Phil whispers, 'It's time for a little something.' He produces some homemade wine and chooses an antique corkscrew from his collection.

* * *

It is March, and still raining. The two quartets meet in Studio One at the CBC to rehearse for the next day's recording.

'Let's play it through and get a bird's-eye view—Jean's coming this afternoon,' says Mick, first violinist of the U of A String Quartet, who all along has been in touch with Jean about this recording. Jan wonders privately how Tom Ralston became Mick. It has never been explained.

'There are questionable notes,' says Normsk. 'Perhaps we should make a list after each movement and ask Jean this afternoon.'

The language of the Octet is formulated around the idea of two distinct quartet personalities, abstract thinking which culminates in the canons of 'The Academicians' and, later, the 'Fugue', where Jean acknowledges her indebtedness to Bach. These are interspersed with movements describing the natural world.

After lunch, the musicians return to the studio to find Jean sitting with David Duke. She's taken off her raincoat and put it to dry on a chair. Her dark umbrella drips in a corner.

With any piece, and especially with premieres, queries abound. 'Getting the bugs out,' says Mick. The players frequently ask Jean about the notation. After each question, Jean confers with David, who usually answers for her. Jan, familiar with Jean's music and this process, speculates whether these changes will be permanent, or whether the manuscript—a casserole of conjectured corrections—will be placed at the CMC to be altered further by subsequent performers.

After the recording session, the two quartets with Jean gather on what Jan calls the 'promenade deck' outside the CBC building for a photograph to be used on the record jacket.

'You excellent fellows,' says Jean. 'Thank you for a fine rendition.'

'I'll give you a ride, Mick,' says Normsk, and Jan watches the two leaders disappear into the parking lot, their heads bowed against the rain, in deep conversation.

∗ ∗ ∗

Many weeks later, on another grey afternoon, Phil and Jan converse on the deck of a small ferry en route to Saltspring Island. Some time ago, Chuckles left the PSQ for the VSO, and ever since, the second violin position has been in flux, with players coming and going. Phil and Jan are surveying their options.

Phil, looking out to sea, says, 'You'll be wanting to call me tomorrow.'

'Whatever for?' asks Jan.

'Believe me, you'll want to call me tomorrow.'

On arrival home, Jan gets a call from Normsk. 'I've been offered Mick's position with the U of A Quartet. What with Fred leaving and the problems we're having with the second violin position, my children getting to university age and other incentives, it's a package I can't pass up. I'm terribly sorry.'

'It's okay, Normsk,' says Jan, aware that this might be the solution to a number of personal difficulties for Normsk.

Jan puts down the phone and dials Phil. 'What are we going to do?'

'There's only one thing we can do,' says Phil, 'and that is to phone Sydney Humphreys.'

'But he lives in Victoria,' says Jan.

'We'll have to make it work.'

Sydney Humphreys is head violin teacher at the Victoria Conservatory. He is well-known to the members of the PSQ who have come of age in England during the 1950s when Sydney as leader of the Aeolian Quartet was a frequent broadcaster on the BBC. A fine violinist, Sydney knows the quartet repertoire cold. With him, the PSQ can expand its programming considerably.

Fortune smiles upon the PSQ. Sydney, with no questions, agrees to join, and Jan and Phil's colleague Bryan King from the Vancouver Opera Orchestra (VOO) agrees to fill the much-needed position of second violin. Sydney stays in Victoria and the remaining three take the ferry once a week to rehearse all day. With Sydney, the PSQ performs a number of concert series—the complete Beethoven, the complete Bartók—in Victoria, as well as at SFU, both on campus and throughout the province.

Returning from Victoria on the ferry one evening after rehearsing Charles Ives, Phil remarks to Jan, 'Funny how we thought it was pushing the envelope to play Borodin in the boonies.'

'Now we're playing Carter in Kamloops,' says Jan, looking at Vancouver's approaching lights.

∗ ∗ ∗

Jean Coulthard was the first composer that Jan met when he arrived in Vancouver. The phone rang and with an accent reminiscent of the Home Counties, Jean asked if Jan would play her Sonata for Cello and Piano. Jan found it quite demanding, though he thought the middle movement—the Sarabande—stretched its relevance a little thin. Jan went to Jean's house to play it through sans piano. Her house, set uphill in an upscale corner of Marine Drive, was sunny and spacious, with a Japanese-themed exterior. Jan noticed an unframed drawing tucked in between two cupboards in the kitchen—a beautiful image of an elderly woman by Joy Finzi, mother of Jan's old school chum Kiffer.

Jan recalls when the CBC Orchestra made a studio recording of Jean's *A Prayer for Elizabeth*. She sat as usual with David Duke and the score. At one point, she turned to Jan and said, 'You are getting a little portly.' This turned out to be her farewell comment to Jan. At the end of the session, Mario Bernardi, trying hard to conceal his frustration with so many queries about doubtful notes, said, 'Jean, how can you let these children of yours out into the world in this condition?' Jean, a lady to the hem of her skirt, brushed his comment aside.

* * *

After Jean dies in 2000, Jan phones David Duke, her executor. 'There's a drawing by Joy Finzi that could be overlooked—it's unframed. I once saw it in her kitchen.' Later, David sends Jan a copy. 'The one you saw isn't an original,' he says. 'The portrait is of Elizabeth Poston's mother, Clementine. Jean and Elizabeth were great friends.'

The print hangs in Jan's studio at LCMS, presiding over a chair used as a shelf for an armful of Jean's music. Jan always chooses some of her pieces for his students to perform at the annual Canadian Music Concert in November.

Jan's cell phone rings.

'Wondering—ahem—what about the Octet?' asks Normsk.

'Jim's still copying it. But there are difficulties because Jean sometimes scores it as two separate quartets and sometimes as a string orchestra in score order. You've got to have a constant format to pull out the parts.'

'Sounds like more money.'

'More money or not, it will be ready by next May for Sooke.'

Profile: Canadian Composers

About the time Jan first meets Jean Coulthard, he also meets Sir Ernest MacMillan, who is visiting Vancouver to judge an international violin competition. In the Vancouver Playhouse, the washrooms are down a flight of stairs, an obstacle course to an elderly man like Sir Ernest. In flight, Jan draws abreast of the great musician. 'Here, boy,' says Sir Ernest, 'help me down the stairs.' Arm in arm, they descend to the Gents together.

Sir Ernest wrote two colourful sketches for string quartet. The PSQ frequently performs one of these, 'À Saint Malo', for schools. A sailing friend once told Jan that the harbour at St Malo is very difficult to negotiate. Once you have sailed out, it's even more difficult to sail back in. Thus, history is made—Jacques Cartier had to keep going.

Musical explorers follow. Jan commissions works for cello, as well as chamber music pieces suitable for the LCMS annual Canadian Music Concert from composers such as Stephen Chatman, Victor Davies and Murray Adaskin. Of all the fine and imaginative works created, *Triptych*—three pieces written for cello and piano by Nikolai Korndorf—has prompted wide interest among cellists.

Korndorf is a Russian émigré establishing himself in Vancouver, well-known in Russia but not in Canada. One of Jan's colleagues has a daughter incarcerated in a Sao Paulo jail. Each year, a vigil is held and one year, Jan is asked to play. Not finding a piece quite suitable for such an occasion, Jan commissions Nikolai to write something. 'That is close to my heart,' Nikolai murmurs. Weeks later, 'Lamentations' is completed and Jan visits Nikolai at his house to be confronted by a bushy-haired and bushy-bearded man with intense eyes. The studio, with an upright piano and a table holding a computer and acoustic technology, barely leaves enough room for Jan to play his cello. At close range, Nikolai's personality is overwhelming. 'You must *prrotestt...*' Nikolai says, turning to Jan from the piano.

'Lamentations' is equally overwhelming with its novel sustained double stops in cross-rhythm to the piano. Over the next two years, for the Canadian Music Concert, Jan commissions the final two pieces—'Response' and 'Glorification'—which alongside 'Lamentations' completes Korndorf's *Triptych*, a glorious addition to the cello repertoire.

A few years later, Nikolai, in his fifties, playing soccer with his son, has a heart attack and dies.

Profile: Sonia Eckhardt-Gramatté

Jan has just returned from Brandon, where he was judging the Eckhardt-Gramatté Competition. 'Ferdinand Eckhardt wanted to be remembered to you,' Jan says to Normsk.

'Good Lord,' says Normsk. 'That comes of playing Sonia's quartets all those times at the art gallery in Winnipeg.'

'The WAG was a special place,' says Jan. 'Ferdinand built it inside and out. It's shaped like an arrowhead and filled with exceptional artworks. I remember Sonia always kept her hair short and wore a tie.'

'Phil, you must shovel your bow. Shovel!' Normsk imitates Sonia. 'That part is important. I am the only person in Canada writing *Kontrapunkt*!'

'All those notes—I've just heard a slew of them. Each competitor had to play a caprice. So many ideas superimposed upon each other. I thought Ferdinand was wonderful after she died. Not only did he publish collections of her works and start a competition to cherish her music, he also honoured his father by publishing a book of his woodcuts.'

'Remember Ferdinand driving that VW?' asks Normsk. 'He was so tall he had the front seat taken out and drove from the back. He was the Austrian consul in Winnipeg. It looked like the back of his neck had had a close encounter with an allied shell.'

'Sad that last time we visited him,' says Jan. 'He served strudel and made coffee and played us old 78s of Sonia playing her own violin caprices. You could hardly hear her for the surface noise.'

'Do you remember that year in Courtenay when they had jazz concerts late at night?' asks Normsk. 'Sonia and Ferdinand were visiting and waited on the bleachers for a full hour while they set up the stage. Then a large group of musicians came out and launched into an Ellington big band number. Sonia and Ferdinand walked out immediately.'

'Such a pity that Sonia's fabled life should end under a bus in Stuttgart.'

INTERLUDE: SYDNEY

The 'new' PSQ has been preparing their Beethoven series at Sydney's house in Victoria. After a long day of rehearsal, Sydney's wife, Mary, insists they stay for a roast beef dinner before catching the ferry home. 'You've got time to wolf it down,' Mary says cheerfully.

'George used to tell a story,' says Sydney, sitting down, 'about a tour he set up in BC for the piano duo Ferrante and Teicher but somewhere along the way, "Teicher" was misspelled as "Streicher". He booked a flight on CP Air for them, and then, realizing they would probably need a piano tuner accompanying them, booked a further seat in the name of "anonymous" because he didn't know which piano tuner he could find. The CP staff interpreted this as a certain Ferrante accompanying a stretcher case, whose name was unknown. They took out two seats to make room.'

'I guess that's not so surprising, travelling the hinterland,' says Jan, anxiously eyeing the mantelpiece clock. The last ferry back to Vancouver is at 9 p.m. 'My cello has shared seats with tool boxes, mountaineering kits and flower arrangements.'

'I can imagine that was only the beginning of George's problems,' says Sydney. 'One piano is bad enough in some of those rural places. Matching two pianos must have been a nightmare. We ran into some awful clunkers when I was playing recitals with Robin Wood—pianos half a tone flat or suffering from water damage, keys that stuck, and then sometimes keys you could press down but not release. Frequently, the same syndromes infected the pedals and invariably one pedal would squeak.' Sydney reaches for the roast potatoes.

'My father was a piano tuner,' he continues. 'It's a machine rather than an instrument. Like a car, it has to be regularly serviced. When Robin and I toured, we travelled with a few tools and tried to arrive at the hall in really good time. We never knew what kind of a monster was going to be there to greet us. I'm sure George could recite a litany of woes about pianos. But then, you had to expect the unexpected when travelling with George.

'I remember, playing bassoon quartets with George, we had to drive to Nelson, a fair distance with a concert at the end of it. Early in the morning, I got a phone call from George. It was snowing heavily down the valley. There would be a change of plan. We would fly down to Spokane, hire a car and drive to Nelson from there. Well, of course, it was snowing in Spokane as well so driving was pretty treacherous. We made slow progress. George found a call box and phoned the local sponsor warning him that we might be late. As the afternoon wore on, George calculated that we would arrive half an hour late and phoned again to tell the sponsor to placate the audience, but the concert would surely take place. Could you pass the mustard?' Jan does so, stealing another look at the clock.

'If you remember,' says Sydney, 'there's a steep descent into Nelson, and the road does an S-bend turning into the main street. It was snowing to beat the band with drifts on either side of the road and George was driving fast. Suddenly, there was a semi coming round the corner up the hill. George did the only thing possible—drove into the snowbank. There was a squeal of metal grinding on metal. There was another car in the ditch hidden by the snow! We were minutes away from the theatre.

'We took our instruments and ran. The audience was still there, waiting. We played the concert and at the end, bowed and walked off. At the back of the stage, there were a couple of cops waiting. They charged George with hit and run and hauled him off to the police station, the applause still in our ears.'

'And now we've got to take our instruments and run,' says Jan.

GZ

TWENTY-NINE

Russia Rossini

The heavenly aroma of stewed meats—*pot au feu*—greets Jan as he walks into Phil's house and takes out his cello.

'What are you making for dessert?' calls Jan to Phil in the kitchen.

'Crème caramel,' says Phil.

'Carmelized custard,' says Jan, acting the philistine.

'No, it's for Marie-Antoine Carême,' Phil corrects Jan. 'He invented it.'

'Ah!' says Jan. 'A famous chef and a close friend of Rossini's. Rossini always had an interest in the kitchen, and in his old age might have invented Tournedos Rossini.'

'He'd have had trouble eating it by then,' says Phil. 'He had no teeth.'

Jan sets his part for Sonata no. 5 on the stand. 'Rossini had only just grown out of his milk teeth when he wrote these sonatas. He was twelve.'

* 1979 *

The musicians have landed in Moscow. They line up to go through security with apprehension. The guards look like young army recruits, with severe haircuts under exaggerated peaked caps. The passage to each cubicle is narrow, with a mirror set at shoulder height obliquely opposite the guard, providing a view of the back of the head. 'To see if you've washed your neck,' supposes Jan.

A visa with photograph is required. Almost two months ago—two days previous to being photographed—Phil, in a moment of self-improvement, took a pre-dawn bike ride accompanied by his dog, who was suddenly attacked by a neighbouring dog. The ensuing skirmish got between the wheels and caused Phil to fall off his bike and bruise his right eye for the visa photograph. Then, just before leaving for Moscow, conducting the North Shore Orchestra and urging them to an orchestral climax, Phil stabbed his left eye with his baton.

The guard looks long and thoughtfully up at Phil and down at the visa several times, which shows a man with a black right eye. The man standing in front of him has a black left eye.

Jan sighs with relief as the guard opens Phil's passport, stamps it and waves him through. Good job Phil washed his neck, thinks Jan.

But security isn't through with Phil. The customs officer opens Phil's viola case and, running his nail over the varnish, makes as if to take the instrument out. Phil holds up his hand. 'Please,' he says softly and courteously. The guard puts it back.

In that moment of calm before Normsk officially left the quartet and Sydney and Bryan joined it, George had offered the PSQ a late autumn tour of the Soviet Union. At that time, with Normsk poised to move to Alberta and no second violin available, it was agreed that an ensemble built around Schubert's 'Trout' Quintet would be practical, comprised of Jan, Phil, Normsk, pianist Linda Lee Thomas and Jan's old buddy Bill Fawcett, bassist from the VSO. (One doesn't just tour the Soviet Union on a whim; arrangements had to be made months in advance. With special permission from the university, Normsk left his new position to fulfill the Russian obligation.)

Practical up to a point. Touring with a double bass is like travelling with a dead body; special arrangements—seats out of the plane, capacious vehicles—have to be provided. The rest of the program contains a Dvořák piano quartet and a Rossini string sonata.

Katerina, a young blond woman, meets the party. She's to be their interpreter for the trip. As they arrive at their hotel, a large digital clock on the wall proclaims it to be 18:12. Katerina excuses herself; she wants to spend the evening with her husband and young boy since she's about to depart. The musicians want to spend the evening visiting the Red Square, and Katerina before leaving gives directions on how to get there by subway. Jan counts six subway stops, trying to make a note of the Cyrillic letters at each station. The Red Square is illuminated, the air clear and cold. The brickwork of the ground rises and then gently slopes towards St Basil's Cathedral. Its deep bells ring sonorously as the guards change at the entrance of Lenin's tomb. ('Who was this guy, Lenin?' someone asks. 'Oh you know, John Lennon,' comes the quip. '"Give Peace a Chance".')

Returning to the subway, the musicians realize that the Red Square is an important interchange and they are faced with a complicated choice. Which line did they take earlier? Jan has visions of getting on a non-stop to the Gulag; a ball of yarn would be useful. The collective wisdom of the group is brought to bear on the problem and somehow, they arrive back at their hotel without incident.

They fly to Arkhangelsk the next day. The airport bus passes miles of industrial pipes but unlike the undeveloped towns of the Canadian north, Arkhangelsk is settled with old stone buildings. The concert takes place at a seemingly abandoned music school. Despite scruffy green rooms, the hall is surprisingly spacious, ornate and well-filled with listeners. The ensemble sits down to play and someone emerges from the wings for introductions and to read out the program. Jan supposes that perhaps some of the proletariat, though used to attending concerts, can't read.

First up is the Rossini Sonata no. 5, from a set of six sonatas he wrote as a boy of twelve. It is essentially silly music, but Rossini's facile style, even as written by a pre-adolescent, has an ephemeral brilliance for the first-time listener. For the performers, the pieces are treacherous. Rossini wrote it for two violins, cello and bass, omitting the viola. In this rescored version, Phil takes over most of the second violin part, leaving the antiphonal virtuosic solos to be played twice by the luckless Normsk.

For each of the instruments, Rossini wrote solos with note lengths that shorten and gather speed as they progress, providing finger twisters that may unseat a musician at any moment. Thus, the string players open this concert highly strung. Although juvenilia, these sonatas contain the seeds of Rossini's style, which is a quick wit and an unerring sense of timing, as well as a melodic invention worthy of Mozart, whom Rossini idolized.

Rossini had written some forty operas by the time he suddenly retired at the age of thirty-eight, after which he tinkered with his *Sins of My Old Age*. The operas were all Italian save two, *Le Comte Ory* and his last, longest and reputedly greatest opera, *William Tell*. This opera points a new path to what we understand today as grand opera, which parallels the *haute cuisine* established by Carême in Paris; the French are masters of style in the arts.

But Rossini—rich, famous and now stout, suffered from mysterious maladies, and with appetite assuaged at La Maison Dorée, Carême's restaurant, satisfied himself in his sunset years not with opera, but with *Sins of My Old Age*. This work is comprised of more than 150 songs, piano solos and other salon pieces characterizing Rossini's unflagging wit, rhythmic verve and melodic invention, and by many titles, his appreciation of food.

The musicians breakfast in Tallinn, where Linda Lee and Bill pursue their quest for *caffe latte*, without success. Black coffee arrives.

'*Slivki?*' Bill asks for cream.

'*Niet,*' comes the refrain.

'At least there's sugar,' says Linda Lee.

Phil turns to Normsk and Jan. 'Carême also had a way with sugar. He had previously worked in a patisserie and would display his famous *pièces montées*, elaborate edifices made out of sugar.'

'Ah, yes!' says Jan. 'For the premiere of *William Tell,* he made a diorama out of sugar—William Tell shooting at the apple on his son's head.'

Reluctant to take '*niet*' for an answer, Linda Lee and Bill pursue *caffe latte* at the Tallinn airport. It seems to Jan that Russian airports are more like converted railway stations. One feature they have in common is a lack of toilets. In one airport, grounded because of weather for several hours, Jan searches in vain for anything resembling a washroom. In desperation, he goes outside and pees on the grass by the runway. Jan marvels at the Russian bladder; its capacity must be limitless. He is grateful for any facility, however primitive. In one airport, washroom users are requested not to drop paper in the toilet. A box outside the stall is available. At Leningrad, the airport is modern and confidently, Jan goes to find the men's washroom. Modern plumbing has been installed. However, the floor slopes towards the entrance and a series of sandbags guide water to an open drain that spills over into the lobby.

The ghosts of Tchaikovsky, Glazunov, Shostakovich, Prokofiev and many more preside in Leningrad. The hall is the biggest and most beautiful venue that they've encountered and is expected to be filled to capacity for the concert. After the rehearsal, Jan searches the empty theatre for a washroom. There is nothing backstage; he visits the foyer. It is very grand with a wide staircase leading to the balcony. No visible washrooms, not even a coat check. Eventually, backstage, Jan opens a closet and there, God be praised, is a toilet set in a space that can barely accommodate a spider monkey. Jan crouches down thankfully. *Spasibo.*

Although Leningrad is the last concert of the tour, the four string players backstage madly warm their fingers for the Rossini, never wanting to tempt providence. 'It's all very well for you guys,' says Linda Lee, 'I can't warm my fingers up. The piano's out there.' After the concert, with the

'Trout' and the Rossini behind them, the group is euphoric as they return to the hotel, only to find the lobby full of suitcases. Jan looks at a luggage label—it belongs to the LSO! The orchestra has arrived for a concert. Colin Davis greets Normsk like a long-lost friend on the stairway. The rest of the orchestra is either in the buffet or in the bar, except for Jack Long, whose cello has been damaged in transit. A local student is bringing an instrument for him.

'It will probably have metal strings. Gut sounds better, don't you think?' asks Jack, seated in the bar with Jan and Normsk.

'Do you remember,' Normsk begins, 'that night in the LSO when we opened with Rossini's overture to *La gazza ladra*? Colin Davis had prepped the sidedrum player to begin the opening roll as soon as Colin walked on stage at the Albert Hall. The entire audience stood up. They thought it was "God Save the Queen".'

In Moscow, they wait for Aeroflot to fly them home. The musicians have piled their instruments and luggage in the centre of the hall. A man driving a polishing machine across the lobby floor growls at them and then yells at Katerina. They move their luggage to one side hurriedly. Poor Katerina, but it is the final conflict for her. Every time they had checked in at airports, there had been great gesticulations over the luggage. The cello had to be strapped into a seat. The bass had to be strapped over three seats. *Niet, niet, niet!*

The musicians hand over all of their rubles to Katerina; the currency cannot be exchanged outside of the Soviet Union. As a final gesture, Linda Lee peels off her sweater and gives it to Katerina. They board the plane.

Dinner is a very pale roast chicken.

Phil prods it with a plastic fork. 'This chicken didn't fly the coop, it flew the oven.'

Jan, chewing his chicken, looks down on the receding lights of Moscow. 'The poultry may prove troublesome. Does anyone know, from *Sins of My Old Age*, the "Castor Oil Waltz"?'

Portrait: Linda Lee Thomas and Gerald Jarvis

Linda Lee Thomas is the most elegant of pianists. Her performances are a guarantee of perfection and tasteful presentation. Her attention to fine detail was honed when, as a director for Masterpiece Concerts, over many years, she enhanced her skills of production, ensuring audience loyalty.

Loyalty is another quality Linda Lee possesses. Gerald Jarvis succeeded Normsk as concertmaster of the VSO. After thirteen years, he moved to Japan to work, returning to New York each summer where he had a cabin at Chautauqua. Having become a guest professor at Musashino University in Japan, he contracted cancer and returned to Vancouver a very ill man. He wanted to see his Chautauqua cabin and hear the birds sing for the last time, so Linda Lee summoned the resources of the musical community to commission a private jet to take him there. Gerald died surrounded by his family soon after his arrival.

A few months later, Linda Lee arranged a memorial reception in Vancouver, inviting those who had contributed to Gerald's travel expenses. Gerald's family was there as well as many of Canada's musicians, including Sergiu Comissiona, then the conductor of the VSO. Several reminiscences of Gerald were shared.

'I remember when I worked with Gerald in London,' said Normsk. 'When not playing the violin, he smoked a Sherlock Holmes pipe. We were given to playing practical jokes on one another. At a rehearsal one morning, during a rapid passage, my fingers flying, I was alarmed to find smoke coming out of my jacket pocket. When I finally had a few bars' rest, I investigated to find Gerry's lit pipe.'

'I remember Gerry Jarvis for one superb moment,' said Jan when it was his turn. 'He and I were to adjudicate a competition with Ida Halpern, the ethnomusicologist. A table, complete with pencils, water jugs, glasses and a small bell had been set up at the back of the Vancouver Playhouse auditorium. The first child came out on stage to play, dressed in white, with black patent shoes and a bow in her hair. She sat down at the piano, adjusted the piano stool and looked up at us expectantly. At that moment, Gerry turned to Ida and whispered, 'Wouldn't you like to have the table a little nearer to you?' He shifted it. Little did he realize that, being in a raked theatre, the table was kept level by a couple of bricks placed under each of its front legs. There was this silent struggle as the table pitched forward. The water jug began sliding. Gerry tried to block it with an arm. The glasses were next. He tried to stop their passage forward. Ida grabbed the little bell. Its tinkle was the cue for the child to play. As she began, there was a hideous crash. At least it was not a resounding one; the Playhouse acoustics are as dead as Louis Riel.'

After the memorial reception, Linda Lee handed a bag of memorabilia to each of the parting guests. Included in the bag was a packet of birdseed signifying Gerald's avian interests. Linda Lee told Jan later, 'Of course, Mr and Mrs Comissiona come from Romania where I guess things are a little different. They rang me up to thank me for the memorabilia, adding that they found the cereal a little hard to chew.'

Portrait: Normsk

'You remember that the ruble was closed currency,' says Normsk. 'I had a couple of rubles left and bought a bowl of Solyanka soup at the airport restaurant.'

'Delicious, that soup,' says Jan. 'Nikolai Korndorf told me it's really a leftovers soup. He wrote me three wonderful cello pieces and his wife made the soup especially when we rehearsed.'

'When we got back to London from Russia that time,' Normsk continues, 'Jenny and I drove out of London and had lunch in some posh restaurant. Brown Windsor soup wasn't on the menu. We drank a nice claret. Later, with the wine coursing through our veins, we parked the car in a leafy lane and made love in the back seat. Twenty minutes later, I awoke with a sense of danger. I craned my neck to look out of the rear window. A man in a cap and uniform smoking a pipe was looking down on us. Behind him was a bus, full of schoolgirls. The bus couldn't get past our car.'

'A Leyland bus, naturally.'

Portrait: Elf

Travels to the Soviet Union include concerts in Scotland en route. Before the concert in Edinburgh, Jan collects Elspeth from the long-term care facility which overlooks rolling fields to Craigmillar Castle, where Mary Queen of Scots spent her first night after her return to Scotland from France. A cheerful nurse shows him how to assemble and disassemble the wheelchair. 'You can put it in the boot of the car,' she says, adding reassuringly, 'Don't worry, we've padded her up.'

After the concert, tea and shortbread are served in the hall. Elspeth is clearly proud and enjoying herself. As she chats to Linda Lee, her eyes are bright, an image that comes to mind a few weeks later when Jan receives the call informing him that she has died. As he puts down the receiver, Jan remembers accompanying her as she played the violin solo for the aria 'Have mercy, Lord' from the *St. Matthew Passion*.

Soon he's boarding the plane again.

INTERLUDE: HEIFETZ

The Soviet tour includes visits to Estonia and Lithuania. In Lithuania's capital, Vilnius, the morning after the concert, a women's committee takes the group on a short tour of the square which includes the cathedral with its famous silver boat hung from the ceiling.

Normsk remarks to Jan, 'Did you know that Heifetz was born in Vilnius?'

'Good Lord, I didn't know.'

Normsk turns to Katerina, the translator. 'Could you ask these ladies to show us the place where the violinist Jascha Heifetz was born?'

Katerina asks the women and they turn to each other, shaking their heads and muttering. She turns back to the musicians. 'They've never heard of Heifetz.'

Later, over dinner, everyone exclaims over this exchange. 'Heifetz has always been my ideal violinist, ever since I was a little boy. Back then I played on the BBC Children's Hour,' recollects Normsk, 'with Uncle Mac, Larry the Lamb and the rest of them. At the end the announcer said, "Thank you, Norman, that sounded very difficult".

'I don't know where I got my perfect pitch—probably from the family piano which must have been flat. My A is below 440, but everybody now plays at least 442, if not 446 in some orchestras. Painful! Boys at school began teasing me when they found out I played the violin. So I took up boxing. It was Sunday—Mass, Monday—boxing, every day—practising.

'We were raised Catholics and it became my turn to be an altar boy. I never knew quite what to do. One Sunday, I was the only boy who turned up. The priest faced away doing his genuflecting and at one point gave me his biretta. I wasn't sure what to do with it, so I laid it on the chair. The priest went on with his mumbo jumbo for the longest time. There seemed to be nothing for me to do so I sat down. He went on raising the Host and stuff, then made a motion to me. I wondered what he wanted. He snapped his fingers irritably behind his back. I realized that he wanted his hat to face the congregation. I looked around for it. I'd sat on it!

'The boxing and the practising, if not the attendance at Mass, paid off—I was eventually sent to Sascha Lasserson for violin lessons. He said I had a big talent and could be a great soloist. I always felt inside that this wasn't true. For one thing, I disliked practising long hours. Lasserson was a very popular teacher. He was a friend of Heifetz and his big hook was that he took his senior student each year to Heifetz's annual recital and would introduce him. Meanwhile, I got disenchanted with the Catholics and began courting Communism. Eventually it was my turn to hear the Great Man and after a wonderful recital, was taken round to the green room. There was a big crowd and I waited in line for my turn: "Oh Maestro, it was a marvellous concert." Then I couldn't think of anything to say. "Oh, er, could I have your autograph?" Heifetz nodded. I found a stump of a pencil in my jacket but no paper. But then I remembered, I had a book in my raincoat. I took it out and opened the flyleaf. "Here, Mr Heifetz." Heifetz looked disdainfully down at the spine, "*Das Kapital!* I couldn't possibly sign that," he said, and turned away. I slunk out and never had another violin lesson.'

THIRTY

Carter Two

Jan once again checks security at Langley Community Music School. Beside an offending open window, there is a framed pencil drawing of the eye-catching community hall on Hornby Island. The front door nestles within a gigantic, upturned tree stump. Jan's eye is also drawn to the facade made of log ends, the sod roof and the wide chimney made of boulders from near the beach.

Jan found the drawing in the grate of the chimney during one of the many summers the PSQ played on Hornby. For all its glorious facade, the hall in those days lacked air conditioning and in the heat, its rustic bathrooms emanated a fetid odour associated with septic tanks.

* 1987 *

On Hornby, the PSQ plays in white jackets with bow ties made by Sydney. Jan has a tailored jacket, streaked with age and lined as if it's a polar bear's coat. Coming off stage at intermission after the musical obstacle race of Elliott Carter's Second Quartet, he is soaking. Armed with a roll of paper towels, Jan strips to the waist and dries himself, but then the clothes, soaking wet, will have to be put back on for the second half of the concert. Playing Elliott Carter in these conditions is a slimming experience.

The stress of losing Normsk to the U of A Quartet and needing to replace two violinists accentuated Phil's and Jan's essential characters. In discussion, Phil made Eeyore-type prognostications; Jan's pragmatism was laced equally with unfounded optimism and despair. Together, they hit on the most practical solution—with Sydney and Bryan, they found a combination that could propel the PSQ through the next decade. Bryan King, bearded, bespectacled and the librarian of the VOO, is knowledge-able and essentially an intellectual; his enthusiasm and dedication to chamber music make him an ideal second fiddle.

Elliott Carter—evidently an astute observer of musicians in action—makes such stock characters the starting point for his Second

String Quartet. Sydney, the first violin, is virtuosic, taking off in flights of fancy unfettered it seems by Bryan, the second fiddle, the martinet, who with his repeated rhythms insists that the rules are observed. Phil, the violist, is dolefully expressive, while Jan, the romantic, ignoring the second violin, is instructed to accelerate or decelerate on whim. Each player has his own motivic units and arrangement of intervals. Each player will earn his spurs with a cadenza and a chance to lead a movement. Carter expresses this scenario with a mathematical precision which would make demands of Einstein's brain capacity.

After the concert, Leigh Cross stumps backstage. 'You boys may be soaking but you really nailed the Carter.' He flicks his program at a passing fly. 'I really heard the piece.'

Leigh is the reason the PSQ is playing on Hornby in the first place. One day, while Jan was teaching at the Vancouver Academy of Music, a man came in wanting cello lessons. Middle-aged, weathered, thickset and with his shock of black hair, he appeared to be a very vital person. When Leigh put bow to string at his first lesson, Jan realized that Leigh's hands were used to manual labour. As the academic year unfolded, Jan began an association with one of the world's most wonderful characters.

Leigh Cross spent his childhood travelling in the southern United States with the carnies, a collection of carnival shows and theatrical performances of a type that is probably extinct by now. He studied composition under Persichetti at Juilliard, learned the bagpipes with the Major Piper at Edinburgh Castle, palled around with Sandy Brown, the Scottish jazz clarinetist, as well as with Sydney Bechet in Paris. He ran a logging enterprise in the Pacific Northwest and saw active service in the Korean War. Disenchanted with American politics, Leigh, his wife and four small boys, close in age, moved to Canada. Looking for real estate in the newspaper, they found and bought a farm without quite realizing where it was situated—on Hornby Island.

They built a house, which according to island custom, began with grand plans that were never completely realized due to creeping disinterest. The kitchen is filled with oversized, industrial culinary tools, capable of feeding an army. The family sits down in the kitchen and, with boarding house stretch, demolishes bowls of salad, fresh bread and beef in cuts of unlikely shapes.

Leigh wanted to learn the cello so that he could play in a chamber group. After some weeks of lessons, he turned to Jan and said, 'Why don't you boys come to the island? I'll set up a concert for you.' At the time, Hornby Island had some six hundred residents in winter, swelling to more than two thousand in summer. The islanders built the unique hall as a community project.

The PSQ happily agreed to the suggestion, confident that Leigh would pull it off. The hall was full for the first concert in 1979, which was accompanied by an exhibit of local paintings. Hornby's residents include potters, photographers, painters and architects, evidenced by the unique variety of outhouses. Afterwards, Leigh said, 'You know, I think the island would support a series.'

And so the Hornby Island Festival was established in 1980. Every year following, in early August, the PSQ plays a week of concerts; series of Beethoven, Bartók, Haydn, Dvořák, second Viennese School and beyond.

'I think the audience is with you, even with the Carter,' says Leigh as Jan hangs up his wet jacket to dry for tomorrow night's concert. 'They've listened to all the Beethovens and the Bartóks. I think we should feature Carter again next year along with some of his contemporaries—Persichetti maybe.'

∗ ∗ ∗

The term used to describe Elliott Carter's language is generally 'metric modulation', a process of fractionalizing a beat—plus or minus—so the music can be propelled forward or slowed down. Metric modulation is not new to music—Gabrieli used it in his canzonas, transforming a duple beat to a triple, usually to a climax. Much in the same way, the stately pavane squeezes its main beat from duple to triple time and becomes a galliard; the old people retreat to the sidelines as the lively younger folks take to the floor.

Carter's use of metric modulation is integrated into his linear writing so one cannot describe an individual movement as either fast or slow, allegro or adagio. The pace is constantly shifting; the instrument you choose to listen to determines the music you hear. If you think the second violin has the beat, it only appears so. There is no fixed reference point. It's like floating around in the cosmos. In addition to this plethora of complications, Carter requests that members of the quartet sit farther apart than usual, tempting providence.

After an intense, hot morning of grappling with Elliott Carter, the PSQ jumps into the sea at Tribune Bay. The water is always cold. Around the corner is Little Tribune Bay. Leigh told them that nudity at Little Tribune was a tradition started by accident. A house had been built on the bay. Its owners—to try to keep the beach to themselves—bathed naked. This had boomeranged because it started a trend, encouraging all the locals to bathe in the buff. The owners had phoned up the police to complain. A police car was dispatched from Courtenay and arrived at Little Tribune two ferries later. Of course, the police had been spotted all the length of their trip and phones had been ringing. The police arrived and there was not a soul on the beach. (One time, the Quartet had gone down there, and respecting tradition, sat on a log in the buff until they heard somebody passing by say, 'Oh, that's the Purcell Quartet.' Eight legs crossed in unison.)

* * *

One year, Phil suggested that the PSQ give a chamber music workshop concurrently with the concerts. Leigh played in a group. The Yawneys came over from Victoria with a group plus their young children. Rosemarin, a violinist from Langley, came with a trio. There was a quartet from Vancouver that included René, the violist, a Dutchwoman. The cellist was Jan's Japanese student Kekko. She was a beautiful woman—delicate, quiet—and possessed exquisite manners.

Before the end of the week, everything had mostly fallen apart. It rained that year. Rosemarin arrived with her boyfriend in a very small camper. It became apparent that his interests lay elsewhere; Rosemarin didn't show for rehearsals, and the local children in the park watched dubiously as the camper rocked to and fro. The Yawney group was tenting. The rain defeated them by day two. They moved four infants, damp towels and soggy diapers, seeking refuge at the elementary school. Leigh said this was strictly *défendu* and the school board would have his hide if they found out, but with the rain pouring down, Leigh, for once, was a defeated man. It wasn't long before Kekko wanted a bath. She had come to the wrong place. She turned to Leigh for help.

'Oh, no problem. Come to our house,' he said cheerfully. Leigh and his family lived in medieval splendour. Leigh's bath, one that stood on claws, suffered from rust around the plug and the handles were missing on the taps. A pair of pliers was left on the soap dish to turn them on. Moreover, something nameless had happened to the drain below the toilet the day before, and Leigh had removed a floorboard behind it to start an archeological dig. Kekko came up for her bath and afterwards thanked Leigh politely as she left. Later, Jan found out that Kekko had taken one look at the bathroom, sat on the toilet seat, ran the taps and made some splashing noises, and emerged unbathed.

To add insult to injury, things were not going well in Kekko's group. They were learning Beethoven's 'Harp' Quartet. Three of the quartet members were Asian students who spoke together in a language René couldn't understand. On the second day, suspecting that they might be criticizing her, she yelled at them in Dutch. After lunch, on day three, it was Jan's turn to coach them. They arrived at the Scherzo. They played through to the Trio, which begins with a cello solo. Kekko played the solo through to the double bar. René turned to Jan and said, 'Don't you think the cellist rushes there?'

This was plainly not just a loaded question, it was a nuclear device. Jan was saved from considering his options. Kekko got up, slowly laid her cello down, unscrewed her bow and shut her music. 'I no play with you.' She put her cello in its case and folded her music stand. 'I no play with you.' She put on her coat. Everyone looked at her mutely. As she went to the door, Jan got up and followed her out. They sat on a log together for a while looking at the sea. 'I no play with her. I go home.' Jan tried to dissuade her, but her mind was made up. 'Ferry tonight.' At the end of the week, Phil in his defence attempted the high road. 'You see,' he said to the groups. 'It's not easy playing in chamber music ensembles and it's less easy staying in one.' The workshop project died in delivery.

Another year, Lindsay, Jan's former student, came over to Hornby for the final concert. She asked Leigh if she could put up her tent in a field. 'Sure,' said Leigh. 'Go to the field on the hillside. There are no cattle there.' Lindsay set up the tent and attended the concert. The next morning she heard noise. She peered out of her tent. Sewage was running down the hill making straight for her tent. Leigh had forgotten that, in order to enrich his field, he had asked the septic tank truck to make deliveries up there.

INTERLUDE: PETER OF VENICE IN CUBA

Leigh has island fever. He's tired of farming and fixing things. He wants to come to the mainland. With a successful festival established on Hornby Island, he's interested in becoming the PSQ's manager just as the quartet is feeling the economic squeeze from SFU.

At SFU, the Department of Fine Arts has a new head—Grant Strate's expertise is in dance. He has a fresh vision for the department. In the time of budget restraints, the resident quartet is the most visible thing moving on Burnaby Mountain. They are called into Grant's office. Jan looks with objective interest at Grant's body language as he stakes out his position. Every time Grant talks about the university, he points his forefinger down and makes circular movements. Every time he mentions the PSQ, he chops the air with the side of his palms. The Canada Council will continue their grant, on condition that the PSQ hire a representative. No manager, no money. Leigh takes it on.

At Vancouver's Expo '86, Cuba has a pavilion. Leigh cultivates a relationship with the Cuban delegation and hatches a master plan. The PSQ has received an invitation to play for the opening of the new Canadian embassy in Mexico City. They will precede this with a Beethoven cycle in Sarasota, then go on to Cuba and after a couple of concerts fly on to Mexico. Leigh hires a small plane to take them from Sarasota to Cuba. This involves notifying the embassies of both countries of the proposed flight plan. Failure to do so probably will result in being shot out of the skies.

After a week in Sarasota, they depart for Cuba on Easter Sunday. The Sarasota airstrip seems deserted. They wait in the sun for a while. Presently, their American pilot turns up. He looks like one of the marching generals from *Evita*. He is unnaturally slim, his brilliant white uniform set off by large black shades and a trim black moustache. They board the Cessna aircraft and it takes off. Half an hour into the journey, the engine begins thumping. 'Trouble!' calls the pilot. 'We'll have to turn back.'

Thirty minutes later, they are back at the Sarasota airstrip. Leigh later maintains that the pilot never intended to go to Cuba. Leigh, who's flown planes, says that you can deliberately create engine knocking and complains to the company about it. For now, he has a crisis to solve. It's Leigh's finest hour. Within an hour and a half, on Easter Sunday, he's found another American company, plane and pilot. He phones Washington and Havana and the flight path remains open. They set forth again. All this excitement goes to Phil's bladder. 'Is there a toilet on the plane?' he asks. It turns out the back seat has a lid, which can be lifted. Phil is in fact sitting on a commode, a *chaise percée*.

Landing in Havana is somewhat unnerving. There's a large airplane wreck beside the runway. Jan suspects it must have crashed several years earlier. The plane taxis to a stop. The pilot gets out and is immediately surrounded by men in battle fatigues with rifles. He's jostled off in the direction of the control tower. The musicians—allowed to go through customs on the other side—survey an empty terminal. The customs men return to their lounge to watch American baseball on TV. (Leigh will later discover that the pilot was incarcerated in his Cessna for three days. He didn't have enough fuel to return home and the Cuban authorities took their time to release him.)

The PSQ was to have been met at the airport and driven to their hotel but the person assigned has long since given up and gone home. The plan was to have dinner at the Canadian consulate. They take a taxi to the hotel and Leigh phones to explain why they will be late. 'No matter,' says the consul, 'take your time.' The Canadian consulate is worthy of a Graham Greene novel. The iron grille gates swing behind them. There is the foliage, the lawn, the swimming pool and beyond—sitting on the patio—is the consul in white ducks, and his wife, knitting. A drink would be welcome before dinner? Margaritas? Would anybody like to swim? An ancient factotum shuffles out with a tray.

Mysterious officials—Jan is never quite sure who they represent—introduce the PSQ to Dolores, their Cuban interpreter, who'd shown around Dizzie Gillespie the previous week. Dolores leads them down Havana's picturesque streets to the concert hall where they play a program of uneasy bedfellows—quartets by Haydn, Dvořák and the Mexican composer Manuel Ponce.

The following morning, Dolores takes them to the TV station. They're to be interviewed on the morning show. Dolores acts as translator. The interviewer seizes on the visual aspect of the quartet's instruments: Are they old? Are they valuable? Sydney is the proud possessor of a Guarneri violin made by Peter of Venice, who only made forty instruments. This one is dated 1695. Sydney holds it up for the camera with a broad smile of satisfaction.

Shortly before the PSQ leaves for Mexico, two men—the still-mysterious organizers of the Cuban trip—introduce themselves at the hotel. The government is not very pleased with Dolores, they confide. 'But why?' choruses the PSQ.

'She makes mistakes,' says one of the men. 'For instance, that TV show, when Mr Humphreys held up his violin, she told the viewers that the instrument was made in 1965.'

THIRTY-ONE

Opera Verismo

Jan and Sue, on holiday in Lucca, Italy, come upon a bronze statue of Puccini in a small square by the via San Paolini. Lucca is the birthplace of Puccini. A few hours earlier, at the open window of their hotel, Jan heard orchestral sounds reminiscent of *Tosca* coming from the Puccini museum, the house of the composer's birth. The statue of Puccini portrays the composer deep in thought, reclining in a chair with his legs crossed. Stepping closer to the statue, Jan notices that Puccini is holding a cigarette.

* 1967 *

Fausto Cleva, in a rage, bangs his head against the concrete wall of the pit and climbs off the podium into the front row for yet another cigarette break. He's in Vancouver from the Met as guest conductor for a production of Puccini's *Girl of the Golden West* for the Vancouver Festival. Jan is leading the cello section of a pickup orchestra—VSO and CBC Orchestra members, as well as other freelance musicians—established just for this event. (The Vancouver Opera Orchestra (VOO) will be established a decade later. Jan will join this orchestra in 1981 and become its principal cello in 1982.)

It's Jan's first time as leader and he's terrified. The whole orchestra is unnerved because this set of parts has never been played and the wrong notes have not been corrected. They're playing the offending notes as Ricordi published them, which triggers numerous tantrums from Maestro Cleva.

Between stubs, there is a personal moment when Cleva, mid-performance, leans over to Jan, clucks his tongue to get his attention, and says *sotto voce*, 'This whole opera is one big wonderful tone poem.'

∗ ∗ ∗

Puccini's undisputed masterpieces are the earlier operas—*La Bohème*, *Madame Butterfly* and *Tosca*. Along with Mozart's *Marriage of Figaro*,

Don Giovanni and *The Magic Flute*, they have risen to the top of the heap and rescue opera companies around the world from bankruptcy. *Tosca* has special significance for cellists; the final act features a cello quartet—the first cello scaling scary heights—while Cavaradossi writes his farewell letter to Tosca. Normally, Jan in the pit pays no attention to plot. He's intent on following singers and not drowning them out while reading music lit by a 25-watt bulb.

On gala occasions, the orchestra sometimes emerges from the pit. For the occasion of the VOO accompanying Luciano Pavarotti in 2006, a stage is built over one end of the hockey arena in Vancouver's GM Place. Jan arrives at the rehearsal to the sound of hammering. Pavarotti's conductor, a timid man, has been sent ahead to rehearse the orchestra. On the afternoon of the second day, men in trench coats begin to file in to the otherwise empty arena. Stylish young women also take seats. A high stool is placed in front of the second violin section. The Great Man can't be far off. As the orchestra rehearses, an enormous man walks slowly up to the stool. He wears a smock outside his pants that suggests he's been painting the outside walls. He has an apple in his hand. The conductor harangues the second violins over intonation. Pavarotti faces them and growls. Several women at the back of their section cross their legs in a hurry. Pavarotti chomps into his apple and, still facing the second violins, begins to sing as bits of apple fly over the section.

Having built the stage, the sponsor's prime preoccupation is to provide sustenance. Pavarotti and his tiny conductor share a green room. Caterers wheel in trolleys with several papers pegged to the sides: *Ravioli Caprese, Risotto di Pesci, Scallopini Milanese, Pesce alla Griglia* and *Bistecca alla Pizzaila*. 'Goodness!' thinks Jan. 'They must be eating for at least three.'

Nor are the slaking vocal chords overlooked. At the back of the stage where the celebrities come on or off, Jan and his cello pass by a gazebo with tables of juices, grapes, plums: 'You musta supporta the voice.' The crowd is satisfied as they leave the stadium to encounter traffic chaos. Rather than join the mess, Jan and his colleagues head to the pub for a beer and scotch eggs before hunting for their cars.

* * *

Traditionally on opening night, the Vancouver Opera holds a reception on stage after the performance. VIPs mingle with the company and crew.

Kim Campbell—during her brief tenure as prime minister—attends such a function. The orchestra, dressed in black, encircle the drinks and eats first; they have a tactical advantage over those who have to hang up their costumes. There is a flurry of movement towards Jan. Men in suits report that Kim Campbell wants to meet him. Kim Campbell once played the cello; the request seems plausible. They escort Jan across the stage to where Kim is talking to a group of people. The two men cough politely and introduce Jan. She turns, looks Jan up and down and says, 'But you're the wrong Jan Hampton!' This confirms everything that Jan suspects about himself—he's been the wrong Hampton all his life!

The orchestra is the servant to the stage. Its job is not to be noticed. The musicians, camouflaged in the gloom below, cannot see the stage and have little idea what goes on up there. Playing *Fidelio*, Chris Catchpole, sharing Jan's music stand, hears the rattle of prison chains: 'Must be near the end of the opera. They're about to take the dog for a walk.'

Since Handel's time, opera companies have been the source of scandals, gossip, speculation and bankruptcies. Operas were the pop culture of their time, occupying much the same position as movies do today. Opera corpses litter the road of history and impresarios surveying the battlefield today can only confidently present about a dozen operas without risking their shirts. It is tempting to inject some novelty into a production that was last presented only three seasons ago.

But novelty can backfire—the Vancouver Opera Association (VOA) loses as many patrons as it receives accolades for staging *Carmen* as a guerrilla piece with the toreador dressed like Elvis Presley, a contradiction in 'bull'. In the fashion of the moment, an advisory on 'some nudity' is printed in the press release for another production. The stage manager rushes three young men in their dressing gowns from the green room to backstage. Effort is made to protect their privacy by providing screens while they take off their dressing gowns. Then they cavort across the stage in front of three thousand people. At a line of ten basins in the green room, the men's chorus, like cattle feeding at the trough, put brown makeup on any exposed skin while in the anteroom, the three young men dab whitening on their wiggerwaggers.

There are operas, such as *Eugene Onegin* and *Salome,* whose emotional intensity drips off the stage into the pit. More tangible things can drip off the stage and the workman's safety board insists that a wire mesh be extended from the footlights over the pit. Apart from helmets, toupées, swords and snowflakes, they must have imagined the spectre of John the Baptist's head rolling off its platter. Nevertheless, you can't control every eventuality. Bob Meyer, the VOO's former principal bassist, remembers playing *Aida* at the Hammersmith Palais. An elephant on stage began to pee. The urine began its epic journey toward the pit orchestra and a uniformed guy rushed in with a bucket to catch the flow before it inundated the musicians. You have to be a quick thinker in opera.

The VSO's music director, Bramwell Tovey, guest conducts the VOA's production of *Die Fledermaus* in 2002. The performance procedure is usually the same—opening is Saturday night and the next performance is Tuesday. In the intervening weekend, Bramwell visits Toronto for a family birthday. On the trip he catches the stomach flu. On the Tuesday night, Jan routinely arrives in the pit early to pick up any Styrofoam coffee cups, water bottles, magazines (brass section) and sheets of last minute directions to the orchestra. A stagehand is tying a bucket to a length of rope by the podium. 'Why the bucket?'

'Oh, the conductor is sick. Can't hold anything down. This is just in case.' The orchestra files in. The viola section sits to the conductor's right with Phil as leader sitting under the bucket. It hangs over Phil the whole evening like Damocles's sword. Luckily, Bramwell has no need to use the bucket, but Phil probably feels the need for champagne more than the characters on the stage.

Profile: O Canada

The Vancouver Opera has a performance the evening of the second referendum on Quebec sovereignty. In anticipation of the result, which is to be announced minutes before the QET's curtain is to rise, the conductor, David Agler, asks Jan to find and distribute the music for 'O Canada'. The decision on whether to play it or not vacillates around the administration. David Agler thinks it should be played anyway, whatever the result. By the time Cam Trowsdale, the concertmaster, walks into the pit and the orchestra is tuning up, there's still no decision.

At the last moment, word comes from the conductor that the orchestra will not be playing it. The manager feels that it might offend the diva, who is Québécoise. The lights are lowered and in the twilight zone, the announcement is made over the PA that the referendum has failed to pass. Somewhere in the balcony someone begins singing 'O Canada'. Gradually, the whole audience joins. Anne-Elise, on her piccolo, is the first in the orchestra to find the pitch and the rest of the orchestra follow her. The anthem ends in a crescendo of harmony.

INTERLUDE: PHANTOM

In *The Phantom of the Opera*, to alleviate eleventh-hour panic, 'swings' are employed. These are singers who can take on any part at a moment's notice. They laze around the shared green room nonchalantly, reading books. Jan, who is employed for *Phantom*'s five-month run in Vancouver, marvels at their coolness. Applying the phantom's makeup is a complicated and lengthy process. On matinee days, the phantom doesn't bother to take it off before the evening performance. Between shows, he eats pizza through half a face. One show, the office finds out late in the afternoon that the phantom has suddenly taken ill. They ring his substitute. No answer. The swing wanders in at his usual time with his book. He's pounced upon by the costume and makeup people. 'While you're having that stuff plastered on your face, you have to collect your wits to play the longest, most complicated part in the production,' thinks Jan, looking up from his datebook.

The music, though not difficult, has sequential traps and everybody is intensively alert and nervous for each premiere. But after a few weeks, Jan catches himself thinking of something else, like what he's going to make for dinner. Alarmed, he wrenches his mind back to the music. As the weeks wear on, so the mind wanders further. At the end of the first month, the brain functions in two places at once. He then realizes that probably everybody in the theatre is going about their tasks, zombie-like, on two planes, from ushers to computer technicians, all thinking about dinner. If a catastrophe overcomes a performance, will everybody snap out of their somnolent state?

'Well,' says Sue, who played with the *Phantom* orchestra from Alaska to Hawaii, 'it happens. A family bereavement took a phantom out of circulation and a substitute phantom was flown from London. He arrived at the last minute for his makeup but the performance began on time. Remember that business in the second act—"The phantom is everywhere"? The proscenium is built to include a gondola over the middle of the stage from which the phantom appears momentarily. To get up there, the phantom is required to climb a vertical ladder bolted to the theatre walls, then crawl along the catwalk horizontally to get into the gondola. They get to this point in the show and the phantom shakes his head. He's not going up there. He suffers from vertigo. Two stagehands jostle him up the ladder. On the catwalk, one stagehand lights the phantom's way holding a flashlight in his mouth. In the scuffle to get the phantom into the gondola on time, the flashlight falls from the stagehand's mouth, centre stage.'

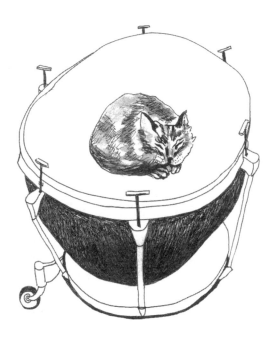

THIRTY-TWO

Brandenburgs

* 1993 *

The CBC Orchestra is to record all six of Bach's *Brandenburg Concertos* in Toronto with a live concert in Roy Thomson Hall as a warm-up. To the principal players' chagrin, the head office decides that all the soloists will be hired in Toronto. Is this a cost-saving measure? Jan speculates—he's heard that the annual orchestra budget is equal to that of a one half-hour TV show. In any case, Jan suspects this won't sit well with the orchestra's conductor, Mario Bernardi, known for his short fuse. Having rehearsed the strings at his leisure in Vancouver, Mario will be required to prepare the entire concert in a single, four-hour rehearsal with the Toronto soloists.

Jan's hunch is right. At Roy Thomson Hall, Mario—worried about the time constraint—asks the continuo players, which of course includes Jan, to rehearse the slow movements for an hour ahead of the orchestra call, extending the whole rehearsal to five hours. They begin the slow movement of Concerto no. 6. This concerto is scored for low instruments—two violas rather than two violins leading the pack. Mario sets a brisk walking pace for the slow movement. Rivka Golani, her long red hair as burnished as her viola, enters at a much slower tempo. 'Too slow,' Mario snaps.

Jan groans inwardly. They are two minutes into a five-hour rehearsal. They begin again, Mario setting the same brisk tempo and again, Rivka, her hair falling over her viola, comes in slower. Mario throws his baton down on his music stand. 'Well, really! If you play like that I'll walk off the platform ... you wouldn't make love that slowly?!'

Rivka looks levelly at him from her viola. 'That's the way I like it,' she says softly.

'Oh well, if that's the case,' says Mario, quickly picking up his baton. The rest of the afternoon passes without incident. It's not often that Mario gets bested.

In appointing Mario as conductor rather than music director, the CBC reserves the right to dictate the programming as well as the dates of recording. Down the years, as CBC's support for its house orchestra wanes, Mario's lack of artistic influence is a contentious point raised by him from time to time. Mario is a wonderful studio conductor. He has an infallible ear for intonation, balance and an unerring sense of rhythm and tempo. When making CDs, the routine is to rehearse and then record a template. Any mistakes are corrected on subsequent takes. Sometimes, a passage hasn't quite satisfied Anton, the producer, who will ask for another take in the dying minutes of a recording session. There might be several short passages up for review and the final session might occur days later. Jan always marvels at how Mario can pluck the appropriate tempo out of thin air.

Back at Roy Thomson Hall as the orchestra performs Concerto no. 6, anxiety over conflicting opinions about tempo and Mario's tantrums does not spoil Jan's delight in playing the slow movement, where the cello and the bass step in tandem—two cello notes to the bassist's one, creating occasional consecutive dissonances—a grinding reminder of one's mortality under the heavenly beauty unfolding above.

* * *

Bach, hardly a mere mortal—composer, violinist, violist and harpsichordist—led the orchestra for all six concertos for their first performance in Cöthen. The Third Concerto uniquely divides the strings into groups of three and its two movements are the lexicon of every string player from high school age onward. Its optimistic rhythmic thrust provides as much joy to the player as it does to the listener and while, it seems, it is subjected to every kind of interpretation—outrageous or otherwise—Bach's music, as always, wins out. The tempestuous character of the last movement runs its course to the very last eighth note of the piece. A ritardando and a pause have to be engineered, though Bach doesn't indicate them, and the awkwardness usually precludes repeating the second half.

(Jan remembers playing the Third Concerto in the LSO at a Promenade Concert in the Albert Hall. Basil Cameron, conducting, suddenly remembered he'd neglected to tell the musicians that for broadcast timings, this repeat needed to be played. In the penultimate bar, cupping hands to his mouth, he shouted, 'Repeat!' There was a squealing of horsehair on gut and a very audible catastrophe was averted. Jan supposed afterwards that during broadcast, heads must have looked up all over the British Isles.

Simon Streatfeild remembers when he was principal viola of the LSO playing the Third Concerto under Casals on his final visit to England. 'We rehearsed the first movement exhaustively,' said Simon. 'Casals kept stopping and saying in a quavery voice, "No, no, gentlemen—de de doo, de de doo." A few minutes later we would stop again, "Gentlemen, no, no, it's de de doo, de de doo." We never did understand what he meant, we just played it as usual.')

The Breitkopf & Härtel editions of the *Brandenburg*s have been worthily editorialized for performance. The bowings usual for Baroque music are simply articulated except for a few isolated bars where slurs have crept in. Jan used to think it was publishers' oversight until, years later, when he was playing Concerto no. 3 in the CBC Radio Orchestra, Jiggy told the strings that the slurs meant 'bowed vibrato'. Jan wonders why he hadn't figured that out, as they so often occur on prolonged, repeated pedal notes.

∗ ∗ ∗

Jiggy, Mario's predecessor, conducts the CBC Orchestra for a few brief, inspiring and disruptive years, from 1980–1982. His most important legacy is to give the orchestra—its string section at least—the capability of performing earlier music in the manner that its composers conceived it. For some years after his departure, the CBC, wanting to extend this legacy, invites a number of distinguished practitioners to Vancouver to work with the orchestra. These guests are usually profiled in live concerts. Not much music is needed in a period performance—there is so much tuning up between the pieces. Between the vulnerabilities of gut strings and the fact that the instruments are tuned half a tone down, nothing ever quite settles. Like inflation, the fact that A rises in pitch over the decades is a mysterious phenomenon. Handel's A was actually our G-sharp. Henry Wood established A at 450 vibrations a second when he started the Promenade Concerts. Now orchestras are closing in on B-flat.

Harpsichords are particularly tiresome. In the cause of authenticity, they are built with wooden frames. They have to be treated like children with bad adenoids—acclimatize them in the hall at least twenty-four hours ahead of time, put a blanket over them at night, tune them in the afternoon of the evening concert, tune them up again before the house is open and touch them up again during intermission. At one concert, the harpsichordist, who lived her life at A 415, forgot to come out with the rest of the orchestra, rendering the exercise, at least up to the intermission, pointless. (There was a reverse situation at about the same time. The CBC Orchestra played Menotti's *The Unicorn, the Gorgon and the Manticore.* It calls for nine players only, omitting the bassoon. Chris Millard, the bassoonist, walked out on stage with his wind colleagues, sat down and asked himself, 'Why am I here?' He sat out the performance and bowed with the rest of them at the end.)

Rehearsals with a distinguished practitioner follow a familiar pattern. The guest arrives with a sheaf of music. The availability of early music has become a cottage industry. An enthusiast has uncovered a rare gem deep in the archives of Versailles or Hampton Court. The score is enlarged, copied, then eviscerated to make single parts, enlarged and copied again. All the original paper blemishes are now enlarged and are as black as the notes, which in any case were very spidery. The music given out looks like aerial photographs of the bombing of Dresden. There is a large improvisatory component to the rehearsals. Dynamics are suggested, then amended. Notes are shortened with dots or lengthened with lines. Stress marks and swung rhythms are also added. At the end of the rehearsals, the notes are buried under interpretive marks.

Frans Brüggen, the great Dutch recorder player and conductor, pays a visit. His pronounced jaws, those of a natural wind player, suggest the look of a Neanderthal. He insists on Mozart's *Eine Kleine Nachtmusik* at A 415, two thirds the speed, plus all the repeats. The string players—who can perform this work in their sleep—find the rehearsals unbearable. All Brüggen's adjectives are violent. 'You have to be brutal,' he admonishes, 'brutal!' At the end of the rehearsals, a second violinist raises her hand: 'Mr Brüggen, the last eighth, two bars before letter C, hasn't got a dot on it.'

'Hasn't got a dot on it? Jesus Christ!' he shouts with his best gutteral Dutch accent.

The most refreshing distinguished practitioner is Monica Huggett. She is completely at ease playing her Baroque violin. Her bow strokes are assured and vigorous on the gut strings. She has a sense of style that is forthright and persuasive and a familiar sense of humour to go with it. Introducing a late piece by Handel to the orchestra: 'He wrote it at the end of his career before he was overcome by wanker's doom.'

Not long after the Toronto recording session, the six *Brandenburg Concertos* appear on a double CD as part of the CBC SM 5000 series. As such, they are safely in the public domain, which one cannot say of many other CBC studio recordings such as Jiggy's memorable reminiscences in 1982 of Percy Grainger. It was hoped after transmission that the recording could be transcribed to a CD. For contractual reasons, this proved impossible. One hopes, in the process of CBC's very own cultural revolution, that its mandarins haven't thrown all its cultural babies out with the bathwater and that this broadcast has been left undisturbed in the archives. In the CBC's race to the bottom, one wonders whether even the archives will survive the pillaging.

Karen Wilson is a creative producer of the CBC Orchestra, full of ideas. She is also an astute politician, who at the beginning of the new century fends off the orchestra's adversaries as they gather in greater numbers. At last she arranges a meeting with Janet Lee, CBC Music Director, and with Mario, at an Italian restaurant in Vancouver. Mario orders risotto. The waiter brings a plate of fried rice and sets it before him. He peers at it with mild distaste. Turning to Janet Lee he says, 'Either the CBC should fund the orchestra adequately or just kill it. It shouldn't starve it to death!'

The CBC takes the third option—they squeeze the life out of the orchestra and in one final machete chop, finish off the last house orchestra in North America after the orchestra's seventieth birthday.

Profile: Max

With Karen Wilson, the CBC Vancouver Orchestra experiences some of its finer moments, none more so than its association with Max—Sir Peter Maxwell Davies. With the help of David Lemon, an entrepreneur whose depth of musical knowledge would shame many a professional musician, the CBC commissions Max's oratorio *Job*. This is recorded live at the premiere and the orchestra stays for one hour after the last of the public leaves the auditorium, recording a couple of patches which are to be inserted. Later, the CD is released on the Collins label.

At a reception after the recording, Jan says to Max, 'I'm amazed that you could write a seventy-minute work for orchestra, chorus and soloists in such a short time. Didn't David only initiate the project three months ago?'

'Oh, it's quite easy,' answers Max. 'I always write in pencil so I can erase right away and of course I do the transpositions straight into the score.' *Oi yoi.*

Max spends half his year on the Island of Hoy in the Orkneys. Here, he lives without a piano or a phone in an old crofter's cottage overlooking the North Atlantic.

At the reception, Max continues, 'Once a week, I walk down the cliff edge to the wharf where Macbrayne steamers bring in provisions. When I return, loaded down with my backpack full of groceries and a bottle of whisky, I get repeatedly mobbed by large seabirds which fly straight at my forehead and then veer upward just at the last second. Unnerving.'

INTERLUDE: DEMISE, 2008

Jan, principal cello of the VOO, is at home practising the cello quartet from Verdi's *Nabucco*, when the phone rings.

'Gene here.'

Gene Ramsbottom's quiet voice conveys danger. 'The CBC has called a special meeting of the orchestra. Can you be there? Georgian Court Hotel at ten tomorrow morning. Bring as many as you can—we need visible support. I think this is it.'

Jan immediately phones Colin Miles. As head of the CMC, Colin is a passionate advocate for Canadian music and musicians. Colin's reaction is immediate. 'The media is sure to be there,' he says. 'We need as many musicians as we can get. I'll get the office to handle the phoning.'

The next morning, driving to town, Jan reflects that this surprisingly dry fall day may mark the end of months of rumour and speculation. Jan feels anxiety; although he retired from the CBC a few years ago, his involvement as principal cello and contractor lasted nearly three decades and he is well aware of strife in the corridors of power. Its trickle-down effects call on much diplomacy as musicians feel the economic impact.

Driving along, Jan anticipates the scene he is about to witness. The musicians will confront a *fait accompli*; the mortal blow has already been dealt in a boardroom in Toronto. Vancouver musicians have been expecting this—the union will whimper, the media will be engaged, there will be public outrage and there will be attempts to save the orchestra. The VOO underwent similar scenes when the VOA wanted to merge its orchestra with the VSO. But in that case, the orchestral members won, becoming a certified orchestra with an exclusive contract and a corresponding meltdown of the opera administration.

Austerity has settled on the city, thinks Jan as he drives past the QET with no billboard advertising a show. The Georgian Court lobby is crowded with musicians and media people. 'The orchestra members are meeting in there,' long-time *Sun* music critic Lloyd Dykk informs Jan. 'The rest of us weren't allowed in.'

Jan notices Colin Miles grandstanding to a television camera. 'Consecutive budget squeezes on the CBC are reducing its impact on all Canadians.' Colin does indignant very well, with a booming voice. 'The loss of the CBC Orchestra would be catastophic to the Vancouver cultural scene. It's not just the orchestral players but the support of conductors, young soloists and composers that would be compromised. That's unacceptable.'

Karen Wilson, who has recently been a casualty herself in the CBC shuffle, turns to Jan. 'This will be the *coup de grâce* of the freelance musician. Membership in the opera orchestra won't supply the lifebelt needed—the VOA hasn't extended its season in all the years I've lived here.'

The door opens. First out is Phil, looking very Eeyore-ish, followed by Bryan King. 'The deed's done,' he says dryly to the general assembly. Bryan, with his clipped speech, also does indignant well. Gene comes up to Jan and says, still talking quietly, 'Our next concert at the Orpheum will be our last.' George Zukerman, on Jan's other side, says, 'It's been coming for thirty years.' The company breaks up into smaller groups, spilling from the small lobby out into the street. Heilwig von Königslöw, violinist and long-time teacher at Langley Community Music School (LCMS), rolls her eyes as she passes Jan on the way to her van. She's hurrying to her first student. She'll teach the rest of the day.

As Jan returns to the parking lot, he glances back at his friends and colleagues still huddled on the street in small groups, turning up the collars of their raincoats against the chill of a Vancouver fall.

THIRTY-THREE

Verklärte Nacht

Jan in his seventies, sitting at the back of Langley Municipality's town hall, eyes the agenda and sighs; LCMS business is scheduled last. Jan and the board president, Tom Scottnicki, are in for a long evening. First, the council has to recognize the local Scout troop, who march in with shirts, flags, scarves and toggles. Decades pass. Finally, the mayor reads the correspondence to the council. 'We've received a letter from the dire …' He hesitates, tries again. 'From the diok …' He clears his throat, tries again, 'From the diocese,' he manages. Jan thinks that for some of these politicians, trying to negotiate polysyllabic words is like trying to spell a word like diarrhea. The council moves on to fret over horse trails and then to sewage lines.

Jan wakes up suddenly to hear somebody asking for the vote on the motion, whatever it is. Passed. At last Tom Scottnicki gets up to speak.

* 2001 *

A young journalist interviews Jan in Langley. 'Well, if you've had such a stellar career,' she asks, 'what the hell are you doing in Langley?'

Jan has to think fast. 'Music is a hard mistress, at every turn needing stewards. Perhaps the young need the most stewardship of all. I owe the Sir James Caird Foundation for a lot of my training—I can repay that debt to the generation embarking on the journey.'

It could be Langley or Lithuania; talent can be awakened anywhere. LCMS was once a cluster of small wooden buildings, which was—by the time of their imminent demise—the largest collection of mould and mildew in western Canada. As more students moved within its walls, which suffered flood, fire and pestilence in turn, it became increasingly urgent to replace the old buildings with a larger, modern structure. After a number of false starts, the president of the LCMS board, Tom Scottnicki, began to chart the murky waters of fundraising and developing political support. Situated in a rural community more interested in horse feed than horsehair, LCMS became the victim of two rival municipalities whose political myopia impeded its progress. Successive LCMS board members attended nearly two decades of mind-blisteringly boring meetings to try to prepare the council for recognition of the school's need.

Tom, the director of an accounting firm in Langley, has a mind like a steel trap. With his political acumen and technical guidance, LCMS finally moved into its beautiful, capacious new quarters in 2001. Unlike the Vancouver Community Music School, which changed its title to 'Academy', the LCMS's success, it feels, owes its allegiance to the community and this value drives some of the school's policies. LCMS was established to create an environment where students, teachers and performers would interact and in so doing, would be a guarantee of a standard of excellence. Langley's disadvantage is that it stands on the perimeter of Vancouver's cultural scene. In spite of this, it has endeavoured to develop programs that bring it an audible voice in the mosaic of Canadian music education. Thus, along with its private lessons and enrichment programs, it has paid attention to the performance and commissioning of Canadian music and the support of Canadian and international artists by running two concert series.

The bigger performance space—the Rose Gellert Hall—has accommodated a number of enterprising projects which reflect a rising standard of performance. Its inauguration was celebrated with a commission of Michael Conway Baker's *A Challenge for the Future* played by the Vancouver Youth Orchestra. In subsequent years, under the guidance of Heilwig von Königslöw, the LCMS string orchestra performed masterpieces of the string repertoire, from Vaughan Williams's *Tallis Fantasia* to Tippett's *Fantasia Concertante on a Theme Of Corelli* and on to Schoenberg's *Verklärte Nacht*. This is to mention a few of the artistic highlights which are the legacy of children who entered the baby program, graduating though the Orff and Suzuki programs to become technically proficient in their late teens, able to play anything put before them. After the performance of *Verklärte Nacht* at the opening of a Suzuki Institute held at LCMS, one of the visiting teacher trainers remarked how extraordinary it was, that these students who had begun their training as toddlers learning by rote could as teenagers tackle such repertoire. Schoenberg's post-Romantic language challenges the most seasoned professional.

* * *

Whether Schoenberg will become a footnote in music history like Stamitz or whether he will acquire the status of a J.S. Bach, posterity, taking its good time, will tell.

Verklärte Nacht, a one-movement work written in three weeks, is based on a poem by Richard Dehmel in which a woman confesses to her lover that she carries another man's child. The man reflects and forgives and the couple walks from darkness into light. While the music is programmatic, exceptional in chamber music, Schoenberg dwells on the transfigured emotions of the couple. The string writing is dense, making considerable demands on the performer. The musical language is post-Wagnerian, though at its reception, the work's chromaticism was nevertheless controversial. In particular, one chord—an inverted ninth—was deemed to be non-existent by the Vienna Music Society, which rejected the work.

* * *

Through the classroom door, Jan hears Heilwig rehearsing *Verklärte Nacht*, admonishing the violas. 'You've got to listen for the triplets. Always listen to the faster notes. Write an arrow going forward. Put it in now. What? You forgot your pencil? Play E-flat melodic minor scale!' Now it's Jan's turn to roll his eyes.

For thirty-six weeks of the year a visitor can walk through the school's corridors to a cacophony of Beethoven's 'Für Elise', Vivaldi's *Spring*, Squire's 'Tarantella' or one of Finzi's *Bagatelles*. At a supreme moment in their lives, it is to be hoped that the students realize that all their efforts are not in vain. Music will govern their inner lives and much of their social lives, bringing them elevation, consolation, love, satisfaction and baptism into a realm that really can't be described. Stewardship of the young musician's journey involves more than scheduling extra rehearsals. It also means making coffee for board meetings, unplugging toilets, pushing pianos about and putting Band-Aids on children's fingers.

LCMS is situated in City Park, and the new facility invites vandalism. Jan is forever anxious about security, often checking doors, windows and lights. The new building is pristine. He clears up cups, bottles and sheets of music. He straightens chairs. At a general recital, one of his students is performing. Jan comes down from his teaching studio to accompany. As he walks on stage to the piano, a small student in the front row turns to her mother and Jan overhears her say, 'Isn't this music school wonderful? Even the janitor plays the piano.'

INTERLUDE: ANNE

Anne Crowden, a former colleague of Jan's from his Edinburgh days and a family friend, founded the Crowden School in Berkeley that now enjoys academic excellence with a distinguished music program. Anne—always concerned for her charges' cultural broadening—travels in the new millennium with her string orchestra up to LCMS from Berkeley. Her students rehearse in the Rose Gellert Hall and before the catered supper arrives, there's time for Jan to give Anne a quick school tour. He makes sure she has her favourite gin and tonic in hand.

'We're very proud of this new facility,' says Jan. 'It took years of politics to achieve.'

'Don't I know it. We inherited a building whereas you built yours from scratch. I love the light, all these windows. Also, you have more grand pianos than we have. And look at all the stacks of chamber music, lucky dog!' She sighs. 'Are you still principal here?'

'No, I've been made Artistic Director Emeritus. This facility requires a principal with more business acumen than I have.'

'Very wise. I can't tell you the relief I felt when I handed over the reins to our new principal. I can holiday this summer in Scotland without worry. In September I'll return to Berkeley. I've given up my apartment. Maybe I'll live in a communal house.' Jan looks at her doubtfully; it doesn't exactly seem to fit Anne, always a strong character—the life and soul of the party. Jan reflects that she probably wouldn't like to live within the confines of a communal house, especially in her late seventies.

Anne helped Colin a lot in his declining years, coming over on Saturday nights to make supper and eat it with him. Colin had taught Anne's daughter, Deirdre, and helped Anne in the establishment of her school.

'I feel there is something wrong with me but I can't deal with it until I get to Scotland,' says Anne. 'Look at my face. Can you see anything wrong?' Jan can't. Her strawberry-blond hair looks faded now with intermingling white strands, but she seems the same ebullient person.

After the concert, Anne looks back at the school, squinting into the setting sun. 'That's a nice hall you have. A good acoustic.'

The students return to their bus, its long shadow cast over the parking lot. Anne turns around. 'Bye, Jansky. Who knows when we'll meet again.'

* * *

The next summer, Deirdre plays for the Vancouver Festival. She is cellist of the Smith Quartet, known for its performances of contemporary string quartets. Jan meets her for lunch. 'Anne got home last summer. One morning at her house in North Berwick, she couldn't get up. She couldn't move. She was diagnosed with pancreatic cancer. She lost weight rapidly and not long after Christmas, she died. We took her into the hospital the night before and she was still laughing and joking.'

Anne's vivid character, joy for life and robust sense of humour had burst into Jan's life fifty years before and now, just as suddenly, had dropped out of it.

THIRTY-FOUR

Elgar Cello Concerto

'Who's that bald guy with his arms outstretched?' asks Jan's student Annelise, pointing with her bow to an old framed photo on the wall.

'That is Pablo Casals, considered to be one of the greatest cellists and musicians of the twentieth century.'

'What's the writing at the bottom of it?'

'It says "To Bonnie and Colin Hampton". Bonnie studied with Casals and Colin thought he was the greatest man he knew.'

'Why are his arms like that?'

'He's giving a masterclass and he's probably saying, "Play with fantasy!" He said that a lot.'

'Did you ever get to hear him play?'

* 1946 *

Jan, age twelve, is sitting next to Colin in the Albert Hall, waiting for Casals to come on stage and perform Elgar's Cello Concerto. Casals has returned to London after a long period of self-exile. This event is considered historic by the English and by cello-kind. The London Cello School is agog. Dilly Dally had turned confidentially to Colin: 'Of course he's asking for soda water but of course we can't get soda water.' Her wattles trembling. A little man with a cello walks onto the platform and a roar of applause breaks out as the entire audience stands up. After several minutes, Jan settles back into his seat and the electric silence is broken by the little man bearing his bow down on the opening chords of the recitative. Jan, hearing a professional soloist for the first time, hasn't realized until this point how beautiful and commanding the cello sound can be.

At the end of the Concerto, the wails of lament subside to a nostalgic whisper. A woman in the seat next to Colin opens her handbag, fetches out a candy and begins fiddling with the wrapper. Colin leans over and puts his elbow over her hands where it remains until Casals finishes.

Amidst the clapping, she complains to Colin, 'I was going to cough.' 'But you didn't, did you?' Colin returns.

Some years later, Casals returns to London to conduct his oratorio, *El Pessebre*. After a rehearsal, Colin takes Jan—in the army at the time—to meet Casals, who has a private suite in a small hotel in Bond Street. Casals, dwarfed in an armchair, tired and with his eyes shut, murmurs, 'I do it for peace.' Around him is a melee of cellists, talking amongst themselves. Within earshot, Maurice Eisenberg demonstrates his golf expertise: 'I clasp the putter just so.' (Maurice will pay for this blasphemy much later, collapsing at a cello lesson he's giving at Juilliard. Jan's colleague Kathleen, a cellist who was a student at Juilliard at the time, will tell Jan: 'There I was in the lobby when Eisenberg was wheeled out on a gurney. I turned to Aldo Parisot who was standing there also and said, "Oh dear, Mr Eisenberg doesn't look very well," and Parisot drawled, "You're damned right, honey, he's dead."')

* * *

Although Elgar's Concerto is a staple in the repertoire of all cellists, it remains quintessentially English. Simple cenotaphs stand in village greens across the Land of Hope and Glory, honouring the local lads who marched to their deaths in the First World War. Their slaughter brought an end to the confident, comfortable Edwardian Age. The music of Elgar—who was never comfortable—might often be associated with that era, but his Cello Concerto, written after the armistice, is an elegy to those young men, a lament for the society as Elgar knew it.

In the first movement he takes a panoramic view of England's pastoral scenery, one touched by love and melancholy. Calm rivers with reeds bristling in a sharp spring breeze flow by banks of green willow, and the first cuckoo is heard between hills where history has marched. There goes Tallis, there goes Purcell, there goes Colin punting his young family down the Thames. One can hear history.

The Concerto opens with a recitative—the first bar of which is nearly always performed twice as fast as Elgar wrote it—affixed with Elgar's favourite adjective, 'Nobilmente'. The cello gives way to the single line of violas who introduce the main melody unadorned. Elgar possibly intended this as a buffer to prepare the audience's ear for the cello's entrance with the tune a tone above the pedal point in the bass. This tune is presented four times in pairs—at the ninth and at the octave. It also disobeys the usual aesthetics; it descends and descends, whereas most melodies are umbrella-shaped, reaching a height somewhere in or after the middle.

The slow movement looks like an interlude but it is deeply compassionate. Elgar has turned his gaze from the horizon to the close-up; he is looking down on the faces of those young men. What if those lads like George Butterworth and Wilfred Owen had lived fulfilled lives like Ralph Vaughan Williams and Arthur Bliss, rather than dying in the mud? Would history have taken a path for the better? The Finale is topped and tailed by the opening recitative and is traditionally assertive, its jingoistic stance undermined by moments of anxiety. Eventually it declines in speed, reduced to a whisper and then Elgar unleashes a passionate wailing that, in its last pages, elevates this concerto to a greatness that rivals all other cello concertos. The music then subsides to a point where we catch a last glimpse of those ashen faces.

The Concerto was not well-received at its premiere in 1919, having been inadequately rehearsed by Albert Coates, the conductor. The soloist, Felix Salmond, was a fine cellist and teacher—he later was associated with both Juilliard and Curtis—and had the distinction of previously premiering Elgar's String Quartet and Piano Quintet. (Colin once told Jan a story about Felix Salmond. 'He resembled a salmon. He had a very long nose. One day, at a railway station he was having an altercation with the ticketmaster. He stuck his nose into the ticket wicket, upon which the man said, "Sir, if you take your elbow out of the window, I'll issue the damn ticket!"')

In early performances, Beatrice Harrison was often associated with the Concerto. Since then, every soloist of note has performed it. The definitive recording is often considered to be that of Jacqueline du Pré who, no doubt, was influenced by her conductor, John Barbirolli, also a cellist. He brought his passion for Elgar and the traditions of English music to Jacqueline's attention. At her demise, a writer—who had little sense of history—pronounced in the obituary that Jacqueline had popularized Elgar's Cello Concerto. But in fact, a legion of famous cellists had preceded her.

During Jan's lifetime, Elgar has transcended his reputation as 'just an English musician' to become an international composer whose language conveys universal meaning. This attainment is a mysterious process, the composer suggesting things that are unobservable. In painting, the image may not be the central idea—it is surrounded by light, air, depth and height, even by scent and sound. Monet and Turner chased these conceptions; Berlioz and Ravel likewise in music.

Elgar's ever-descending melody may convey nostalgia for the Edwardian Age that had been violently torn apart but it contains a melancholy that each of us feels sometimes when we contemplate our place in the world. To a Britisher, that melody conveys a pastoral landscape, civilized by cool weather and implacable history. The gentle breezes carry suggestions of people who have contemplated in this place—King Harold, Thomas Becket, Jane Austen, Queen Victoria, Benjamin Britten. They, along with all the children, skipped through the beech woods, squelched in the streams, smelled the farmyard and heard the cock crow.

* * *

Jan is wearing his own squelching gumboots as he rehearses Elgar's Concerto with Meredith Davies and the VSO in 1968. It snows the night before the first rehearsal and by morning the slopes of the Coastal Range are covered in eight inches of snow. The show must go on. Jan drives his car cautiously, slithering down the North Shore into the city. He rehearses Elgar in a padded jacket and a toque. By the time the dress rehearsal comes along, the snow is gone.

Interestingly, there are only rare instances of Rostropovich performing the Elgar. Elgar's Concerto is among a handful of cello concertos regularly performed, but Rostropovich was intent on enriching the cello repertoire, and over his career commissioned or premiered some 200 works. There is room for just so many heroes in one's life. For Colin, Casals was the greatest musician of the century. But Rostropovich with his formidable technique is Jan's hero. No one he's heard has such a command over the instrument or such a rapport with his audience.

Through Colin's influence, the University of California hosts a week's master classes at Berkeley in 1974 with Rostropovich, an event that was preceded some years earlier by master classes with Casals. Jan and Judy travel down with several students from the Vancouver Academy. Rostropovich is about to record the two Haydn cello concertos and he requests of the Bay Area cello fraternity as many different recordings—for listening purposes—of these concertos as they can muster.

Rostropovich doesn't touch the cello at the master classes. He demonstrates his points from the piano, and for the entire week doesn't refer to the printed page. Particularly impressive is his coaching of the Debussy Sonata, with the student cellist and his accompanist downstage and Rostropovich slightly upstage at a second piano. No music. Rostropovich makes his musical points, always playing from memory the spirit of Debussy's harmonies, if not exactly the way Debussy notated them.

One afternoon, Bonnie and Jan collect Rostropovich from San Francisco to drive him back to Colin's for supper. He had been having tea with a Russian lady. He asks to sit in the back seat with a little basket that holds his miniature dog, Puchs. (Puchs always travelled with Rostropovich on the plane. Once the aircraft was airborne, Rostropovich would release this little animal from its basket and nobody could do much about it. That was in the good old days.) While Bonnie drives across the Bay, Rostropovich is very silent. Conversation between Bonnie and Jan is desultory; Jan is in awe of the great man in the back seat. When they arrive at Colin's house, Rostropovich asks for manuscript paper and disappears into the bedroom. Emerging for supper half an hour later, he's written his cadenza to Haydn's D Major Concerto.

* * *

Over the decades, many lesser cellists than Rostropovich march through Colin's house. His support for his students remains strong, but as their numbers dwindle down the years, support instead for Colin becomes a concern of his friends Anne Crowden and Tony Lepire.

It is 1996. The phone interrupts Jan's practice.

It's Tony. 'Colin's been getting these terrible headaches. They are putting him in hospital. He wants to speak with you.'

'Don't worry, son,' says Colin. 'They think it might be cancer but I'm not depressed.'

'I'll be down early next week.' Jan feels the familiar tug between family and professionalism. 'I have concerts on the weekend.'

Jan catches a plane from Vancouver. He tiptoes into the ward at the Kaiser Hospital in Oakland. It's a bright August day. Colin lies quiet, his face suddenly gaunt. A clipboard at the end of the bed says, 'No interventions.' ('I've had a good life, son,' he said a few times on Jan's previous visits.) Jan sits by the bed but Colin doesn't open his eyes, nor does he speak. Andy is flying out from Scotland and will arrive tomorrow.

Later, Anne drops in. 'Some ex-student of Colin's showed up yesterday with her cello, insisted on playing the Bach suites in here,' says Anne. 'Never did a cello sound so loud—there's a guy dying of AIDS in the ward next door.'

'I can imagine Colin raging inside.'

'He didn't stir—the last words he said were the day before—"Dying isn't so bad."'

The doctors keep draining Colin's lungs long enough for Andy to arrive and say goodbye. Both sons are quiet by his bedside as Colin keeps lifting his right arm in the air, as Beethoven was purported to have done. Then, with a last guttural sound, Colin's breathing stops. The blood, stopped in his arm, interlaces under the skin, which to Jan from his bedside view looks like a jigsaw puzzle.

Anne, Andy and Jan return to the house to prepare for a wake that is a general invitation to the musical community to come and say goodbye. In those few days there is a curious levity between the three of them as they clean up the house. Andy opens the fridge door; a single bottle of beer graces the top shelf. 'Tony told me that he and Colin opened a beer while they were waiting for the ambulance.' There is relief that Colin's struggles are all over but for months after Jan can't talk about it and tears well up as John Tavener's *The Protecting Veil* comes unbidden into his consciousness. The CBC Radio Orchestra had recently performed this with Steven Isserlis. The opening sounds are spellbinding, the solo cello sings with long, tenuto tones in a high register where many cellists fear to venture, accompanied by the string orchestra, which opens downward to the double basses. The effect suggests immensity and eternity—a huge canvas of widely spaced tones interrupted eventually by splashes of sound like paint flicked from a brush.

Colin's passion, along with his resinous cello tone, are captured, thankfully, on vinyl. Colin once said, 'Somehow, I don't think electricity and music are a good mix.'

Oh, but sometimes.

INTERLUDE: CREMAINS

The door to the crematorium office is open. A young woman sits on a desk, paring her nails.

'Yeah, this is the place.' She produces a long form. 'You have to fill this in. How are you going to pay? Credit cards are okay. They never refuse payment on cremations. You can collect the ashes in five days. There may be some ceramic chips in with your loved one. The result of heat exposure. California has strict rules about depositing ashes. What will you do with the cremains?'

Colin is to be buried at the Starcross community, a lay Catholic community run by Brother Toby and Sisters Martha and Julie. Brother Toby's adoptive son had attended the Crowden School where, between concerts, Colin and Brother Toby struck up a friendship. Colin's soul, in need of reassurance, was sustained by Brother Toby's pragmatic Catholicism. At the height of the AIDS scare, the community had elected to give love and shelter to babies orphaned by the disease for the short time that they were expected to live. Miraculously, a few children became clean of their infection.

Jan returns to the office to collect the ashes. In the intervening days, he's wrestled with the problem of finding an urn for them. The same young woman, now chewing gum, hands Jan a transparent plastic bag half full of grey ash with no visible identification. Except for her glistening crimson nails, she might have been cleaning out the grate. Jan looks at the contents. All that is left of Colin is two pounds of fine ash.

As he's leaving, Jan notices a shelf above the door.

'You want an urn?' asks the young lady, snapping her gum. 'The most expensive ones are on the left, then they go down in price.'

Jan chooses a tasteful metal box from the right.

Sitting next to Andy in the back seat of Bonnie's car, Jan holds the box on his lap. Once the cortège leaves the Bay Area, the fog thins and Bonnie, driving, picks up speed in the brightening August sunlight. The Starcross farm nestles in gorgeous countryside with orchards of ripening apples and plums.

Brother Toby, after a simple service in the chapel, holding a large cross, leads the party down the hill to the orchard which serves as the eternal resting place for so many short lives. Jan places the box and, with a shovel handed to him by Brother Toby, begins to fill in the earth with eyes blinded by tears.

Outside the farmhouse, lunch has been set up on a trestle—local wine, salads plucked from the vegetable garden nearby and drizzled with the community's cold-pressed olive oil, tarts with eggs and nuts garnished with red peppers, plums from the tree that is providing the shade while they eat this feast. Bonnie produces a cassette of the Grillers playing Beethoven's A-Minor Quartet, the tenuous paragraphs of Beethoven's 'Hymn of Thanksgiving' for recovery of health. The Lydian mode creates an ambiguity between the keys of C and F major, interrupted by the certitude of D major. Jan pauses amidst the table clatter to hear the hymn subside into a chord of F major, Colin with his Amati cello providing the fundamental F—a quiet, reassuring, resonant F—a rare juxtaposition, in the sunshine, of the senses.

THIRTY-FIVE

Chaconne

The reunited PSQ—the old boys, Normsk, Fred, Phil and Jan—is rehearsing the Chaconne from Britten's Second Quartet in Normsk's cottage at Sooke Harbour. 'Linger a little more there,' suggests Normsk. 'It's a heavenly moment.'

In 1975, Normsk contacted Britten to ask whether he would write the PSQ a quartet and Britten wrote back, declining: 'I may have a quartet on the stocks for the future, but nothing can be promised. Everything at the moment is very uncertain.' He had just finished his Third Quartet for the Amadeus, a public performance that he did not live to hear. Under Normsk's guidance, the original PSQ in their active years performed Britten's Second Quartet scores of times. Tonight, they will play it for the last time.

Normsk is nervous. They know they won't play it as well as they did thirty years ago, but they also know they'll be forgiven. The point is to impart the greatness and the beauty of Britten's music to the amateur musicians at the Sooke Chamber Music Workshop, an audience that may not have heard this work. Normsk retired from university life in Edmonton in the mid-eighties and moved to the warmer climes of Sooke on the west coast of Vancouver Island. He had honed his conducting skills at the university, and had previously taken conducting lessons from Sir Colin Davis. With his acute ear, Normsk was a natural for a sunset career as a conductor. Thus, the Sooke Philharmonic Orchestra sprang up, a vibrant organization with an annual season of concerts of a scope and artistic standard that would be the envy of much larger towns. Sooke, just far enough away from Victoria, has an ephemeral charm that attracts professional retirees, many of them competent amateur musicians.

'Those down bows on the sixteenths are still damn awkward,' says Fred, who hasn't played the violin much for twenty years. 'More tiring than selling real estate.'

'Don't let's open that old argument again. We haven't got time,' says Phil.

Bowings are not critical to Jan. He exercises the cellist's prerogative of bowing opposite from the upper strings and gazes out at a line of goslings, protected forward and aft by their parents shielding them from marauding eagles looking for a *bonne bouche.* He's drawn back by Normsk, who with an air of finality says softly, 'They're Britten's bowings and they facilitate the crescendo.'

The Chaconne is the glory of Britten's Second Quartet, which commemorates the 250th anniversary of the death of Purcell. The chaconne—a form associated with Purcell—is a piece elaborated over a harmonic progression that is repeated continually. A dotted rhythm provides the spine to procedures that feature the whole quartet, instruments in tandem, individual solos and cadenzas from Jan, Normsk and Phil.

Phil's cadenza is catapulted out of a frenzied paragraph played by the whole quartet. He descends from the nostril position to calmer middle ground and descends still further to introduce the serene second violin solo.

'Phil, I think you could draw out those last double stops more. Britten says lento and it will help to profile Fred,' interrupts Normsk.

'Oh, gee, I'm dying holding on to this high C forever,' says Fred.

Phil brushes this exchange aside. 'My old viola sounded better in the high range than the one I'm playing now.' Phil wasn't at Sooke the previous year because he didn't like to leave his wife, Margarita, alone. She suffers from Parkinson's disease. This year his daughter persuaded him that it was okay to come. Caregiving has not affected Phil's professional life; he still freelances and in between refines his motor skills by making exquisite silver and gold jewellery.

Despite his complaints, Fred plays his solo beautifully. Later he's joined by Normsk playing in thirds above him, after which the quartet subsides to *pianissimo* trills which seem to Jan to mimic the fluttering wings of the hummingbirds paying repeat visits to the rhododendrons close by.

After Normsk's cadenza, the Chaconne ends with multiple crashes of C major chords. 'I'm bushed,' declares Fred.

'Let's crack open a bottle of h-h-huh,' suggests Normsk, reaching for the corkscrew. Jenny produces a cheeseboard and the rehearsal room becomes a sitting room. They watch a video of Britten conducting his

Nocturne with the CBC Orchestra. Britten had visited Vancouver a year before Jan arrived. There, forty years younger, play Arthur Polson, George Zukerman, et al. 'We're going to play the *Nocturne* here next season,' says Normsk.

'Speaking of Britten, will you visit the Aldeburgh Festival when you go to England next month?' asks Phil.

'Not this year, but that reminds me—we'll meet Hugh Maguire at Manningtree Station on his way to the Festival,' says Normsk.

'Why Manningtree?' asks Jan.

'It's convenient. A group of us old farts like to meet there to play chamber music.'

'Good Lord! Who?' asks Jan.

'People you know—Denis Vigay, Trevor Connor, Kenneth Essex. We always play in the waiting room. Ken is ninety-two and still driving. The trunk of his car serves as a cocktail cabinet. Not that we need it—the station has a wonderful bar and a restaurant that serves very good lamb chops all day.'

Jan is getting mellow. 'Phil, remember when we played Kodály at UBC for a midday concert? Madame Kodály was the honoured guest. They took us for lunch in a private room at the faculty club. The conversation flowed as if we were in a Trappist monastery and, in desperation, you told that joke, "Could I but express in song", and at the punch line, "Kodály: Buttocks-pressing song", Madame Kodály gave you a broad smile of total incomprehension and everybody burst into conversation.'

'Like that other time'—Phil is getting into his cups—'in Montreal, when we played all the Beethovens. After the last concert, the concert committee took us for a drink at a private club. For Montreal, it was ultra-stuffy British with Stubbs's pictures of horses around the walls. We sat at a long mahogany table and nobody could think of anything to say except you, Jan, talking and laughing with the woman next to you.'

Jan replies. 'We got on to the subject of Russian toilets. Then, she told me this extraordinary story. She had taken a children's choir to New Zealand. "We arrived in the evening in a town," she recollected, "after a long bus journey. It had been raining all day. The billeting people had gathered in a school gym to meet the visitors. It took forever to sort out which child went with which billet. The evening wore on and the gym gradually emptied. At last, I was the one person left. A local woman

looked me up and down and said, 'Well, I guess I must be billeting you.'"'
Jan pauses to sip his wine.

'The woman went on, "We took off in her old VW, the rain pelting down on the windscreen. You couldn't see out. We drove for hours, it seemed. Eventually, the road petered out and we bumped along what seemed a very long drive. She stopped the car. 'Wait here,' she ordered. She went into the house, returning to the car after five minutes. 'I'll show you to your room.' Her husband, or whatever he was, was in the kitchen, looking tousled. I suspect he'd been sleeping in what was to be my bed and had got thrown out.

'"'You can brush your teeth in the kitchen,'" she said. Well, frankly, it had been a long day and I needed the bathroom.

'"'The outhouse is at the end of the lawn.'" She pointed. I went out in the rain and halfway across, I fell into a pit! She never told me that they'd moved the outhouse to a new location!" the woman finished.'

Jan moves out to the kitchen to refill his glass. 'There was that reception in Glasgow,' says Phil, 'in a room in a pub, given by the girl who organized the concert.'

'She kept talking about urinals,' calls Jan from the kitchen. 'She pronounced it "uriynals" for some reason.'

'Well, she had a tale to tell,' says Phil, tilting his wineglass dangerously. 'She'd gone to Saudi Arabia or somewhere and she'd been approached by a man who wanted to come to England and obtain a passport. Would she marry him? And she agreed and she said that from that moment, everything changed. She was in this village as a tourist and straight away she became a chattel. She wasn't allowed out of the village or even the house.' Phil takes a deep draft of his wine.

'After a week or so, a European photographer had come to the village to shoot pictures of a famous ruin nearby. He asked her if she knew where it was and she answered yes. Would she show him and she said yes. They left the village and at the site, the photographer spent much time, using rolls of film. It was sunset when they returned and the villagers were talking in undertones. They were looking at her, pointing at her and acting very hostile. That night, she decided she had to get out, so in the middle of the night, she got up and left, leaving her suitcase behind her. She literally walked her way back to Western civilization.'

From the kitchen, Jan watches a scene unfolding before him almost as if in slow motion—Phil reaches from the depths of his armchair and places his wineglass on what he thinks must be the tabletop beside him. The stem tips on the edge of a book and smashes to the floor, leaving red wine raining down the wallpaper, the carpet and everything in between. 'Oh my God!' moans Phil. 'I'll get the paper towels.'

Phil leans against the table to get out of the armchair, little realizing that the table is hinged. The tabletop crashes and a myriad of objects on it fall to the floor while Phil, unbalanced, is thrown against the sideboard. Normsk has joined Jan in the kitchen; both are heaving with suppressed hysterics.

'Don't worry, Phil,' says Jenny evenly, 'let me do it.'

* * *

Concert night, the former PSQ negotiates the steps down to Soiree Lane ahead of the students for a sound check and to rearrange the hall from workshop mode to concert formality. The house clings like a mountain goat to a steep bluff and has been extended to include a room of recital hall proportions by its owner, Don Chrysler, for his cellist wife, Janette. A long bookcase camouflages a hinged door which accesses the private quarters. Every year, Jan searches for the right segment of bookcase to enter the bedroom which serves as a green room. After the sound check, they warm up in the cramped bedroom and wait for the audience to arrive.

The workshop students have always been a captive audience but the thrill and dread of performing tightens nerve endings, a professional hazard one cannot outgrow. The quartet walks out through the bookcase to enthusiastic applause. They sit, poised to begin Britten's Second Quartet, waiting for the audience to become quiet and attentive. The opening is languid, serene even. Around Phil, calmly bowing the interval of a tenth, the others play in octaves assuredly anticipating Normsk's rubato as it colours the phrase. They haven't performed together for so long but old habits and reactions intuitively return. Even the Scherzo, whose rhythm makes inhuman demands on reactive time, twitters like an aviary to a safe conclusion. Its comparative brevity makes way for the monumental announcement of the Chaconne, strings in unison, rising in fourths and falling in fifths.

Some twenty minutes later, Normsk has the last take on the Chaconne; his cadenza makes way to multiple double stops. The others join him and with the last ringing chords of C major, the music seems to run into the applause. They walk back through the door in the bookcase. Jan is soaked. 'Sorry about that missed note in the Scherzo,' he says.

'Phil and I were too busy chasing our offbeats to notice,' says Fred, wiping the sweat off his chin rest.

Beyond the bookcase, the crowd is heading for the refreshments. Jan overhears a former student: 'Those old boys can still play up a storm.'

PSQ

Surround Sound

June is moving into July. Sue and Jan sit on the deck in the warmth of the long evening sun. Their two cats sit too, on the balustrade looking down on their territory. Jan keeps his eye on the sun. It has just reached its summer solstice, setting over a dimple behind Mount Seymour. Sue and the cats look for birds flying in and out of the cherry trees. The cats twitch when they see quick movements in between the branches. Sue is listening; she can hear the goldfinches, the bushtits, the robins and the white-crowned sparrows.

Jan can only hear the blue jays, crows and the two ravens that call to each other high over the neighbouring woods. Jan's loss of hearing can partially be attributed to the internal noises in his head, like the white noise of a television set or the wind whistling through telegraph wires. It's distracting but doesn't prevent him from hearing real sound.

It has been a hot day. Hundreds of cars have driven to the beaches of Belcarra, Bunsen and Sasamat. Sunset arrives a little earlier in some of those areas, hidden in the valley. Cars are beginning to head for home. They pass the drive every few seconds; the bass thumps of their stereos, like a distant air raid, can be heard two blocks from either side of the driveway. There seem to be two species of thumps—fast at 130 beats to the minute and slow at forty-eight to the minute.

The worse the music, the louder it's played, thinks Jan. Will they be deafer than me at half my age? Motorbikes add their unnecessary noise to the din. Motorbikes also seem to come in two species—the deep roar or the mosquito-like whine. The latter can be heard as they rev their engines up the Barnet Highway on the opposite shore of the inlet. Like the trains, they can be heard as far as Capitol Hill. Unlike the trains, their sound offers no redeeming features. The boats begin to return at sunset. People who ride motorbikes also, one supposes, ride jet skis. Sound carries easily over the water.

Machinery clanks as freighters at the opposite shore are loaded. Boxcars are shunted to the pile of sulphur and from time to time, the thermal plant lets off steam with a noise that suggests the preamble to a cataclysmic explosion. The sun has gone and the last sailboat majestically arrives at Rocky Point, a calm scene on a darkening vista. The moon rises, the cacophony subsides. The cats will go in, followed by Sue and Jan. Jan will go to bed, put earphones on and listen to Dutilleux. His musical journey is not over yet; he has found an exciting new composer. Later, he will lie awake listening for the resident bear, for the deer, which ate the strawberry plants, and for the mother raccoon, who will bring her three kits to drink at the birdbath. In the small hours, at high tide, the freighter, now loading, will announce to its crew and the waiting tugs that it is about to sail halfway round the world. Its long, low horn will break the silence and anybody still awake, if they listen carefully, can follow its attenuating echo as it passes from nearby mountains to ones farther down the valley, disappearing into the Coastal Range.

Acknowledgements

For readings, commentaries, advice and support, many thanks to Don Mowatt, Barry Hill, Cam Trowsdale, Susan Round, John Elsen, Holly Duff, Alan Crane, Warren Sommer, David Gordon Duke, Angela Goddard and her students at West Point Grey Academy, Arnold and Lorene Nickel, Sylvie Ingram, Mark Abley, Stephanie Bolster, Christopher Patton, Stephen Partridge and the late Elise Partridge. Thanks to Chris Round for typing the first draft and to Langley Community Music School for work space and support. Special thanks to Bramwell Tovey for the Foreword. Thanks also to Bevan, Nicholas and William Voth for understanding and patience. A huge thanks to everyone at The Porcupine's Quill—Stephanie Small, Chandra Wohleber and Tim and Elke Inkster—for making this book possible. I owe a debt of gratitude to Barbara Nickel, author, musician and friend, who, as editor, generously gave her time to wrestle this book into readable shape. Working with Barbara has been a fun, illuminating and creative journey.

DONALD FRANCIS TOVEY

About the Author

Ian (Jan) Hampton was born at London in 1935 and became a naturalized Canadian in 1974. Ian was educated at Bedales School (Hampshire). He studied cello with Joan Dickson in Edinburgh 1952–4, with William Pleeth at the Guildhall School of Music 1954–7, and with Paul Tortelier in Paris in 1958. He was a founding member (1959) of the Academy of St Martin in the Fields, and a member (1956–9) of the London Symphony. Hampton was the cellist (1959–65) of the Edinburgh String Quartet, taught at the University of California at Davis, the San Francisco Institute of the Arts and at Sacramento State College and was cellist of the Oakland Symphony and the Persinger String Trio. He moved to Vancouver in 1966 to become principal cellist (1967–73) of the Vancouver Symphony Orchestra and also of the CBC Vancouver Chamber Orchestra (from 1966). In 1967 he also became a founder and cellist of the Baroque Strings (to 1988), and also of the Purcell String Quartet, remaining with the latter group until 1989. In 1979, Hampton became principal of the Langley Community Music School and, in 1982, principal cellist of the Vancouver Opera Orchestra along with his role as principal cello of the CBC Vancouver Orchestra. He feels strongly that his best work has been with what might be called 'musical pioneering' (i.e. his work with the Purcell String Quartet and the Langley Community Music School) and that more attention needs to be paid to works by contemporary composers. In recognition of his contribution to Canadian new music, in 2009 Hampton was named a Canadian Music Centre ambassador. He blogs at hungdrawnandcultured.com.